QUIET WATER

MASSACHUSETTS, CONNECTICUT, AND RHODE ISLAND

AMC'S CANOE AND KAYAK GUIDE TO 100 OF THE BEST PONDS, LAKES, AND EASY RIVERS

4th Edition • Alex Wilson and John Hayes

Appalachian Mountain Club Books
Boston, Massachusetts

AMC is a 501(c)3 nonprofit, and sales of AMC Books fund our mission to foster the protection, enjoyment, and understanding of the outdoors. If you appreciate our efforts and would like to become a member or make a donation to AMC, visit outdoors.org, call 603-466-2727, or contact us at Appalachian Mountain Club, 10 City Square, Boston, MA 02129

outdoors.org/books-maps

Distributed by National Book Network.

Front cover and title page photographs of Tully Lake and River and back cover photograph of Long Cove on Martha's Vineyard © Alex Wilson
Interior photographs © Alex Wilson and John Hayes, except where noted
Maps design by Nadav Malin and Vanessa Gray, © Alex Wilson and John Hayes
Book design by Abigail Coyle

Library of Congress Cataloging-in-Publication Data

Names: Wilson, Alex, 1955- author. | Hayes, John, 1944- author. | Appalachian Mountain Club.
Title: Quiet water Massachusetts, Connecticut, and Rhode Island : AMC's canoe and kayak guide to 100 of the best ponds, lakes, and easy rivers / Alex Wilson and John Hayes.
Description: Fourth edition. | Boston, Massachusetts : Appalachian Mountain Club Books, 2024. | Includes bibliographical references and index. | Summary: "Paddlers of all skill and experience level can enjoy the trips described in this guide to the best quiet water paddling in the southern New England states of Massachusetts, Rhode Island, and Connecticut"-- Provided by publisher.
Identifiers: LCCN 2024009683 | ISBN 9781628421767 (trade paperback) | ISBN 9781628421774 (epub) | ISBN 9781628421781 (mobi)
Subjects: LCSH: Canoes and canoeing--Massachusetts--Guidebooks. | Canoes and canoeing--Rhode Island--Guidebooks. | Canoes and canoeing--Connecticut--Guidebooks. | Massachusetts--Guidebooks. | Rhode Island--Guidebooks. | Connecticut--Guidebooks. | BISAC: SPORTS & RECREATION / Water Sports / Canoeing | TRAVEL / Special Interest / Ecotourism
Classification: LCC GV776.M4 W55 2024 | DDC 797.1220974--dc23/eng/20240301
LC record available at https://lccn.loc.gov/2024009683

The paper used in this publication meets the minimum requirements of the American National Standard for Information Sciences-Permanence of Paper for Printed Library Materials, ANSI Z39.48-1984. ∞

Outdoor recreation activities by their very nature are potentially hazardous. This book is not a substitute for good personal judgment and training in outdoor skills. Due to changes in conditions, use of the information in this book is at the sole risk of the user. The author and the Appalachian Mountain Club assume no liability for accidents happening to, or injuries sustained by, readers who engage in the activities described in this book.

Interior pages and cover are printed on responsibly harvested paper stock certified by The Forest Stewardship Council*, an independent auditor of responsible forestry practices. Printed in the United States of America, using vegetable-based inks.

5 4 3 2 1   24 25 26 27 28 29 30 31 32 33

MAP LEGEND

⌂ Tent site

◀ Lean-to

⊤ Picnic area

[△] Campground

⊟ Boat access

[P] Parking area

Marsh

Peak

▬ Dam

Interstate highway ════════

State highway ─────────

Paved road ▬▬▬▬▬▬

Less-traveled road ═════════

Rough dirt road · · · · · · · ·

Foot path - - - - - - - -

River

Stream

} arrow indicates direction of flow

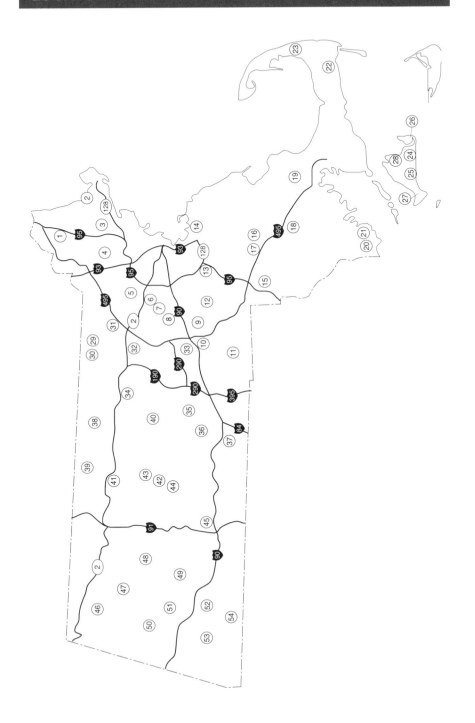

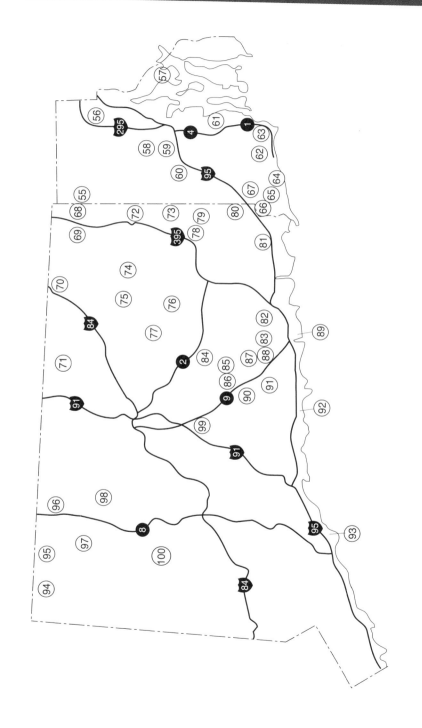

CONTENTS

SECTION 2: SOUTHEASTERN MASSACHUSETTS AND CAPE COD

SECTION 3: MARTHA'S VINEYARD

SECTION 4: CENTRAL MASSACHUSETTS

SECTION 5: WESTERN MASSACHUSETTS

SECTION 6: RHODE ISLAND

SECTION 7: EASTERN CONNECTICUT

SECTION 8: SOUTHERN CONNECTICUT

SECTION 9: WESTERN CONNECTICUT

NATURE ESSAYS

AT-A-GLANCE TRIP PLANNER

Trip number	Trip name and access location	Area/ One-way length	Estimated time
SECTION 1 | EASTERN MASSACHUSETTS			
1	Crane Pond and Parker River *Georgetown, Groveland, and Newbury, MA*	3 miles one way	6 hours
2	Essex Marsh and Choate (Hog) Island *Essex and Ipswich, MA*	3,000 acres	All day
3	Ipswich River and Wenham Swamp *Hamilton, Ipswich, Topsfield, and Wenham, MA*	8 miles one way	1 to 2 days
4	Stearns Pond and Field Pond *Andover and North Andover, MA*	Stearns Pond 41 acres; Field Pond 59 acres	3 hours
5	Concord River and Great Meadows National Wildlife Refuge *Bedford, Billerica, Carlisle, and Concord, MA*	6.5 miles one way	6 hours
6	Walden Pond *Concord, MA*	61 acres	2 hours
7	Sudbury River *Concord, Lincoln, Sudbury, and Wayland, MA*	10.6 miles one way	All day
8	Assabet River *Maynard and Stow, MA*	5.5 miles one way	6 hours
9	Ashland Reservoir *Ashland, MA*	157 acres	2 hours
10	Whitehall Reservoir *Hopkinton, MA*	592 acres	4–6 hours
11	Blackstone River *Northbridge and Uxbridge, MA*	4 miles one way	5 hours
12	Charles River *Dover, Medfield, Millis, Natick, Norfolk, and Sherborn, MA*	13.4 miles one way	All day
13	Neponset River *Boston, Canton, Dedham, Milton, Norwood, MA*	8 miles one way	All day

Hiking trails	Swimming	Motorboats	Permit required	Trip highlights
			NO	Shallow, marshy stream and out-of-the-way pond
🚶		🚤	NO	Salt marsh estuary with winds, tides; island wildlife refuge, hiking trails
🚶			**YES**	Shallow, marshy stream, wildlife refuge; permit needed for camping
🚶			NO	Shallow, marshy ponds within state forest
🚶		🚤 *10 MPH limit*	NO	Slow-flowing, historic river; wildlife refuge with rare plants and turtles
🚶	🏊		NO	Small, deep, protected, historic pond
🚶		🚤	NO	Slow-flowing, historic river; wildlife refuge
🚶		🚤 *few motors*	NO	Slow-flowing, historic river; wildlife refuge; rails-to-trail
🚶	🏊	🚤 *10 MPH limit; no personal watercraft*	NO	Wooded reservoir within state park
🚶		🚤 *12 MPH limit; no personal watercraft; no water-skiing*	NO	Large, former water-supply reservoir with protected coves and islands
🚶			NO	Historic canal and slow-flowing river
			NO	Shallow, wooded, historic, mostly protected river
🚶			NO	Shallow, wooded, historic, mostly protected river

Trip number	Trip name and access location	Area/ One-way length	Estimated time
14	Weymouth Back River *Hingham and Weymouth, MA*	3.6 miles one way	4 hours

SECTION 2 | SOUTHEASTERN MASSACHUSETTS AND CAPE COD

Trip number	Trip name and access location	Area/ One-way length	Estimated time
15	Bungay River *Attleboro and North Attleborough, MA*	2 miles	3 hours
16	Lake Nippenicket, Hockomock Swamp, and Town River *Bridgewater and West Bridgewater, MA*	Hockomock Swamp 16,950 acres; Lake Nippenicket 354 acres; Town River 2 miles one way	8 hours
17	Snake River *Taunton, MA*	3.5 miles one way	8 hours
18	Lake Rico and Big Bearhole Pond *Taunton, MA*	Lake Rico 250 acres; Big Bearhole Pond 37 acres	4 hours
19	East Head Pond *Carver and Plymouth, MA*	92 acres	2 hours
20	Westport River East Branch *Westport, MA*	4 miles one way	4 hours
21	Slocums River *Dartmouth, MA*	4 miles one way	4 hours
22	Herring River and West Reservoir *Harwich, MA*	4.5 miles one way; West Reservoir 47 acres	4 hours
23	Nauset Marsh and Salt Pond Bay *Eastham, MA*	1,300 acres	4 hours

SECTION 3 | MARTHA'S VINEYARD

Trip number	Trip name and access location	Area/ One-way length	Estimated time
24	Edgartown Great Pond *Edgartown, MA*	890 acres	8 hours
25	Tisbury Great Pond *Chilmark and West Tisbury, MA*	790 acres	8 hours
26	Pocha Pond *Edgartown, MA*	210 acres	2 hours
27	Menemsha Pond and Quitsa Pond *Chilmark and Gay Head, MA*	Menemsha Pond 665 acres	4 hours
28	Sengekontacket Pond *Edgartown and Oak Bluffs, MA*	726 acres	5 hours

SECTION 4 | CENTRAL MASSACHUSETTS

Trip number	Trip name and access location	Area/ One-way length	Estimated time
29	Nashua River and Pepperell Pond *Groton and Pepperell, MA*	5 miles one way	6 hours

Hiking trails	Swimming	Motorboats	Permit required	Trip highlights
		🚤 *no personal watercraft; no water-skiing*	NO	Salt marsh estuary, shallow at low tide
			NO	Shallow, meandering, marshy, wooded stream
	🏊	🚤	NO	Lake provides access to huge, wild Hockomock Swamp; separate Town River section
		🚤	NO	Winding river through thick vegetation
🚶	🏊		NO	Shallow lakes and ponds within state park
🚶	🏊		NO	Small, shallow lake; rare species; within huge forest with rare habitat
🚶		🚤	NO	Tidal estuary with shallow coves
🚶	🏊	🚤 *few motors*	NO	Shallow, marshy estuary; hiking, swimming at state park
🚶		🚤	NO	Shallow, marshy estuary; hiking on Cape Cod Rail Trail nearby
🚶		🚤 *few motors*	NO	Huge salt marsh; shallow at low tide
🚶	🏊	🚤	NO	Large, salt water to brackish pond
🚶	🏊	🚤	NO	Large, salt water to brackish pond
🚶	🏊	🚤	NO	Small, salt water pond that connects to Cape Pogue Bay; wildlife refuge
🚶		🚤	NO	Large, salt water pond open to sea
🚶		🚤	NO	Large, salt water pond open to sea; wildlife refuge
🚶		🚤 *22 MPH limit*	NO	Dammed-up river section with protected bays, inlets, and islands

Trip number	Trip name and access location	Area/ One-way length	Estimated time
30	Squannacook River *Groton and Shirley, MA*	3 miles one way	3 hours
31	Beaver Brook *Littleton and Westford, MA*	3 miles one way	4 hours
32	Nashua River and Oxbow National Wildlife Refuge *Bolton, Harvard, Lancaster, and Shirley, MA*	9.5 miles one way	7 hours
33	Assabet River Reservoir (Mill Pond, A-1 Site) *Westborough, MA*	333 acres	3 hours
34	Paradise Pond *Princeton, MA*	61 acres	2 hours
35	Eames Pond *Paxton, MA*	74 acres	2 hours
36	Quaboag Pond, Quaboag River, and East Brookfield River *Brookfield, East Brookfield, Warren, and West Brookfield, MA*	Quaboag Pond 541 acres; Quaboag River 9 miles one way; East Brookfield River 2 miles one way	8 hours
37	East Brimfield Lake, Quinebaug River, Holland Pond, and Long Pond *Brimfield, Holland, and Sturbridge, MA*	Holland Pond 85 acres; East Brimfield Lake and Long Pond 420 acres; Quinebaug River 4.5 miles one way	8 hours
38	Millers River, Otter River, and Lake Denison *Templeton and Winchendon, MA*	Lake Denison 82 acres; Millers River 7.5 miles one way; Otter River 3 miles one way	8 hours
39	Tully Lake and East Branch Tully River *Athol and Royalston, MA*	Tully Lake 243 acres; East Branch Tully River 3 miles one way	Tully Lake 4 hours; East Branch Tully River 3 hours round trip
40	Ware River and East Branch Ware River *Barre and Rutland, MA*	3 sections of 2 miles, 2.3 miles, and 3 miles one way	3 hours each section
41	Lake Rohunta *Athol, New Salem, and Orange, MA*	383 acres	4 hours
42	Muddy Brook and Hardwick Pond *Hardwick, MA*	Hardwick Pond 66 acres; Muddy Brook 1.6 miles one way	3 hours
43	Pottapoag Pond *Hardwick and Petersham, MA*	570 acres	4 hours

Hiking trails	Swimming	Motorboats	Permit required	Trip highlights
			NO	Shallow, marshy, meandering river; within wildlife management area
			NO	Shallow, meandering, marshy stream
🚶		🚤 *few motors*	NO	Marshy river through national wildlife refuge
🚶		🚤	NO	Shallow, marshy, stump-filled reservoir
			NO	Small, shallow, wooded pond
🚶			NO	Small, shallow, marshy pond; partly within state park
		🚤 *few motors on rivers*	NO	Shallow, meandering, marshy rivers
🚶		🚤	NO	Lakes connected by canoe trail through swamp
🚶	🏊		NO	Shallow, marshy, meandering river; within wildlife management area, state park, and state forest
🚶	🏊	🚤 *10 MPH limit on Tully Lake; no motors on river*	NO	Reservoir with protected islands and bays; marshy, slow-flowing river
🚶			NO	Mostly marshy, protected, slow-flowing rivers
		🚤	NO	Shallow, marshy, elongated lake
		🚤 *no personal watercraft*	NO	Small, marshy pond and brook
🚶			NO	Wilderness pond, part of Quabbin Reservoir

Trip number	Trip name and access location	Area/ One-way length	Estimated time
44	Swift River *Belchertown and Ware, MA*	4.5 miles one way	4 hours
45	Chicopee River Reservoir *Wilbraham, Ludlow, and Palmer, MA*	106 acres; 1.2 miles one way	4 hours

SECTION 5 | WESTERN MASSACHUSETTS

Trip number	Trip name and access location	Area/ One-way length	Estimated time
46	Bog Pond and Burnett Pond *Savoy, MA*	Bog Pond 40 acres; Burnett Pond 30 acres	1 hour each pond
47	Plainfield Pond *Plainfield, MA*	65 acres	2 hours
48	Upper Highland Lake *Goshen, MA*	56 acres	2 hours
49	Littleville Lake *Chester and Huntington, MA*	275 acres	3 hours
50	Housatonic River *Lee, Lenox, Pittsfield, and Washington, MA*	10 miles one way	8 hours
51	Buckley Dunton lake *Becket, MA*	195 acres	3 hours
52	Upper Spectacle Pond *Otis and Sandisfield, MA*	72 acres	2 hours
53	Three Mile Pond *Sheffield, MA*	81 acres	2 hours
54	Thousand Acre Swamp and East Indies Pond *New Marlborough, MA*	Thousand Acre Swamp 155 acres; East Indies Pond 69 acres	4 hours

SECTION 6 | RHODE ISLAND

Trip number	Trip name and access location	Area/ One-way length	Estimated time
55	Bowdish Reservoir *Glocester, RI*	226 acres	4 hours
56	Olney Pond *Lincoln, RI*	120 acres	2 hours
57	Brickyard Pond *Barrington, RI*	102 acres	2 hours
58	North Branch Pawtuxet River *Scituate, RI*	2.5 miles one way	3 hours
59	South Branch Pawtuxet River *Coventry, RI*	1.5 miles one way	2 hours

Hiking trails	Swimming	Motorboats	Permit required	Trip highlights
🚶		*few motors; no personal watercraft*	NO	Small stream; outflow from Quabbin Reservoir
		🛥	NO	Small reservoir, scenic river with wooded shores
🚶			NO	Small, marshy northern fens within state forest
🚶			NO	Small, marshy, protected pond
🚶	🏊		NO	Small, wooded pond within state forest
		10 HP limit	NO	Elongated, wooded reservoir
			NO	Slow-flowing river
🚶			NO	Medium-sized pond within state forest
🚶		*few motors*	NO	Small, shallow, marshy pond
		shallow water; aquatic plants limit motors	NO	Small, shallow, marshy pond within wildlife management aea
🚶		*few motors*	NO	Shallow, marshy ponds within state park
🚶	🏊	*10 HP limit*	NO	Shallow, marshy pond
🚶	🏊		NO	Small pond within Lincoln Woods State Park
🚶		*few motors*	NO	Shallow, marshy, wooded pond
			NO	Clear-flowing outlet of water-supply reservoir
🚶			NO	Narrow, meandering river flowing through urban area; hiking/biking path starts at access

Trip number	Trip name and access location	Area/ One-way length	Estimated time
60	Big River *Coventry and West Greenwich, RI*	2.3 miles one way	3 hours
61	Belleville Pond *North Kingstown, RI*	159 acres	3 hours
62	Worden Pond, Great Swamp, Chipuxet River, and Pawcatuck River *South Kingston, RI*	Worden Pond 1,075 acres; Chipuxet and Pawcatuck rivers 9 miles one way	8 hours
63	Tucker Pond *South Kingston, RI*	101 acres	2 hours
64	Ninigret Pond *Charlestown, RI*	1,700 acres	8 hours
65	Watchaug Pond and Poquiant Brook *Charlestown, RI*	Watchaug Pond 573 acres; Poquiant Brook 0.75 mile one way	4 hours
66	Pawcatuck River *Charlestown, Hopkinton, and Westerly, RI*	8 miles one way	All day, round trip
67	Wood River and Alton Pond *Hopkinton and Richmond, RI*	6.5 miles one way	All day, round trip

SECTION 7 | EASTERN CONNECTICUT

Trip number	Trip name and access location	Area/ One-way length	Estimated time
68	Quaddick Reservoir and Stump Pond *Thompson, CT*	467 acres	2 hours for Stump Pond
69	West Thompson Lake and Quinebaug River *Thompson, CT*	West Thompson Lake 239 acres; Quinebaug River 3 miles one way	5 hours
70	Mashapaug Lake and Bigelow Pond *Union, CT*	Mashapaug Lake 287 acres; Bigelow Pond 26 acres	4 hours
71	Somersville Mill Pond and Scantic River *Somers, CT*	Somersville Mill Pond 41 acres; Scantic River 3 miles one way	3 hours
72	Ross Marsh *Killingly and Sterling, CT*	55 acres	2 hours
73	Moosup River and Oneco Pond *Sterling, CT, and Coventry, RI*	2–4 miles one way	2–4 hours
74	Mansfield Hollow Lake *Mansfield and Windham, CT*	500 acres	8 hours

Hiking trails	Swimming	Motorboats	Permit required	Trip highlights
		few motors	NO	Slow-flowing river through broad marsh
hiking		few motors	NO	Shallow, marshy pond
		no motors on river	NO	Large, shallow pond; small, shallow, meandering streams
		10 HP limit	NO	Small, natural kettle pond
hiking			NO	Large estuary with winds and tides
hiking	swimming		NO	Large pond within state park; nearby wildlife refuge
		few motors	NO	Wide, undeveloped river
			NO	Marshy, meandering river
	swimming	motorboats	NO	Shallow, marshy pond; parts lie within state forest and state park
hiking		motorboats	NO	Flood-control reservoir and protected river stretch
hiking	swimming	10 MPH limit; no motors on Bigelow Pond	NO	Deep, clear lake with islands; shallow, marshy pond; partially within state park
		6 MPH limit	NO	Shallow, marshy, meandering stream
			NO	Small, shallow, marshy pond
		few motors	NO	Small, wooded, meandering stream
hiking	swimming	8 MPH limit	NO	Wooded reservoir, deep coves, islands, and inlet rivers

Trip number	Trip name and access location	Area/ One-way length	Estimated time
75	Eagleville Pond and Willimantic River *Coventry and Mansfield, CT*	Eagleville Pond 80 acres; Willimantic River 1.5 miles one way	3 hours
76	Mono Pond *Columbia, CT*	113 acres	2 hours
77	Bishop Swamp *Andover, CT*	53 acres	2 hours

SECTION 8 | SOUTHERN CONNECTICUT

Trip number	Trip name and access location	Area/ One-way length	Estimated time
78	Hopeville Pond and Pachaug River *Griswold, CT*	Hopeville Pond 150 acres; Pachaug River 3.6 miles one way	4 hours
79	Pachaug River and Beachdale Pond *Voluntown, CT*	Beachdale Pond 46 acres; Pachaug River 2.5 miles one way	4 hours
80	Green Falls Pond *Voluntown, CT*	48 acres	2 hours
81	Mystic River *Stonington and Groton, CT*	3.2 miles one way	4 hours
82	Powers Lake *East Lyme, CT*	144 acres	3 hours
83	Uncas Pond *Lyme, CT*	69 acres	2 hours
84	Babcock Pond *Colchester, CT*	147 acres	3 hours
85	Moodus Reservoir *East Haddam, CT*	486 acres	5 hours
86	Salmon River *East Haddam and Haddam, CT*	4 miles one way	4 hours
87	Whalebone Creek and Selden Creek *Lyme, CT*	Whalebone Creek 1 mile one way; Selden Creek 2.7 miles one way	All day
88	Lord Cove *Lyme and Old Lyme, CT*	351 acres; 5-mile maze of waterways	5 hours
89	Great Island Estuary and Roger Tory Peterson Wildlife Area *Old Lyme, CT*	wildlife area 588 acres; Lieutenant River 3.5 miles one way; Blackhall River 3 miles one way	8 hours
90	Pattaconk Reservoir *Chester, CT*	56 acres	2 hours

Hiking trails	Swimming	Motorboats	Permit required	Trip highlights
		8 MPH limit	NO	Shallow, marshy pond and river
		8 MPH limit	NO	Shallow, marshy pond
			NO	Small, shallow, marshy pond
🚶	🏊	8 MPH limit	NO	Dammed-up meandering river
🚶		8 MPH limit	NO	Dammed-up meandering river
🚶			NO	Small, wooded, mountain pond
			NO	Tidal river with boat traffic and historic museum
		8 MPH limit	NO	Small, wooded, protected pond
🚶			NO	Small, elongated, wooded pond, partially within a state forest
🚶		8 MPH limit	NO	Shallow, marshy pond within wildlife management area
		35 MPH limit	NO	Large reservoir
🚶			NO	Shallow, marshy, tidal estuary
			YES	Tidal estuary channel of Connecticut River; small, marshy, inlet stream; permit needed for camping
			NO	Tidal estuary, brackish marshland, protected islands and coves
		no motors in wildlife refuge	NO	Salt marsh estuary, partially within wildlife refuge
🚶	🏊		NO	Shallow, marshy pond within state forest

Trip number	Trip name and access location	Area/ One-way length	Estimated time
91	Messerschmidt Pond *Deep River and Westbrook, CT*	73 acres	2 hours
92	East River *Guilford and Madison, CT*	6 miles one way	5 hours
93	Charles E. Wheeler Wildlife Management Area, Housatonic River Estuary *Milford, CT*	812 acres in wildlife management area	4 hours

SECTION 9 | WESTERN CONNECTICUT

Trip number	Trip name and access location	Area/ One-way length	Estimated time
94	Housatonic River *Canaan, North Canaan, Salisbury, CT, and Sheffield, MA*	11.5 miles one way	8 hours
95	Wood Creek Pond *Norfolk, CT*	151 acres	3 hours
96	West Branch Reservoir *Colebrook and Hartland, CT*	201 acres	3 hours
97	Lake Winchester *Winchester, CT*	246 acres	3 hours
98	Lake McDonough *Barkhamsted, CT*	391 acres	5 hours
99	Mattabesset River, Coginchaug River, and Cromwell Meadows State Wildlife Area *Cromwell and Middletown, CT*	Mattabesset River 5 miles one way; Coginchaug River 2 miles one way	6 hours
100	Bantam River, Bantam Lake, and Little Pond *Litchfield and Morris, CT*	Bantam Lake 933 acres; Bantam River 2 miles one way	3 hours for river trip

Hiking trails	Swimming	Motorboats	Permit required	Trip highlights
			NO	Shallow, marshy pond within wildlife management area
		🛥	NO	Salt marsh estuary and tidal river
🥾		🛥 *no motors before September 1*	NO	Salt marsh estuary, partially within wildlife refuge
		🛥 *few motors*	NO	Large, slow-flowing river
🥾		🛥 *few motors*	NO	Shallow, marshy pond
🥾		🛥 *few motors*	NO	Deep, elongated, wooded reservoir
		🛥 *8 MPH limit*	NO	Midsized, wooded lake with protected bays
🥾	🏊	🛥 *10 MPH limit*	YES	Midsized, wooded lake with clear water
		🛥 *few motors*	NO	Rivers through extensive marshlands with bays and side channels
🥾	🏊	🛥 *no motors on river*	NO	Large, natural lake; small, marshy stream

PREFACE

The first edition of *Quiet Water Canoe Guide: Massachusetts, Connecticut, and Rhode Island*, written by Alex Wilson and published in 1993, was the second in a series that now includes guides to New Hampshire/Vermont, Maine, New York, and the Mid-Atlantic region. John Hayes, coauthor with Alex Wilson of the New Hampshire/Vermont, Maine, and New York guides, has coauthored the second, third, and fourth editions of this guide as well.

We took the opportunity in subsequent editions to add new material, nearly doubling the amount of water covered. The first edition contained 64 entries covering 93 bodies of water. In each of the second, third, and fourth editions, we dropped several entries because of limited or challenging access, shoreline development, overuse, invasion of exotic weeds, and paddling difficulty. The fourth edition has expanded to 100 entries and 140 bodies of water, a gain of more than 50 percent from that first edition.

Because descriptions inevitably go out of date, we also rechecked all bodies of water to ensure that new development had not crowded the shores, revised directions to reflect new road names, and added Global Positioning System (GPS) coordinates to access points. When possible, we avoided places with substantial development, but we focused more on the effect of personal (motorized) watercraft and high-speed boating on safety, the quietwater experience, and the environment.

We thank blogger Erik Eckilson and Kevin Klyberg of the National Park Service for their help in identifying places to paddle on the Blackstone River, and we thank David Hodgdon of Blue Hill Adventure for pointing out the paddling available on the Neponset River. Thanks also to Allyn Copp, Malcolm Moore, and Steve Shriner for their valuable insights and participation in research.

INTRODUCTION

Quiet waters—lakes, ponds, estuaries, and slow-flowing streams—receive much less attention than whitewater rivers. If you seek the adrenaline rush of paddling cascading waterways, plenty of excellent resources exist—but this is not one of them. The peaceful solitude of out-of-the-way lakes and ponds lures us to quietwater paddling. This guide will lead you to wood ducks swimming through early morning mists. Rounding a bend on a winding inlet channel, you may encounter the playful antics of river otters. If you spend any substantial time paddling, you are sure to see an osprey diving into the water before soaring upward, a silvery fish grasped in its talons. You may also spot some old-growth white pine towering above crystal-clear ponds that help you imagine what forests looked like centuries ago.

With quietwater paddling, you can focus on being there instead of *getting* there. You don't need a lot of fancy high-tech equipment, although a light canoe or kayak makes portaging over beaver dams a lot easier. Binoculars and field guides to fauna and flora make up the most important gear—after boats, paddles, and personal flotation devices (PFDs).

This guide will lead you to a body of water and describe why you might want to paddle it. We tried to include places that have abundant wildlife or extensive marshlands or beautiful scenery; most entries have all three. Some entries feature historical and cultural resources. We hope that our research will allow you to spend your valuable time paddling instead of driving around for hours, trying to find elusive accesses. We designed the Quiet Water series for paddlers of all experience levels to help you better enjoy the Northeast's wonderful water resources.

THE SELECTION PROCESS

This guide includes only a small percentage of the lakes, ponds, estuaries, and slow-flowing rivers in Massachusetts, Connecticut, and Rhode Island. In the selection process, we looked for attractive scenery; limited development; few motorboats and personal watercraft; a varied shoreline with lots of coves and inlets; and interesting plants, animals, and geological formations.

We included a variety of water types: big lakes and rivers for longer excursions and smaller, protected ponds and marshes for when you have limited time or when weather conditions preclude paddling larger bodies of water. This book is not only for vacationers planning a weeklong trip hundreds of miles from home but also for local residents wanting to do some paddling on their afternoon off.

The book contains a wide geographic spread of small and large bodies of water from the tri-state region. We asked people about the best places to paddle; we consulted DeLorme's *Massachusetts Atlas & Gazetteer* and *Connecticut and Rhode Island Atlas & Gazetteer*; we read other books about paddling; and we systematically searched the United States Geological Survey (USGS) 7.5-minute topographical maps of the states.

Although we tried to include the very best places to paddle, we doubtless missed some worthwhile locations. If you have suggestions, please write to Alex Wilson at alex@atwilson.com.

SAFETY, EQUIPMENT, AND TECHNIQUE

We all long to glide on mist-filled, mirror-smooth surfaces of quiet ponds at daybreak. But if you spend any time paddling lakes and tidal rivers, you will also encounter far less tranquil conditions. Swift estuary tides, coupled with wind, make for dangerous conditions. On larger bodies of water, strong winds can arise quickly, whipping up 2- to 4-foot waves in no time—waves big enough to swamp an open boat. If you capsize in cold water even a moderate distance from shore, hypothermia—a cooling of the body's core that can lead to mental and physical collapse—may set in quickly. If you have just driven a long way to reach a particular lake and find it dangerously windy, choose a more protected body of water or go hiking instead.

SAFETY FIRST

All Northeast states require each boater to carry a U.S. Coast Guard–approved (Type I, II, or III) personal flotation device (PFD). A good PFD keeps a person's face above water, even if that person has lost consciousness. A foam- or kapok-filled PFD will also help keep you warm in cold water.

Children 12 and younger must wear their PFDs at all times. Adult PFDs are not acceptable for children—if they are too large, they might slip off. Although the law does not usually require adults to wear PFDs, we strongly recommend that you do so, especially when paddling with children. If you do not normally wear your PFD while paddling, at least don it in windy conditions, when crossing large lakes, or when you may encounter substantial motorboat wakes. It could save your life. (*Note*: Connecticut requires all persons in manually propelled craft to wear PFDs from October 1 through May 31. Massachusetts requires all canoeists and kayakers to wear PFDs from

September 15 through May 15. As of 2023, Rhode Island requires all paddlers, regardless of age, to wear a PFD at all times.)

You should also bring along a waterproof first-aid kit. The best kit is one that you assemble yourself. Make sure that it has bandages and moleskin for blisters, an antihistamine for allergic reactions, sunscreen, an extra hat, a pain reliever, and any special medications that you might need.

As for clothing, plan for the unexpected. Even with a sunny-day forecast, a shower can appear by afternoon. On trips of more than a few hours, we bring along rain gear and dry clothes in a waterproof stuff sack as a matter of course. Along with unpredicted rain, temperatures can drop quickly, especially in spring or fall, making conditions ripe for hypothermia. Avoid wearing cotton. Lightweight nylon or polypropylene clothing dries more quickly than cotton, and wool slows heat loss even when wet. Remember that heads lose heat faster than torsos. Bring a hat.

Also, bring a whistle, which you may need to summon help. The sound of a whistle travels farther than the sound of a human voice, especially in windy conditions. Bring enough food to maintain your energy level, and carry 1 liter of water for short trips and 2 or more liters for long trips. Avoid shallow, marshy waters during waterfowl hunting season. For hunting season dates, check the states' fish and wildlife websites: mass.gov/eea, ct.gov/deep, and dem.ri.gov.

Other safety tips include:

- Get off the water during lightning storms; lightning usually strikes the highest object in the vicinity. When you're in a boat on a lake, that means you.

- Know what to do if you capsize—and have experience doing it.

- Avoid dehydration by drinking plenty of liquids.

- Avoid areas with a lot of high-speed boating.

- Check the weather forecast before going out.

- If appropriate, check times of low and high tides.

EQUIPMENT

For quietwater paddling, avoid high-performance racing or tippy whitewater canoes and kayaks. Rent or borrow a boat before buying; selection will be easier with a little experience. Whether you prefer a canoe or kayak, look for a model with good initial and secondary stability. A boat with good initial stability and poor secondary stability will tip slowly, but once it starts, it may keep going. The best canoes for lakes and ponds have a keel or shallow V-shaped hull, and the bottoms are fairly flat from bow to stern. This helps them track in a straight line, even in a breeze. Kayaks perform extremely well in rough water, particularly if equipped with a foot-operated rudder and a sprayskirt to keep from taking on water.

If you like out-of-the-way paddling requiring portages, get a Kevlar (strong, lightweight carbon fiber) boat if you can afford it. We paddle a rugged, high-capacity 18-foot, 4-inch Mad River Lamoille canoe that weighs just 60 pounds; a 15-foot, 9-inch Mad River Independence solo canoe that weighs less than 40 pounds; a 14-foot Wenonah Wigeon kayak that weighs 38 pounds; and a 14-foot Wilderness Systems Tchaika kayak that weighs 32 pounds. (Manufacturers have replaced these with newer, similar models.) If you plan to paddle alone, consider a sea kayak or a solo canoe in which you sit (or kneel) close to the boat's center. Paddling a well-designed solo canoe is far easier than paddling a two-seater by yourself. The touring or sea kayak—with its long, narrow design, low profile to the wind, and two-bladed paddling style—is faster and more efficient to paddle than a canoe.

A padded portage yoke in place of the center thwart (a crosswise, left-to-right strut) on a canoe is essential if you plan on much carrying. With unpadded yokes, wear a life vest with padded shoulders. Attach a rope—called a painter—to the bow so that you can secure the boat when you stop for lunch, line it up or down a stream, and—if the need ever arises—grab on to it in an emergency. We both have embarrassing stories about not using a painter to secure the boat. Wind can cause Kevlar boats to disappear very quickly, and it's not fun to watch your boat bobbing away in a stiff wind!

Choose light, comfortable paddles. For canoeing, we use a relatively short (48- or 50-inch), laminated, bent-shaft paddle. The paddle, a composite of various woods to give it strength, has a synthetic tip to protect the blade. Straight-shaft paddles work well, but bent-shaft paddles allow more efficient paddling because the downward force converts more directly into forward thrust. Always carry at least one spare paddle per group, particularly on longer trips, in case you break a paddle or a porcupine gets hold of one.

PADDLING TECHNIQUE

On a quiet pond, does it matter if you use the proper J-stroke, the sweep stroke, or the draw? No. Learning some of these strokes, however, can make paddling more relaxing and enjoyable. We watch lots of novices zigzagging along, frantically switching sides, shouting orders fore and aft. People have told us about marriage counseling sessions devoted to paddling technique!

If you are new to the sport and want to learn canoeing or kayaking techniques, buy a book or participate in a paddling workshop, such as those offered by the Appalachian Mountain Club (activities.outdoors.org), equipment retailers, and boat manufacturers. See Appendix B (page 321) for some recommended books on canoeing and kayaking.

Start out on small ponds. Practice paddling into, with, and across the wind. On a warm day, close to shore, with your PFD on and others to help you if needed, practice capsizing. Intentionally tipping your boat will give you an idea of how easily it can upend. Try to get back into the boat away from shore.

Bailing water out of a kayak while treading water is impossible. Use a hand pump—either a boat-mounted permanent one or a portable one. Two people should be able to right a canoe, bailing out most of the water. (Keep a bailer fastened to a thwart.) Getting back in the boat is another story. Try climbing in simultaneously from opposite sides. If that doesn't work, grab onto the boat from opposite sides, and kick your way to shore. Good luck!

PADDLING WITH KIDS

When canoeing with kids, keep calm and try to make it fun. Even though you may be plenty warm from paddling, children can get cold while sitting in the boat. Remember that everyone should wear PFDs at all times, and PFDs will help keep children warm. Kids especially also need protection from sun and biting insects. Watch for signs of discomfort. Set up a cozy place where youngsters can sleep; after the initial excitement of paddling fades, a gently rolling canoe often makes children drowsy, especially near the end of a long day. For lengthy excursions, make sure to bring a waterproof sack with dry clothes for everyone.

HOW TO USE THIS BOOK

For each trip in the book, we provide a list of basic information, a map, directions, and a short description of what you'll see.

TRIP INFORMATION

At the start of each trip description, we include the location, DeLorme and U.S. Geological Survey (USGS) map information, area covered by the trip, an estimate of time required for a leisurely paddle, habitat type (that is, type of environment you will encounter), types of game fish, predominant animals and kinds of vegetation you should expect to see, public campgrounds, contact details, camping information, and notes about development or hazards to avoid. For information on private campgrounds, see the extensive lists in the DeLorme atlases.

Choose larger bodies of water and longer rivers when you have more time and a good weather forecast. Under windy conditions, opt for smaller waterways. Most entries include substantial shallow-water marshlands.

Note that although we list fish species for each destination, specific or general advisories against eating or reducing consumption of caught fish from all bodies of water exist, particularly for pregnant and nursing women and for children. Advisories do not apply to stocked hatchery fish. We include specific and general advisories in Appendix A on page 319.

MAPS

In addition to the maps included in this guide, we recommend that you use the most recent editions of DeLorme's *Massachusetts Atlas & Gazetteer* (6th edition) and *Connecticut/Rhode Island Atlas & Gazetteer* (5th edition), available at bookstores, outdoor retailers, and delorme.com. Note that these editions use page numbering that differs from the atlases in previous editions of this guide. We key each entry to the respective DeLorme atlas, which divides Massachusetts into 54 detailed 10″ x 14″ maps at a scale of 1:80,000, divides Connecticut into 42 maps, and divides Rhode Island into 12 maps, both at a scale of 1:65,000. The maps include most—but not all—access locations, campsites, road names, campgrounds, and parks, as well as other pertinent information. For more details on topography, marsh areas, and so on, refer to the 7.5-minute, 1:24,000-scale USGS topographical maps listed in each section. Google Maps and Google Earth also provide a wealth of data about waterways, especially using satellite view.

GETTING THERE

We give directions from the nearest city or major highway to the access location, providing distances between points, with the cumulative distance given in parentheses. We assume you will use a detailed highway map, such as DeLorme's atlases. We also include Global Positioning System (GPS) coordinates, with latitude and longitude values reported in degrees and minutes. If it's more convenient to use degrees as one number with decimals, instead of degrees and minutes, just divide the minutes by 60 to get a decimal. For example, to convert 42° 44.704', divide 44.704 minutes by 60 minutes per degree to get 0.745067°. Then add this decimal to 42° to get 42.745067°. You can use these coordinates on your cell phone to get directions to an access. For example, if you enter longitude 42° 44.704' N and latitude 70° 58.931' W into the search function on the iPhone Maps app or Google Maps app (as 42 44.704'n 70 58.931'w or as 42.745067n 70.982183w), you'll get directions to the Crane Pond/Parker River access.

WHAT YOU'LL SEE

The trip descriptions, each a few paragraphs long, give details about the area's natural features. Those details include birds, animals, and plants that you will likely see and, in some cases, prominent geological or historical features. Bringing field guides to birds, plants, and animals—along with waterproof binoculars—would be a great help in identifying and enjoying what you see.

Happy paddling!

STEWARDSHIP AND CONSERVATION

Diverse wetlands—among the richest, most readily accessible ecosystems—provide wonderful opportunities for paddlers to learn about nature. You can visit crystal-clear mountain ponds, slow-flowing rivers, and fascinating bog habitats. You can observe hundreds of species of birds; dozens of mammal, turtle, and snake species; and hundreds of plant and insect species. Some quite rare species, such as a delicate bog orchid or a family of otters, offer a real treat. But even ordinary plants and animals lead to exciting discoveries and hours of enjoyment.

In essays separate from the trip descriptions, we describe a few interesting plants and animals you might encounter, along with more general topics. The essays and accompanying pen-and-ink illustrations by Cathy Johnson appear throughout the book. We hope this additional information will enhance your own observations.

DO WE REALLY WANT TO TELL PEOPLE ABOUT THE BEST PLACES?

People have asked us how we could, in good conscience, tell others about remote, unspoiled places. After all, increased visitation would make these locations less idyllic. After spending many an hour grappling with this difficult issue as we paddled along, we concluded that people who experience wild, remote areas firsthand will come to value them and to build support for their protection.

For many lakes and ponds, protection means purchase of threatened surrounding areas by state or local governments or by private organizations such as The Nature Conservancy. On other bodies of water, restricting high-speed boating offers the best form of protection.

Wetlands perform extremely important functions, including recharging groundwater, helping control floods, supporting fishing and waterfowl hunting, and providing habitat for hundreds of species, including many that are rare and endangered. Even low-impact uses, such as canoeing and kayaking, can substantially affect fragile marsh habitat. Paddling can disturb nesting loons and eagles, rare turtles, and delicate bog orchids. Canoes and kayaks can carry invasive plants and other harmful organisms from one body of water to another. Be sure to clean off your boat before you visit other water bodies.

You can go even further than the adage "Take only photographs, leave only footprints." Carry along a trash bag and clean up after less thoughtful individuals. If each of us did the same, we would all enjoy more attractive places to paddle. Motorboat users tend to have a bad reputation when it comes to leaving trash; paddlers should have the opposite reputation, which could come in handy when seeking restrictions on high-impact resource use.

For information on low-impact camping and other uses of fragile habitats, see *Soft Paths: How to Enjoy the Wilderness without Harming It*, 4th edition, by Rich Brame and David Cole (Stackpole Books, 2011). Also, visit the website of Leave No Trace (lnt.org), an organization dedicated to teaching people how to minimize their outdoor impact; read a brief outline on page xxxvii.

Besides reducing our impact on the environment, we can actively work to protect fragile populations of bald eagle, osprey, otter, and other wildlife. If we want to preserve these species and their habitats for future generations, we must demand that elected and appointed officials make wildlife preservation and ecosystem protection a higher priority. We can also join conservation organizations—such as AMC, Sierra Club, The Nature Conservancy, Audubon Society, and many others—so that when those organizations speak about preserving the environment, their voices carry the weight of tens of thousands of like-minded members.

Some of the waters featured in this book have more protection now than when the first edition was published in 1993. Many bodies of water in the three states now impose a 10 HP limit on motors, or prohibit internal combustion motors, or prohibit personal watercraft, or impose speed limits. The land around several of our most treasured water resources has received protection from development forever. However, while various land trusts continue to protect more of the shoreline along a few key ponds and lakes, most other bodies of water suffer from continued development and more high-speed boating. When we update this guide in a few years, we hope to report a lot more progress in protecting these lakes and ponds.

We heartily applaud Massachusetts for banning lead sinkers and jigs weighing less than 1 ounce, although it seems unlikely that Connecticut and Rhode Island will follow suit in the near future.

AMC'S CONSERVATION EFFORTS

Because the lakes and ponds of New England are beautiful, their real estate value is high, which can lead to excess development and harm to the environment. In response, the Appalachian Mountain Club has worked hard to protect the undeveloped shorelines of the Northeast. AMC, with other environmental organizations and land trusts, has successfully secured millions of dollars in funding from federal and state open space programs to protect critical lands with high aesthetic, recreational, and ecological waterfront values. AMC has been a leader in protecting riparian lands during the licensing of hydropower projects, knowing that in return for using the public waters, the hydroelectric dam owners have an obligation to create shoreline management plans and mitigate their operational effects on the watershed.

Freshwater streams, lakes, and ponds provide beauty and habitat across the northeastern landscape that AMC works to protect and understand. AMC's Research team conducts freshwater science and monitoring that span mountain lakes and streams to large urban rivers. For example, the Merrimack River Watershed is among the largest in New England, covering over 5,000 square miles. AMC has monitored remote ponds and streams in this watershed's headwaters in the Pemigewasset Wilderness area in the White Mountain National Forest to understand how climate change and pollutants like acid rain are affecting freshwater ecosystems. Continuing downstream, AMC works in freshwaters in the urbanized communities of Manchester, New Hampshire and Lowell and Lawrence, Massachusetts, to understand how mercury has accumulated from air pollution and a legacy of industrialization. Specifically, in the Dragonfly Mercury Project, it engages community members—including youth, school groups, and families—in collecting dragonflies that serve as biological indicators for mercury pollution. Mercury manifests in foodwebs, where it can present risks to wildlife and humans. With partners, AMC extends the mercury research to the Concord, Assabet, and Sudbury Rivers along with the Nashua River. The information gathered can help resource managers and community members inform the people who live and recreate in these rivers and freshwaters, and it underpins AMC's ongoing efforts to address air pollution and climate change through policy and advocacy.

PUBLIC ACCESS

Private land abuts many waterways. To ensure continued access, please respect this property. Never camp or picnic on private land without permission. In many places, adjacent landowners also own the riverbed or lake bed, which means that even if you have the right to paddle there, you may not have the right to fish there.

The southern New England states have done a commendable job of providing public access to waterways, either by establishing conservation easements or by purchasing land and water outright. We have listed only public access locations, but private property bounds most bodies of water. Never launch your boat from private land without getting permission first, and do not get out along the shore on land posted as private. Cooperation will help keep waterways open to paddlers.

LEAVE NO TRACE

The Appalachian Mountain Club is a national educational partner of the Leave No Trace Center for Outdoor Ethics. The center is an international nonprofit organization dedicated to responsible enjoyment and active stewardship of the outdoors by all people, worldwide. The organization teaches children and adults vital skills to minimize their impacts when they are outdoors. Leave No Trace is the most widely accepted outdoor ethics program used today on public lands across the nation by all types of outdoor recreationists. Leave No Trace unites five federal land management agencies—United States Forest Service, National Park Service, Bureau of Land Management, Army Corps of Engineers, and U. S. Fish and Wildlife Service—with manufacturers, outdoor retailers, user groups, educators, organizations such as AMC, and individuals.

These seven principles guide the Leave No Trace ethic:

- **Plan ahead and prepare.** Know the terrain and any regulations applicable to the area you're planning to visit, and be prepared for extreme weather or other emergencies. This will enhance your enjoyment and ensure that you've chosen an appropriate destination. Small groups have less impact on resources and the experience of other backcountry visitors.

- **Travel and camp on durable surfaces.** Travel and camp on established trails and campsites, rock, gravel, dry grasses, or snow. Good campsites are found, not made. Camp at least 200 feet from lakes and streams, and focus activities on areas where vegetation is absent. In pristine areas, disperse use to prevent the creation of campsites and trails.

- **Dispose of waste properly.** Pack it in, pack it out. Inspect your camp for trash or food scraps. Deposit solid human waste in catholes dug 6 to 8 inches deep, at least 200 feet from water, camp, and trails. Pack out toilet paper and hygiene products. To wash yourself or your dishes, carry water 200 feet away from streams or lakes and use small amounts of biodegradable soap. Scatter strained dishwater.

- **Leave what you find.** Cultural or historic artifacts, as well as natural objects such as plants or rocks, should be left as found.

- **Minimize campfire impacts.** Cook on a stove. Use established fire rings, fire pans, or mound fires. If a campfire is built, keep it small and use dead sticks found on the ground.

- **Respect wildlife.** Observe wildlife from a distance. Feeding wildlife alters their natural behavior. Protect wildlife from your food by storing rations and trash securely.

- **Be considerate of other visitors.** Be courteous, respect the quality of other visitors' backcountry experience, and let nature's sounds prevail.

AMC is a national provider of the Leave No Trace Master Educator course. AMC offers this five-day course, designed especially for outdoor professionals and land managers, as well as the shorter two-day Leave No Trace Trainer course, at locations throughout the Northeast. For Leave No Trace information and materials, contact the Leave No Trace Center for Outdoor Ethics at 800-332-4100, or visit lnt.org. For a schedule of AMC Leave No Trace courses, see activities.outdoors.org.

SECTION 1

EASTERN MASSACHUSETTS

The Eastern Massachusetts bodies of water included here range from the New Hampshire border to just south of Boston, and westward to I-495. This section includes truly historic areas—such as Walden Pond and the Charles, Concord, and Sudbury rivers—along with rivers and ponds that drain into Massachusetts Bay and into bays along the North Shore.

Although this book focuses primarily on ponds and lakes, in this section the major portions of ten entries include rivers. Much of early United States history unfolded on these rivers, as did the history of American Indians. The Charles, Concord, Sudbury, Assabet, Neponset, and Blackstone rivers provided opportunities for navigation, mill sites, shipbuilding, and more. The Blackstone included a canal with locks and powered the Stanley Woolen Mill. Today, you can paddle sections of the Blackstone River and the Blackstone Canal, as well as walk or bike the old towpath. Perhaps surprisingly, much of these river corridors remains free from development. The lengthy upper Charles River section undulates through forests rich with birds, deer, and other wildlife, as well as myriad trees and shrubs; every time we visit the Charles, we revel in its wildness.

Along the North Shore, we include a coastal river estuary, as well as more inland locations. Essex Marsh provides a great opportunity to paddle an extensive estuary and to hike on an island loaded with wildlife. The marsh presents a challenge because of strong tides and winds that often blow unimpeded across the low terrain.

Inland from there, you can paddle an upper Parker River section that flows on a barely perceptible current through Crane Pond Wildlife Management Area, a swamp that stands in marked contrast to the coastal rivers. Although not quite as swampy, the Ipswich River and Wenham Swamp offer another great wilderness paddling experience; because of the slightly stronger currents and an 8-mile length, many people use two vehicles, making this a one-way trip.

We also include Ashland and Whitehall reservoirs, dammed up originally to provide water for a burgeoning population. No longer used as water supplies, they now provide excellent recreation opportunities.

At some point, all Northeast paddlers should make a pilgrimage to Walden Pond to stand where Thoreau stood and to breathe in the air hovering over the pond that inspired so much transcendentalist literature.

TRIP 1

CRANE POND AND PARKER RIVER

Narrow, marshy Parker River flows through a wildlife management area filled with birds and wetlands plants. High water levels, especially in spring, make paddling through meandering channels much easier. Use shorter boats here. You will see many waterfowl, a diverse array of aquatic plants, and more.

LOCATION Georgetown, Groveland, and Newbury, MA

MAPS *Massachusetts Atlas & Gazetteer*, Map 19: C4, Map 29: A6; USGS Exeter, Georgetown

LENGTH 3 miles one way

TIME 6 hours round trip

HABITAT TYPE Narrow, shallow, marshy stream

FISH Trout, largemouth bass, pickerel (see fish advisory, Appendix A)

INFORMATION Crane Pond Wildlife Management Area, mass.gov/info-details/crane-pond-wma

CAMPING Salisbury Beach State Reservation

GETTING THERE

Southern Access From I-95, Exit 81, go west on Central Street, and turn left on Main Street at the stop sign. Go 1.8 miles, and turn right on Thurlow Street. Go 1.0 mile (2.8 miles) to the access on the right. Park just before the bridge. It's easier to put in on the far side of the bridge. This is the preferred access. **42° 44.704' N, 70° 58.931' W**

Northern Access From I-95, Exit 81, go west on Central Street, and turn left on Main Street at the stop sign. Go 0.3 mile to the access on the right. **42° 45.328' N, 70° 56.971' W**

WHAT YOU'LL SEE

Crane Pond Wildlife Management Area, which surrounds this section of the Parker River, offers a superb paddling environment. The river, more like a creek here, varies from canoe width to about 20 feet as it wanders through an extensive marsh; beaver keep most of the channel open. When we paddled here in the first week of August, sunfish redds (shallow depressions) indicated that the fish were spawning.

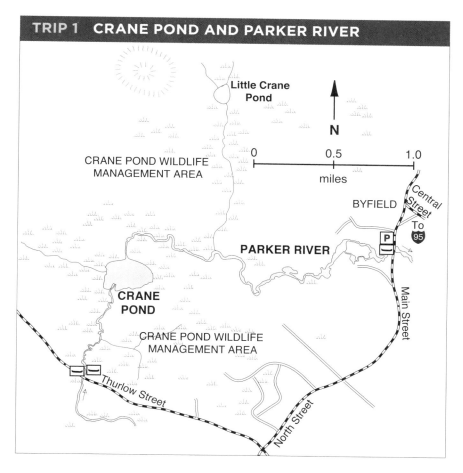

TRIP 1   CRANE POND AND PARKER RIVER

Axillary flowers and three-leaved whorls make swamp loosestrife easy to identify.

With its sharp bends and 180-degree turns, the waterway will test your paddling skills. Kayakers may have a difficult time here, except maybe during times of high water when the channels widen; use a short boat and short paddle. To make any kind of reasonable progress, the bow person in a canoe should have a perfected draw stroke; even then, a certain amount of backing and filling will be necessary to negotiate tight turns. We also prefer using a short canoe here. Whatever type of craft you choose, paddling this portion of river will be well worth the effort.

Aquatic plants dominate this environment. Pickerelweed lines the shore in most areas, along with abundant swamp loosestrife, with its graceful arching bows that drape out over the waterway. The dominant underwater plant, at least in early August, seemed to be a species of yellow-flowered bladderwort. Widely dispersed dwarf red maples stand on slightly higher ground throughout the swamp. Look for clumps of arrowhead, sweetgale, narrow-leaved cattail, buttonbush, yellow pondlily, and American white waterlily. The floating leaves of pondweed, watershield, and lesser amounts of smartweed occur sporadically throughout. In places, especially in open areas subject to wind, rafts of duckweed pile up and seriously impede paddling later in summer. The duckweed is another reason to paddle here during spring high water.

We saw only small amounts of one invasive species, purple loosestrife. We also noticed patches of an interesting parasitic plant, common dodder (*Cus-*

cuta gronovii), a native plant that grows throughout most of the United States and Canada. Its orange, leafless, parasitic stems entwine around marshland shrubs, from which dodder absorbs its nutrients. Many other species of dodder, most of them invasive, occur throughout the United States. Few species, however, inhabit wetlands, and *C. gronovii* is by far the most abundant dodder in the Northeast, especially in wetlands.

After flowing through Crane Pond, the river narrows, bumping up against some large boulders and nearby banks, whose main tree species include white pine, red oak, red maple, and hemlock. We paddled over two drowned-out beaver dams and observed downy woodpeckers here, along with nuthatches, cardinals, robins, crows, and more. Out on the open water, look for other bird species, such as red-winged blackbird, eastern kingbird, tree swallow, Canada goose, black duck, and wood duck.

We recommend starting from the Thurlow Road access, paddling out and back. That way, depending on water levels, the amount of surface-clogging vegetation, and your paddling skill, you can decide to turn around at the appropriate time.

TRIP 2

ESSEX MARSH AND CHOATE (HOG) ISLAND

Essex Marsh is a large saltwater estuary that harbors a large island wildlife refuge with hiking trails. This is a wonderful place to explore and to study saltwater species. At times, tides and wind can cause difficult paddling conditions; novice paddlers should steer clear of Essex Marsh.

LOCATION Essex and Ipswich, MA

MAPS *Massachusetts Atlas & Gazetteer*, Map 30: A2, B2; USGS Ipswich, Rockport

AREA 3,000 acres

TIME All day

HABITAT TYPE Salt marsh estuary; island hiking; dunes

FISH Striped bass, saltwater species (see fish advisory, Appendix A)

INFORMATION Crane Wildlife Refuge, The Trustees of Reservations,

617-542-7696, thetrustees.org; excellent description in *Nature Walks along the Seacoast* (see Appendix B); Great Marsh Coalition, greatmarsh.org; tide charts, usharbors.com

CAMPING Salisbury Beach State Reservation

TAKE NOTE Some development; lots of main-channel boat traffic in summer; watch out for wind, waves, and tides, especially near Route 133 bridge and in Castle Neck River; always wear your PFD; not recommended for novice paddlers

GETTING THERE

From Route 128, Exit 53, go west on Route 133 for 3.3 miles to the access in Essex, on the right, across from Woodman's Restaurant. After unloading your boat, park at a small roadside park behind the restaurant. **42° 37.859' N, 70° 43.48' W**

Parking downtown is sometimes difficult. You can also launch from Clammer's Beach at the end of Conomo Point Road. From Woodman's, go east on Route 133 for 1.5 miles, and turn left on Harlow Street. Go 0.6 mile (2.1 miles), and turn left on Conomo Point Road. Go 0.9 mile (3.0 miles) to the access on the right. **42° 39.065' N, 70° 44.744' W**

WHAT YOU'LL SEE
ESSEX MARSH

Essex Marsh, just an hour north of Boston, offers splendid paddling and hiking. Spend a few hours or an entire day exploring this interesting area. The Essex and Castle rivers and several thousand acres of tidal creek and salt marsh compose Essex Marsh, part of the 20,000-acre Great Marsh. Castle Neck's sand dunes, beach plum, and bayberry highlands protect the marsh from open ocean. In the middle of the marsh, Choate Island (also known as Hog Island), a rather dramatic drumlin—a rock and soil deposit formed by a receding glacier—dominates the local topography. It rises steeply on the western side to 177 feet and then slopes gradually east. The Trustees of Reservations owns 697 acres that include Choate Island, Long Island, and three smaller islands, maintaining them as Crane Wildlife Refuge.

We love visiting here, especially during the week, when there's less boat traffic in the main channels. With an 8-foot tide differential and extensive mud flats at low tide, try to avoid paddling at low tide.

Paddling to the left on the Essex River will shortly take you to the Route 133 bridge. While the salt marsh on the inland side of the bridge offers enjoyable exploration, the tidal current under the bridge, where the channel constricts, causes very fast and tricky currents. Use caution!

We prefer going to the right to Choate Island, following the widening channel, rounding successive curves, and proceeding generally north. Look back periodically, noting landmarks that will guide your return. As water levels change, the area can look quite different. We recommend taking along a compass and a photocopy of the map in this book.

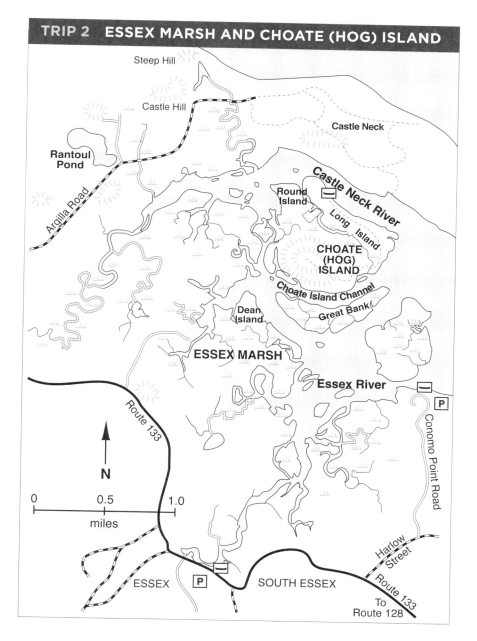

TRIP 2 ESSEX MARSH AND CHOATE (HOG) ISLAND

Steep Hill

Castle Hill

Castle Neck

Rantoul Pond

Argilla Road

Castle Neck River

Round Island

Long Island

CHOATE (HOG) ISLAND

Choate Island Channel

Dean Island

Great Bank

ESSEX MARSH

Essex River

P

Conomo Point Road

Route 133

N

0   0.5   1.0
miles

ESSEX   P   SOUTH ESSEX

Harlow Street

Route 133

To Route 128

To hike on the islands and through Crane Wildlife Refuge, approach the boat landing on the north side of Long Island. Aim initially for the steeper, western end of Choate Island. As you get near, head off into Choate Island Channel right in front of the island, following it to the right and then around the island, or—if the tide is high enough—continue around the island's west side. The more direct western route suffers from exposed tidal flats on either side of low tide. Visitors can land their boats at Long Island between 8 A.M. and sunset year-round.

You can venture a little way into Lee's Creek between Choate Island and Round Island, but much of this area is protected as bird nesting habitat. The water around the island is exceptionally clear, with white sand visible even 10 or 15 feet down. Paddling across to Castle Neck, explore the sand dunes and Crane Beach, also owned by The Trustees of Reservations. If you pull your boat up on Castle Neck, watch for rising tide, and be careful not to damage the fragile dune ecosystem.

You could also explore Castle Neck River and the inlet creeks and channels that reach into the salt marsh, an extremely interesting ecosystem dominated by smooth cordgrass (*Spartina alterniflora*) and saltmeadow cordgrass (*S. patens*). At high tide you can travel deeply into the little side creeks and look out over thousands of acres of *Spartina*. At low tide, watch for mussels clinging to the sod banks, fiddler crabs, perhaps horseshoe crabs, and clumps of seaweed clinging to rocks. On the mud flats, keep an eye out for various sandpipers and gulls. You should also see osprey and many other bird species here, especially during migration.

From the south, Choate Island's distinct profile rises above the salt marsh.

Wind, blowing across a fairly broad expanse of water and low salt marsh, can present even more of a problem than tidal currents, generating sizable waves. Wear your PFD here; novice paddlers should avoid this area.

CHOATE ISLAND

A wonderful trail extends southeast from the Long Island dock and across to Choate Island. Maintained by The Trustees of Reservations, the route goes past a large barn on Long Island, a newer Cape Cod–style cottage, and the original Choate House on the main island. Thomas Choate built the house, a beautiful example of early eighteenth-century architecture, between 1725 and 1740. From Choate House, the trail extends uphill to the island's peak, passing through the oddly out-of-place 95-acre spruce forest planted in the 1930s by Richard Crane, the Chicago plumbing magnate, who purchased the island and much of the surrounding land in the early 1900s.

Until recently Crane Wildlife Refuge hosted a large deer population, typically numbering from 50 to 75. With no hunting, and native predators long gone, the deer became quite tame. Since the mid-1980s, however, Lyme disease, borne by deer ticks, has become a major problem on isolated islands such as this. To reduce the deer population in an effort to control deer ticks, the refuge has permitted limited bow hunting in recent years; numbers have decreased, and deer have become much more wary of humans.

TRIP 3

IPSWICH RIVER AND WENHAM SWAMP

Wenham Swamp offers one of a few opportunities in Massachusetts for an on-site canoe and kayak camping trip. This pristine swamp is a favorite of bird-watchers.

LOCATION Hamilton, Ipswich, Topsfield, and Wenham, MA

MAPS *Massachusetts Atlas & Gazetteer*, Map 29: B6, Map 30: B1; USGS Ipswich, Salem

LENGTH 8 miles one way; can be paddled both directions

TIME 1 to 2 days; shorter trips possible

HABITAT TYPE Slow, meandering river through vast marshland; some islands; overhanging trees and vines

FISH Brook, brown, and rainbow trout; largemouth bass; white perch (see fish advisory, Appendix A)

INFORMATION massaudubon.org/places-to-explore/wildlife-sanctuaries /ipswich-river

CAMPING Ipswich River, Perkins Island (Perkins Camping limited to Mass Audubon members)

TAKE NOTE No development; no motors

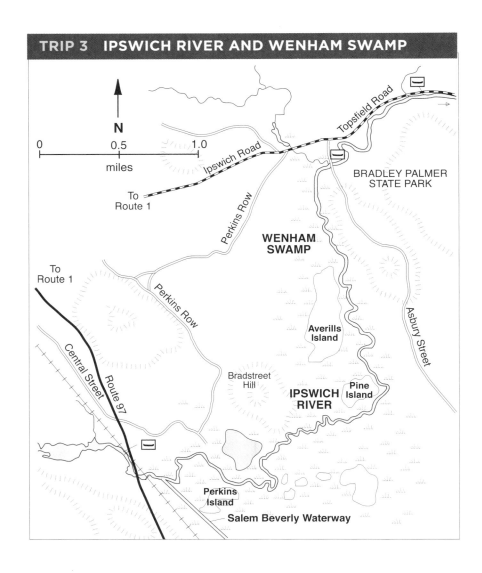

TRIP 3   IPSWICH RIVER AND WENHAM SWAMP

GETTING THERE

Route 97 From the junction of Routes 1 and 97 in Topsfield, go 0.7 mile south on Route 97 to the access on the right. **42° 37.539′ N, 70° 56.175′ W**

Asbury Street From the junction of Route 1 and Ipswich Road, go 1.2 miles east on Ipswich Road, and turn right on Asbury Street. Go 0.2 mile (1.4 miles total) to the access by the bridge. We do not recommend this access because of limited parking and because you can't get your car completely off the road. **42° 39.238′ N, 70° 54.718′ W**

Ipswich Road From the junction of Asbury Street and Ipswich Road, go 0.3 mile east on Ipswich Road to the access on the right. This and the Asbury Street access are part of Bradley Palmer State Park. **42° 39.539′ N, 70° 54.42′ W**

WHAT YOU'LL SEE

We love following the Ipswich River's narrow twists and turns as it meanders through vast, tree-filled Wenham Swamp. Silver maple dominates the shoreline, interspersed with large swamp white oak, willow, red maple, cherry, and white pine. Trees reach out over the water, lending a closed-in, protected feeling. The section included here courses for 8 miles, which could easily require a full day or more to paddle, especially if you explore side channels and hidden coves and stop for a picnic lunch.

We especially enjoyed Perkins Island—where Mass Audubon members can reserve a campsite—with its huge straight-trunked trees. Its relatively clear understory stands in stark contrast to the brushy banks and encroaching vegetation along most of the streambed. Prominent shrubs and vines include

A great egret stalks the shallows.

dogwood, wild grape, arrowwood, and poison ivy. Royal and sensitive ferns share the banks with cardinal flower, while patches of American eelgrass and pondweed undulate in the gentle current.

Damselflies and painted turtles sun on the many deadfalls, and the constant presence of flitting songbirds holds one's attention for much of the way. We paddled right up to a rather unconcerned great egret and found a couple of cormorants fishing in one of the more open areas. Paddling back to the Route 97 access, retracing our route, we saw the swamp from a new perspective and continued to glimpse new things. We vowed to return to this wonderful spot soon . . . and often.

TRIP 4

STEARNS POND AND FIELD POND

Stearns and Field ponds, though relatively small, provide opportunities for a broad study of aquatic and shoreline plants. Extensive hiking trails lead to nine other ponds within Harold Parker State Forest. Camping is available on-site.

LOCATION Andover and North Andover, MA

MAPS *Massachusetts Atlas & Gazetteer*, Map 29: B4, B5; USGS Reading Area: Stearns Pond, 41 acres; Field Pond, 59 acres

TIME 3 hours, more if you study the plants or portage into other ponds

HABITAT TYPE Shallow, marshy ponds; hiking trails

FISH Largemouth bass, yellow perch (see fish advisory, Appendix A)

INFORMATION mass.gov/doc/harold-parker-state-forest-trail-map/download

CAMPING Harold Parker State Forest

TAKE NOTE No development; no motors

GETTING THERE

From Lawrence, go south on Route 114. When Routes 114 and 125 split, go 3.8 miles on Route 114, and turn right into Harold Parker State Forest. Go 0.8 mile (4.6 miles) to the Stearns Pond access on the left. **42° 37.142′ N, 71° 4.351′ W**

For Field Pond, go another 0.3 mile (4.9 miles), and turn right on Middleton Road at the T. Go 1.1 miles (6.0 miles), and turn left on Jenkins Road. Continue 0.8 mile (6.8 miles), and turn right on Harold Parker Road. The access is on the left in another 1.2 miles (8.0 miles). **42° 36.628′ N, 71° 6.492′ W**

From Salem, go north on Route 114 for 3.4 miles past the intersection with Route 62, turn left into the state forest entrance, and follow directions as above.

From I-93, Exit 35, go 2.6 miles north on Route 125, and turn right on Harold Parker Road (a hard right leads to Gould Road). Go 0.6 mile (3.2 miles) to Field Pond on the right. For Stearns Pond, continue 1.2 miles (4.4 miles), and turn left on Jenkins Road. Drive 0.8 mile (5.2 miles), and turn right on Middleton Road. Go 1.1 miles (6.3 miles), and turn left on Harold Parker Road. Continue 0.3 mile (6.6 miles) to the access on the right.

WHAT YOU'LL SEE

A collection of small ponds in Harold Parker State Forest, a half hour north of Boston, provides opportunity for very relaxing quietwater paddling. Of the eleven ponds in the forest, we focus on the two largest: Stearns Pond and Field Pond.

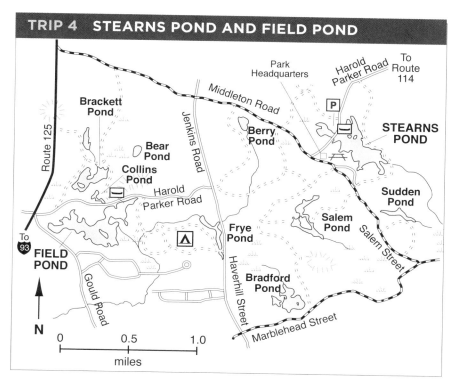

TRIP 4 STEARNS POND AND FIELD POND

The puffy, white, ball-like flowers of buttonbush, a shrub that can withstand root immersion for periods of time, bloom in summer.

Both ponds have highly varied shorelines—full of coves, inlets, and islands—so despite their small sizes, you can do a surprising amount of exploration. White pine; red and sugar maples; red, white, and scarlet oaks; and gray birch cloak the hillsides. Sweet pepperbush, highbush blueberry, winterberry, sheep laurel, and other shrubs form a dense tangle for most of the shoreline, but intermittent patches of needle-carpeted forest floor allow you to stretch your legs or to enjoy a picnic lunch.

Floating pond vegetation dominates the surface, particularly on Stearns Pond, and bur-reed, purple loosestrife, and cattail occur in the marshy spots. Bladderwort and other submerged plants provide hiding places for largemouth bass. Mossy hillocks of tree stumps remain from years ago when dams raised water levels. Small, carnivorous sundews grow amid the sphagnum moss on these stumps. Along the shallow, sandy shores, look for freshwater mussel shells left behind by industrious raccoons. The forest's vernal pools also provide habitat for rare blue-spotted salamanders (*Ambystoma laterale*).

The 3,500-acre state forest provides plenty of opportunities for exploring, especially if you don't mind a small portage. You can paddle any of the ponds as long as you park off the pavement. You can put in across the road from Field Pond into Collins Pond, for example, paddle to the north end, and then carry over to Brackett Pond. Getting to Salem Pond, the most remote, requires a considerable carry. To investigate these areas, use the Harold Parker State Forest trail map, which shows the forest's network of trails and unpaved roads, most closed to vehicles.

TRIP 5

CONCORD RIVER AND GREAT MEADOWS NATIONAL WILDLIFE REFUGE

Paddling this section of the historic Concord River, although not a wilderness experience, transports us back to the time of Ralph Waldo Emerson and Henry David Thoreau. This slow-flowing waterway can be paddled in both directions. Look for orioles and lots of other bird species in the tall trees lining the river.

LOCATION Bedford, Billerica, Carlisle, and Concord, MA

MAPS *Massachusetts Atlas & Gazetteer*, Map 28: C2, Map 40: A1, A2; USGS Billerica, Maynard

LENGTH 6.5 miles one way; shorter trips possible

TIME 6 hours round trip

HABITAT TYPE Slow-flowing river through wildlife refuge; shrubby marshlands

FISH Largemouth, smallmouth, and calico bass; yellow perch; pickerel; northern pike (see fish advisory, Appendix A)

INFORMATION *The Concord, Sudbury, and Assabet Rivers,* 2nd edition, by Ron McAdow (Bliss Publishing, 2000); Great Meadows National Wildlife Refuge, fws.gov/refuge/great-meadows, 978-443-4661; Sudbury, Assabet & Concord Wild & Scenic River Stewardship Council, sudbury-assabet -concord.org

CAMPING Harold Parker State Forest

TAKE NOTE Limited development; motors allowed, 10 MPH speed limit

GETTING THERE

From Route 62 in Concord, go 0.4 mile north on Lowell Road to the access on the left before the bridge. Drop your boat, and park along the street. **42° 27.971′ N, 71° 21.331′ W**

From the junction of Routes 4, 62, and 225, go 1.5 miles northwest on Route 225, and bear diagonally right on the access road, well before the bridge. **42° 30.546′ N, 71° 18.7′ W**

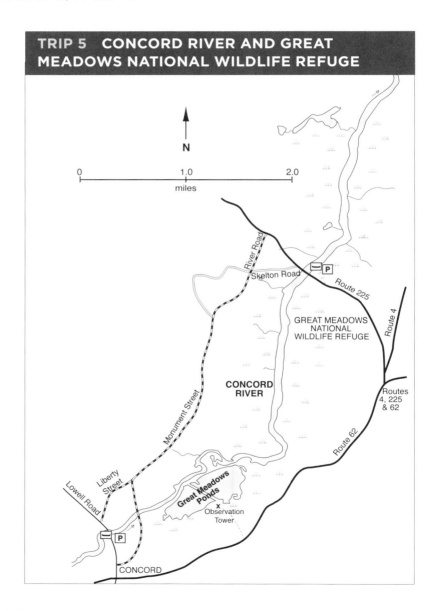

TRIP 5   CONCORD RIVER AND GREAT MEADOWS NATIONAL WILDLIFE REFUGE

WHAT YOU'LL SEE

The Concord River flows generally north with imperceptible current from the confluence of the Assabet and Sudbury rivers in Concord until it reaches Lowell and the Merrimack River. We focus here on a 6.5-mile section that flows through Great Meadows National Wildlife Refuge. Thoreau wrote about his travels on the Concord in 1839 in *A Week on the Concord and Merrimack Rivers.* This historic area includes the Old North Bridge, about which Emerson penned:

> By the rude bridge that arched the flood,
> Their flag to April's breeze unfurled,
> Here once the embattled farmers stood,
> And fired the shot heard round the world.

—Concord Hymn, *The Complete Works
of Ralph Waldo Emerson* (1904)

Motorboats use this section of the river but must comply with a 10 MPH speed limit. Paddling here on a June weekend, we saw more canoes and kayaks than motorboats. Because of the narrowness of the wildlife refuge on the river's west side, you will see a few large houses perched on lots above the riverbank, but they do not impinge much on this mostly undeveloped section of river.

High plant diversity characterizes this area, including American lotus (*Nelumbo lutea*), with its enormous yellow flowers, growing in impoundments within the wildlife refuge. This unusual plant is found in only a few New England locations but may be spreading (see "Waterlilies: Beautiful and Fascinating Flowers of the Pond," below). Dominant plants along the shrubby shoreline include buttonbush, smartweed, silver maple, pickerelweed, and invasive purple loosestrife. Towering oaks and white pines occur on higher ground. We also noticed patches of invasive watermilfoil and water chestnut. Common yellowthroats, white-throated sparrows, eastern kingbirds, grackles, and yellow warblers called from the underbrush, while crows, orioles, red-eyed vireos, chickadees, and robins called from the treetops. Tree swallows fed their nearly fully fledged young on a bare branch overhanging the river.

WATERLILIES: BEAUTIFUL AND FASCINATING FLOWERS OF THE POND

Various species of floating-leaved waterlilies (order Nymphaeales; families Nymphaeaceae and Cabombaceae) occur on most of the Northeast's shallow ponds, lakes, and slow-flowing rivers. These beautiful and ecologically important plants have fascinating physiologies.

We discuss three very common species here: American white waterlily (*Nymphaea odorata*) and yellow pondlily (genus *Nuphar*), both in the Nymphaeaceae, and watershield (*Brassenia schreberi*) in the Cabombaceae. Botanists believed until recently that two separate white waterlily species existed, but with the advent of rapid DNA fingerprinting, they determined that the two represented subspecies of the same plant. One form has green leaf undersides (*N.o. tuberosa*), the other purple (*N.o. odorata*).

Taxonomy of yellow pondlily has not been settled. Some botanists believe that the United States has as many as eight separate species, while others believe that it may be as few as one, with several subspecies. Time, and DNA fingerprinting, will tell.

Until very recently, botanists placed watershield in the Nymphaeaceae family. They have now placed it in the closely related Cabombaceae family.

We also describe here a larger and more dramatic member of this family, usually found farther south, that may be expanding its range into New England: American lotus (*Nelumbo lutea*).

Most waterlilies can grow in water as shallow as 6 inches or as deep as 15 feet—as long as the water is clear enough for sunlight to penetrate to the bottom, where photosynthesis occurs until leaves reach the surface in spring. The long, hollow petioles (stems) on waterlilies play an interesting role in transporting gases to and from underwater rhizomes. The plant somehow causes air to travel downward for respiration and pushes carbon dioxide upward. This process and the mechanisms driving it are not well understood. (We wonder if the "popping" or "snapping" sound we frequently hear when paddling on sunny days in shallow ponds might somehow be attributed to this air flow, instead of to the fish we had previously assumed to be the source.) Such mysteries make one realize how much people have yet to discover about the natural world, including some of the most common wetlands plants.

Numerous insects, snails, and amphibians are closely associated with waterlilies. You can often find speckled, sausage-shaped, jellied egg masses of pond snails on the undersides of leaves. You may see frogs and even young painted turtles sunning on larger leaves, and bass and pickerel often lurk in the shade just beneath the leaves.

American white waterlily. Gorgeous white (occasionally pink) flowers of this waterlily grace the surface of ponds throughout New England and well beyond. As with other waterlilies, stomata (microscopic leaf openings for CO_2 and O_2 exchange) occur on top of the leaf, while stomata of most other plants reside on the bottom. You will see its round leaves with a slit on one side growing almost anywhere, including the most polluted, stagnant ponds, its fragrant flowers often competing against the aroma of fouled water. The beauty of a pond whose surface is covered with white blossoms from this waterlily can thus belie the pond's true condition.

As with other members of the family, American white waterlily's underwater stems end in rhizomes that anchor the plant in the mud, with its leaves extending to the surface. We had observed this plant for years, unaware of a remarkable aspect of its physiology. After blooming on three of four successive days, during which the flowers open each morning and close in the afternoon, a coiling action of the stem pulls the flower head back underwater. There, the seeds develop in the fertilized flower head, taking three to four weeks to mature. The flower head becomes a sort of seed capsule, called an aril, which eventually breaks off and floats to the surface. After a few days, during which the aril could drift to the far reaches of the pond, it decomposes, releasing the seeds, which sink; some of them take root in the bottom mud.

Yellow pondlily. Large oblong leaves and a bright yellow, waxy, cuplike flower that may extend slightly above the water's surface characterize this genus. We're fascinated by the flower. What look like yellow petals are actually sepals, and what look like small yellow stamens are actually petals. A disklike stigma is in the center. Take a close-up photo with your phone, or, in a pinch, turn your binoculars around and look through the big end as a sort of magnifying glass to get a really detailed look at this flower. Of course, try to stay in your boat when you do this, and try not to drop your phone or binocs into the water.

As you might expect from their leaf size, yellow pondlily rhizomes can grow quite large. Sometimes they dislodge from the bottom through wave action, especially where motorboats zoom about at high speed. Huge mats sometimes form, which can provide significant obstacles to your boat's progress.

Watershield. This plant does not look anything like the species described above. It lacks showy flowers, and its small, oval leaves bear no slit. The petiole (stem) joins the leaf in the center, and a gelatinous, slimy film covers the stems and the reddish undersides of leaves.

Its small, obscure, reddish flowers actually change sex in order for the plant to reproduce. During a two-day period, the plant first functions as female, then as male. On the first day, the flower's stigmas (female reproductive part that transfers pollen to the ovary) accept pollen from other plants; at the day's end, the plant draws the flower underwater. The flower emerges on the second day, and the anthers (male reproductive part) release pollen into the wind. At the end of the second day, the flower submerges again to allow for seed development.

Aquatic biologists (no, not biologists who swim) have studied watershield's effects on blue-green algae, which release toxins into the water, and on aquatic plant species. They have learned that watershield exhibits allelopathy, which means that the plant releases chemicals into the environment that affect other species. In this case, the allelochemicals inhibit blue-green algae growth and the proliferation of other aquatic plant species. Toxic algae blooms have become increasingly prevalent in a warming, more polluted world, and the use of naturally occurring plant chemicals as biological controls would certainly be a positive step.

American lotus. Perhaps the most fascinating of all the species described here, this plant—native to the southeastern United States—has shown up in New England in recent years. An extensive stand occurs just north of the Massachusetts border in Brattleboro, Vermont, and the plants are found in several impoundments within Great Meadows National Wildlife Refuge just north of Concord, Massachusetts. Botanists believe these northern populations were introduced and may be spreading, which could become an invasive species problem.

American lotus sports huge, round, floating leaves—up to 24 inches in diameter—coated with microscopic hairs that prevent wetting. Water landing on the leaves beads up and runs off, keeping the leaves largely dry. The dramatic yellow flowers, among the largest of any North American plant—up to 10 inches in diameter—extend well above the water's surface. These thermogenic flowers generate heat that may help attract pollinating beetles. The pods that form after blooming contain hard, thick-walled, remarkably durable seeds (the dried seedpods are often used in flower arrangements). Lotus seeds discovered in Egyptian tombs thousands of years old have germinated and produced viable plants.

WALDEN POND

All paddlers in the Northeast, at some point, should make a pilgrimage to Walden Pond. Here we revere Henry David Thoreau, who penned in Walden *the reason why many of us seek solitude in nature:*

> *I went to the woods because I wished to live deliberately, to front only the essential facts of life, and see if I could not learn what it had to teach, and not, when I came to die, discover that I had not lived.*
> —Walden *(1854)*

LOCATION Concord, MA

MAPS *Massachusetts Atlas & Gazetteer*, Map 40: A1; USGS Maynard

AREA 61 acres

TIME 2 hours

HABITAT TYPE Historical glacial kettle-hole pond; hiking trails

FISH Rainbow and brown trout, largemouth and smallmouth bass (see fish advisory, Appendix A)

INFORMATION Walden Pond State Reservation, mass.gov/locations /walden-pond-state-reservation, 978-369-3254; $5 launch fee; Thoreau Society, thoreausociety.org

TAKE NOTE Recreation area development only; no internal combustion motors

GETTING THERE

From the Route 2 rotary in Concord, go 3.5 miles east, and turn right on Route 126. Go 0.5 mile (4.0 miles) to the access on the right. **42° 26.258′ N, 71° 20.12′ W**

From I-95, Exit 45, go about 4.5 miles west on Route 2, and turn left on Route 126. Go 0.5 mile (5.0 miles) to the access on the right.

WHAT YOU'LL SEE

Walden Pond has come a long way since the first edition of this book. In the intervening 30 years, a major revegetation effort has added tens of thousands of new native plants, restoring the shoreline and nearby trails to a condition not seen in 85 years.

The pond, a "kettle hole," formed 12,000 years ago when receding glaciers left behind a large chunk of ice buried in glacial till. Melting ice created a 100-foot-deep, sandy-bottomed pond, which provides superb swimming. The absence of any major inlet streams keeps Walden Pond relatively sterile, though; without stocking, it would provide little in the way of fishing.

We include the pond primarily for its historic significance. Simply paddling the same water that Thoreau and Ralph Waldo Emerson (two founders of the environmental movement) knew so well can give you—we have to say it—a transcendental experience. Henry David Thoreau lived at Walden Pond, on land owned by Emerson, from July 4, 1845, until September 1847, and he later reflected on the experience in *Walden*, published in 1854.

At the time Thoreau lived here, Walden Pond's woods were among the last in the Concord area not cleared for farming. He built a small one-room cabin near the pond's northern tip and spent his days studying natural history, gardening, reading, writing, and entertaining guests. His writing career began here, penning *A Week on the Concord and Merrimack Rivers*. In this book, he wrote about Walden and other ponds:

> A lake is the landscape's most beautiful and expressive feature.
> It is Earth's eye; looking into which the beholder measures the
> depth of his own nature.

Society's destruction of forests deeply affected Thoreau. In *Walden*, he wrote: "When I first paddled a boat on Walden it was completely surrounded

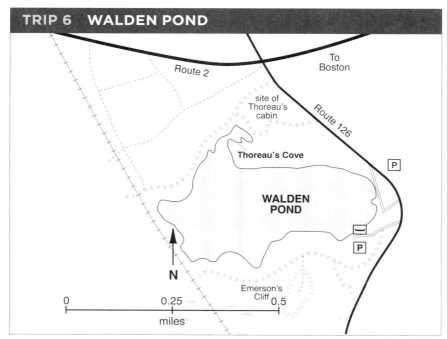

TRIP 6 WALDEN POND

SECTION 1: EASTERN MASSACHUSETTS

by thick and lofty pine and oak woods . . . but since I left those shores, the woodcutters have still further laid them waste." To compensate, Thoreau planted 400 white pines, but the great hurricane of 1938 knocked them down; look for the few remaining stumps above the house site.

When Thoreau lived here, loons occasionally visited the pond, but they disappeared, pushed away by encroaching civilization and a lack of fish. After the birds had been absent from Massachusetts for more than a century, a loon chick hatched in Fall River in 2020, the result of an intensive reintroduction program.

In the twentieth century, Walden became far more crowded than Thoreau could have imagined, in part from the fame he himself brought to the pond. In the early 1900s, as many as 2,000 tourists visited the pond per day. By the summer of 1935, after an 80-acre parcel of land around the pond had been granted to the commonwealth as a public park, as many as 485,000 people visited the pond each summer, with up to 25,000 visitors on a single Sunday. Today, visitors number 600,000 annually, with folks turned away on warm summer afternoons when the park reaches capacity.

Since 1975, the Massachusetts Department of Environmental Management has managed Walden Pond and has worked to restore its eroded banks and trails. If your schedule permits, come midweek after Labor Day or before Memorial Day or perhaps on a drizzly day that will help you reflect on the pond's historic past as you paddle the deserted shores.

TRIP 7

SUDBURY RIVER

The Sudbury River flows lazily through Great Meadows National Wildlife Refuge, making it easy to paddle both directions. Revel in the abundant birdlife and observe a variety of interesting aquatic plants.

LOCATION Concord, Lincoln, Sudbury, and Wayland, MA

MAPS *Massachusetts Atlas & Gazetteer*, Map 40: A1, B1; USGS Framingham, Maynard

LENGTH 10.6 miles one way; shorter trips possible

TIME All day

HABITAT TYPE Slow-flowing river through wildlife refuge; broad, shrubby marshlands

FISH Largemouth, smallmouth, and calico bass; yellow perch; pickerel; northern pike (see fish advisory, Appendix A)

INFORMATION *The Concord, Sudbury, and Assabet Rivers*, 2nd edition, by Ron McAdow (Bliss Publishing, 2000); Great Meadows National Wildlife Refuge, fws.gov/refuge/great-meadows, 978-443-4661; Sudbury, Assabet & Concord Wild & Scenic River Stewardship Council, sudbury-assabet -concord.org

TAKE NOTE Some development; motors allowed, 10 MPH speed limit

GETTING THERE

Access points are given in order, starting upstream (south end).

Pelham Island Road From the junction of Routes 20, 27, and 126 in Wayland, go west on Route 20. Turn immediately diagonally left on Pelham Island Road. Go 0.4 mile to the access on the right, just across the bridge. **42° 21.526' N, 71° 22.153' W**

Route 20/Boston Post Road From the junction of Routes 20, 27, and 126, go 0.7 mile west on Route 20 to the access on the right, just before the bridge. **42° 21.806' N, 71° 22.458' W**

River Road From the junction of Routes 20, 27, and 126, go 1.3 miles north on Route 27, and turn left on River Road. Access is immediately on the left. **42° 22.147' N, 71° 22.917' W**

Route 27/Old Sudbury Road From the junction of Routes 20, 27, and 126, go 1.3 miles north on Route 27; access is on the right, just before the bridge. **42° 22.452' N, 71° 22.867' W**

Sherman Bridge From the junction of Routes 117 and 126 in Lincoln, go 1.5 miles south on Route 126, and turn right on Lincoln Road. Go 0.7 mile (2.2 miles) to the access on either side. **42° 23.791' N, 71° 21.867' W**

Route 117/South Great Road From the junction of Routes 117 and 126, go 1.1 miles west on Route 117 to the access on the right, just before the bridge. **42° 25.205' N, 71° 21.853' W**

WHAT YOU'LL SEE

This section of the Sudbury River from Heard Pond downstream to Sudbury Road offers wonderful paddling through broad expanses of Great Meadows National Wildlife Refuge (Great Meadows NWR). In another 2.4 miles downstream from Sudbury Road, the Sudbury joins the Assabet to form the Concord River. You can paddle the Sudbury (and the Concord, which flows through another section of Great Meadows NWR) both directions through the lazy current.

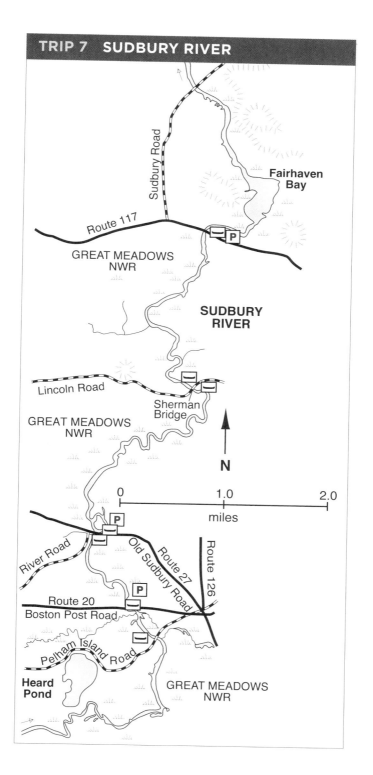

A mechanical harvester prepares to unload a few thousand pounds of water chestnut, a very destructive invasive plant.

The Sudbury lacks the breadth of the Concord but has broader surrounding meadows, filled with low-growing grasses and other marsh plants.

At times of high water, you can paddle up the Heard Pond outlet and explore the prime birding habitat of this small pond and the surrounding marshes and woods (part conservation lands, part Great Meadows NWR). At the other end of this section of the Sudbury, in Fairhaven Bay, look for ospreys fishing alongside the human anglers. In between, you can spend hours paddling along, enjoying the surrounding marshlands with their abundant birdlife and plants.

Look for buttonbush (*Cephalanthus occidentalis*), with its spherical white flowers and seed heads, growing along the banks and in the water. Purple loosestrife (*Lythrum salicaria*), an introduced species, grows on slightly higher ground. We found small patches of four-leaved water clover—aptly named *Marsilea quadrifolia*—an aquatic fern introduced into New England from Europe, along with larger patches of water chestnut, *Trapa natans*, another alien and far more destructive species. When we paddled here twenty years ago, the towns of Lincoln and Concord were harvesting truckloads of water chestnut from Fairhaven Bay, using a huge, floating harvesting machine.

The birds impressed us most, however, as they called from their streamside perches. We saw or heard many species, including bobolink, white-throated and song sparrows, barn and tree swallows, wood duck, eastern kingbird, red-winged blackbird, Baltimore oriole, grackle, tufted titmouse, common yellowthroat, yellow warbler, chickadee, cedar waxwing, mourning dove, killdeer, catbird, and cardinal.

ASSABET RIVER

This slow-flowing section of the Assabet River travels through an extensive marshland with inlets, islands, and multiple channels to explore. Look for typical wetlands species, especially great blue heron; we saw many fishing here, along with lots of other wetlands birds.

LOCATION Maynard and Stow, MA

MAPS *Massachusetts Atlas & Gazetteer*, Map 39: A6, B5; USGS Framingham, Hudson, Marlborough, Maynard

LENGTH 5.5 miles one way

TIME 6 hours round trip

HABITAT TYPE Slow-flowing marshy river

FISH Largemouth bass, yellow perch, pickerel (see fish advisory, Appendix A)

INFORMATION Assabet River National Wildlife Refuge, fws.gov/refuge/assabet-river; *The Concord, Sudbury, and Assabet Rivers*, 2nd edition, by Ron McAdow (Bliss Publishing, 2000)

TAKE NOTE Limited development; hiking trail

GETTING THERE

Sudbury/Boon Road From the junction of Routes 27 and 62 in Maynard, go 1.0 mile west on Route 62, and turn right on Routes 62 and 117. Go 1.9 miles (2.9 miles), and turn left on Route 62. Continue 1.1 mile (4.0 miles), and turn left on Whitman Street. After 0.9 mile (4.9 miles), turn left on Boon Road (immediately becomes Sudbury Road), and go 0.2 mile (5.1 miles) to the access at Magazu's Landing on the right, just after the bridge. **42° 24.698′ N, 71° 30.487′ W**

White Pond Road From the junction of Routes 27 and 62 in Maynard, go 1.0 mile west on Route 62, and turn right on Routes 62 and 117. Go 0.4 mile (1.4 miles), and turn left on Hastings Street. In 0.3 mile (1.7 miles), turn left on White Pond Road, and go 0.2 mile (1.9 miles) to the access on the left, just before the bridge. **42° 25.418′ N, 71° 28.502′ W**

Ice House Landing From the junction of Routes 27 and 62 in Maynard, go 1.0 mile west on Route 62, and turn left on Route 117. Go 0.2 mile (1.2 miles), turn right on Winter Street, and go 0.2 mile (1.4 miles) to Ice House Landing on the right. **42° 24.526′ N, 71° 28.096′ W**

WHAT YOU'LL SEE

Marshy Assabet River, on its way to join the Sudbury River at Concord, flows lazily through extensive marshlands upstream from the small Ben Smith Dam at Ice House Landing in Maynard. If time is limited, we prefer putting in at Boon Road or White Pond Road and paddling upstream. (You can paddle all the way upstream to the dam at Route 62.) Regardless of where you start, the Assabet offers a fabulous trip, with portions bordered by Assabet National

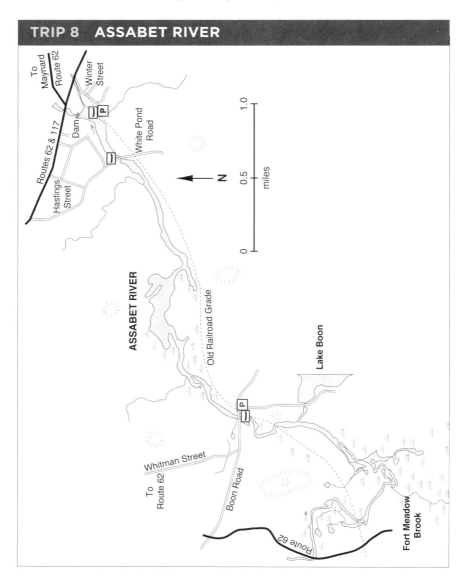

TRIP 8   ASSABET RIVER

To Maynard
Route 62
Winter Street
Dam
Routes 62 & 117
Hastings Street
White Pond Road
N
1.0
0.5
0
miles
ASSABET RIVER
Old Railroad Grade
Lake Boon
Whitman Street
To Route 62
Boon Road
Route 62
Fort Meadow Brook

Wildlife Refuge. It's also worth reading the kiosk information at Ice House Landing, maintained by the Maynard Conservation Commission. One of the kiosks contains this quote from Nathaniel Hawthorne in *Mosses from an Old Manse*:

> Running our boat against the current, between wide meadows, we turn aside into the Assabeth. A more lovely stream than this, for a mile above its junction with the Concord, has never flowed on earth—nowhere, indeed, except to lave the interior of a poet's imagination.

Hawthorne's river selection, like the section covered here, flows through extensive marshlands. The most interesting paddling lies upstream of Boon Road among the islands, marshy inlets, and multiple river channels. A little less than a mile downstream from Route 62, you can paddle south under a culvert up Fort Meadow Brook into a broad beaver marsh.

We didn't keep a great blue heron count, but we watched many of them fish the shallows and shorelines. Large groups of barn, bank, and tree swallows darted across the water, gathering insects. We also saw or heard white-breasted nuthatches, common yellowthroats, red-winged blackbirds, brown thrashers, cardinals, song sparrows, eastern kingbirds, spotted sandpipers, eastern phoebes, red-tailed hawks, turkey vultures, Canada geese, and robins.

Red maple, red oak, and other trees rim the marsh, while small amounts of jewelweed, yellow pondlily, American white waterlily, and pickerelweed appear along the grass-lined banks. Cattails sprout up here and there throughout the wetlands. Painted turtles perch on logs, plummeting into the water as you pass, and frogs dive down through the floating aquatic vegetation.

Although we saw some clumps of invasive purple loosestrife, we were more distressed to find large clumps of Japanese knotweed at the Boon Road access. In the last twenty years, the amount of this super-invasive plant has increased dramatically, particularly along Connecticut and Rhode Island waterways. An ornamental escape, knotweed thrives in disturbed areas, spreading easily through root rhizomes and from pieces of dislodged stems carried downstream by flowing water. These plant parts easily take root and then grow in dense patches that crowd out all native vegetation.

While you're here, you can bike or hike the former Boston and Maine Railroad railway bed. Groups involved with the Assabet River Rail Trail hope to acquire the remaining sections to complete the 12-mile Acton to Marlborough trail.

ASHLAND RESERVOIR

Ashland Reservoir offers a few hours of pleasant paddling along wooded shorelines over deep, clear water. The scenic shoreline harbors many tree species, with white pine and red oak in plentiful supply. Expect to see ducks and cormorant, along with other bird species.

LOCATION Ashland, MA

MAPS *Massachusetts Atlas & Gazetteer*, Map 51: A6; USGS Medfield

AREA 157 acres

TIME 2 hours, longer if you go for a swim

HABITAT TYPE Deep reservoir; wooded shoreline

FISH Brook, brown, and rainbow trout; largemouth and calico bass; yellow perch (see fish advisory, Appendix A)

INFORMATION Ashland State Park, mass.gov/locations/ashland-state -park, 508-881-4092, 508-435-4303 (off-season)

TAKE NOTE Little development; motors allowed up to 10 HP/10 MPH; no personal watercraft

GETTING THERE

From I-495, Exit 54A, go 5.5 miles east on West Main Street, which joins Route 135, and turn right on Main Street. Go 0.6 mile (6.1 miles), and veer right on Chestnut Street. Follow it for 1.3 miles (7.4 miles), and then turn right on South Street (unmarked). Go 0.4 mile (7.8 miles), and turn right on East Street to the access. **42° 13.938′ N, 71° 28.121′ W**

WHAT YOU'LL SEE

Ashland Reservoir, popular with canoers and kayakers, provides an excellent spot for a quiet morning or afternoon paddle. With a largely undeveloped shoreline, a 10 MPH limit for motors, and attractive woods surrounding the reservoir, Ashland offers some of the best lake paddling within the I-495 loop. A little more than 1 mile long and about 0.25 mile wide, the reservoir is quite deep, with little aquatic vegetation. Ashland State Park, at the north end off Route 135, offers picnic and swim areas, hiking trails, and a boat launch (open seasonally).

As you paddle north, the reservoir quickly opens up, with some deep coves on the west shore. (The west shore—with more variation—provides more interesting paddling than the east shore.) Red oak and white pine dominate the heavily wooded shoreline, but you will also see red maple, American chestnut, scarlet and white oaks, gray and black birches, sassafras, black gum, and pitch pine. Shrubs—sweet pepperbush, alder, blueberry, and winterberry—grow densely along the shore. During a mid-September paddle, we found some edible grapes overhanging the water along the east shore.

In places, you will see numerous shallow depressions in the sand a foot or two in diameter. Spawning sunfish keep these locations free of debris and organic matter. During summer, adult males valiantly guard these depressions, fanning the eggs that their mates deposited to provide adequate aeration. Along with lots of sunfish, Ashland Reservoir features healthy populations of largemouth bass, yellow perch, and stocked rainbow trout.

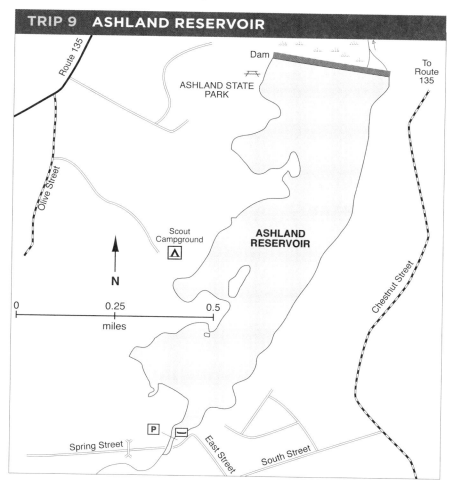

TRIP 9 ASHLAND RESERVOIR

WHITEHALL RESERVOIR

Whitehall Reservoir features several islands and protected bays, making it seem larger than it is. Plan for half a day or more to explore the various passageways surrounded by gorgeous forests. Islands contain unusual tree species for this latitude. Avoid this popular lake on busy summer weekends.

LOCATION Hopkinton, MA

MAPS *Massachusetts Atlas & Gazetteer*, Map 51: A4, A5; USGS Milford

AREA 592 acres

TIME 4 hours; 6 hours for thorough exploration and a picnic

HABITAT TYPE Reservoir; many islands and protected bays

FISH Trout, largemouth bass, white and yellow perch, pickerel, northern pike (see fish advisory, Appendix A)

INFORMATION Whitehall State Park, mass.gov/locations/whitehall-state -park, 508-435-4303

TAKE NOTE Little development; motors allowed, 12 MPH limit; no personal watercraft

GETTING THERE

From I-495, Exit 54A, go 1.2 miles east on West Main Street, and turn left on Route 135/Wood Street. Drive 2.7 miles (3.9 miles) to the access on the left. **42° 14.46′ N, 71° 34.338′ W**

WHAT YOU'LL SEE

Whitehall Reservoir at one time served as a water supply for areas west of Boston, but with Quabbin Reservoir's creation in 1939, drinking water from Whitehall was no longer needed, and the property eventually got turned into a state park. Its years of restricted access mean great boating today. Whitehall State Park encompasses the reservoir's entire shoreline but allows homeowners to erect small docks. From the water, the reservoir feels undeveloped and wild. Visitors sometimes see bald eagles here, and black bears have been spotted in the surrounding woods.

The highly varied, heavily wooded shoreline includes numerous deep coves and dozens of wonderful islands to explore, along with a few marshy areas.

The open woods invite picnicking. Mixed deciduous trees and conifers grow along the shore, as do mountain laurel and highbush blueberry, all typical southern Massachusetts plant species. Near the center of the reservoir on the west side, however, a fantastic grouping of islands sports far different vegetation, including Atlantic white cedar, tamarack, and black spruce—trees you would expect to see much farther north. On a quiet weekday morning, weaving in and out of these almost magical islands on the channels that cut through them, the rest of the world can seem pretty far away.

While the wetness of the islands near the reservoir's center precludes exploration on foot, the higher islands on the reservoir's north end present a perfect place for a picnic or a blueberry-picking excursion. Also, near the dam at the northeastern tip, some gorgeous open woodlands—tall white pines with a thick carpet of pine needles underfoot—invite closer inspection.

While Whitehall Reservoir's 592 acres offer some great paddling for a half-day or more, we recommend avoiding it on busy summer weekends.

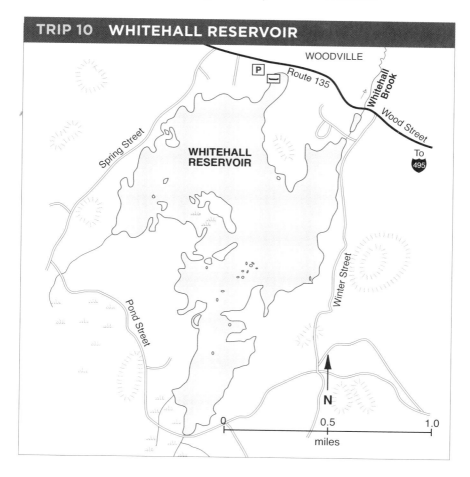

TRIP 10   WHITEHALL RESERVOIR

WOODVILLE

Route 135

Whitehall Brook

Wood Street

To 495

WHITEHALL RESERVOIR

Spring Street

Winter Street

Pond Street

N

0   0.5   1.0

miles

BLACKSTONE RIVER

This is a rare trip where you can paddle in a loop: downstream on a river and then upstream on a canal. In addition to historical sights, you will see great blue heron, kingfisher, and osprey, along with myriad wetlands plant species. You can also hike or bike the historic towpath.

LOCATION Northbridge and Uxbridge, MA

MAPS *Massachusetts Atlas & Gazetteer*, Map 51: B4; USGS Blackstone, Uxbridge

LENGTH 4 miles one way

TIME 5 hours round trip

HABITAT TYPE Moderate-flowing river and parallel canal with no current

FISH Largemouth, smallmouth, and calico bass; yellow perch; pickerel; northern pike (see fish advisory, Appendix A)

INFORMATION Blackstone River and Canal Heritage State Park, mass.gov/locations/blackstone-river-and-canal-heritage-state-park; Slater Mill, nps.gov/blrv/learn/historyculture/slatermill.htm

TAKE NOTE Limited development; current on Blackstone River below dam can be significant; inexperienced paddlers should avoid river; always wear PFD on the river

GETTING THERE

From the junction of Routes 16 and 146, go 2.6 miles east on Route 16, and turn left on Oak Street. Drive 0.8 mile (3.4 miles) to the access on the right at River Bend Farm Visitor Center. **42° 5.651′ N, 71° 37.396′ W**

WHAT YOU'LL SEE

Paddling on the Blackstone River and Blackstone Canal allows not just an exploration of natural history but also a tour through some of our nation's extraordinary cultural history. America's industrial revolution, in many ways, began on the Blackstone River, where the first water-powered mills began to spin cotton. The Slater Mill, America's first true factory, built in 1793, is on the river in Pawtucket, Rhode Island, and is open as a museum dedicated to the American Industrial Revolution.

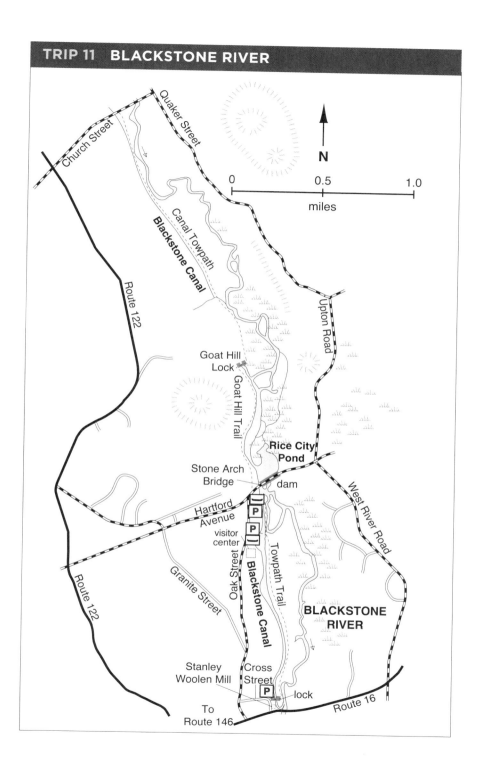

The Blackstone River passes under the historic Stone Arch Bridge, constructed in 1869 from precisely fitted granite stones.

The Blackstone River extends from Worcester to Providence, dropping 438 feet over its 45-mile length. Its 34 dams use 409 feet of the river's drop for the many mills along here. From 1828 to 1848, a canal paralleled portions of the river, allowing horse-drawn boats and barges to carry freight and people between Providence and Worcester.

This entire stretch of the river and canal lies within the John H. Chafee Blackstone River Valley National Heritage Corridor. We address only one small segment, but dozens of other places await exploration by canoe or kayak—as well as by foot or bicycle on the many miles of pathways created here, including the restored towpath that paralleled the Blackstone Canal; a bicycle path will eventually connect Worcester and Providence.

This segment of river and canal, both upriver and downriver from the River Bend Farm Visitor Center, offers one of the best places to explore this region by canoe or kayak. As you leave the visitor center, paddle to the left (north), crossing under a pedestrian bridge and into the canal. Paddling up this non-flowing canal, which will be pea green with floating vegetation by midsummer, you will quickly reach a wall and steps where you can portage into the river, beneath the dam, or above the dam into the combined canal and river.

On a visit one beautiful early August day, we launched into the river, paddling north under the Hartford Avenue Stone Arch Bridge (admire the construction of the 1869 bridge with tightly fitting, precisely cut granite) into Rice City Pond, a large wetlands. Be aware of the dam to the right, keeping your distance.

A wide range of marsh plants, including cattail, bulrush, pickerelweed, arrowhead, bur-reed, phragmites, and wild rice populate the pond's shoreline. In late summer, look for elderberry bushes laden with fruit. On more solid ground, you will see gray birch and red maple in profusion; look carefully for some catalpa, swamp white oak, and black gum trees. In early August, you may smell the flowers of very common sweet pepperbush; look for elongated clusters of small white flowers.

The very shallow, muddy-bottomed water contains huge carp; we caught glimpses of just a few but saw the trails of stirred-up mud left by dozens of these large fish as they fled before us. Anglers have caught carp of more than 30 pounds here, but consuming Blackstone fish carries risk, as this was once one of the nation's most polluted rivers. In Rice City Pond and continuing northward, we saw great blue herons, kingfishers, cormorants, and ospreys; earlier in the season, one would see more waterfowl. Moving along quietly, glimpse painted turtles sunning on logs before they retreat into the water as you approach.

Sticking to the western shore, enter the canal, and about a mile north from Hartford Avenue, find the remnants of the Goat Hill Lock, built in 1827, one of only four of the original 48 locks that remain visible.

Explore the extensive coves north of the pond—to the extent vegetation allows. Eventually, stronger current and shallow water impede your travel. We got about 2 miles upstream from the Hartford Avenue bridge before continuing our explorations southward, back to the bridge and portage around the dam. Note the water level at the portage just south of the Hartford Avenue bridge. When water goes over the spillway, the water level is too high for paddling south on the river—except by experienced whitewater paddlers. On the river, use caution and wear your PFD. Even at low water, strong current and downed trees may cause strainers that can roll or trap a boat.

With the water level down, we portaged over to the river put-in and paddled with the current about 2 miles down to a portage across to the canal and the Stanley Woolen Mill, built in 1853. Look for the portage sign fairly high on a tree to the right, marking the easy carry across a mowed field to the dam. Before getting back in your boat, consider walking down the towpath trail to observe the well-preserved Stanley Woolen Mill.

Launch your boat into the canal for an easy paddle on still water back up to the River Bend Farm Visitor Center. Duckweed can cover the fairly stagnant water here, making paddling not quite as pleasant as earlier in the season.

CHARLES RIVER

The upper Charles River carves a narrow, undulating path through generally wooded shores, offering solitude and beauty. Watch for muskrat and myriad bird species. If you're quiet, you may see deer in the early morning or evening.

LOCATION Dover, Medfield, Millis, Natick, Norfolk, and Sherborn, MA

MAPS *Massachusetts Atlas & Gazetteer*, Map 40: C2, Map 52: A1, A2, B1, B2; USGS Framingham, Medfield

LENGTH 13.4 miles one way; shorter trips possible

TIME All day

HABITAT TYPE Meandering, slow-flowing river through mostly preserved land; marshlands

FISH Largemouth, smallmouth, and calico bass; white and yellow perch; pickerel; northern pike (see fish advisory, Appendix A)

INFORMATION The Charles River (see Appendix B); The Trustees of Reservations, thetrustees.org, 617-542-7696; Massachusetts Audubon Society, massaudubon.org, 781-259-9500; Charles River Watershed Association, crwa.org

TAKE NOTE Limited development; too shallow for motors

GETTING THERE

Access points are given in order, starting upstream (south end).

Route 115 Use only for a one-way trip downstream. From the junction of Routes 109 and 115 in Millis, go 1.8 miles south on Route 115 to the access on the left, just over the bridge. **42° 8.584′ N, 71° 20.929′ W**

Forest Road From the junction of Routes 109 and 115, go 0.7 mile east on Route 109, and turn right on Village Street. Go 0.8 mile (1.5 miles), and turn left on Forest Road. Continue 0.8 mile (2.3 miles) to the access on the left, just before the bridge. **42° 9.48′ N, 71° 19.977′ W**

Dwight Street From the junction of Routes 109 and 115, go 1.4 miles east on Route 109, and turn right on Dwight Street. Go 0.5 mile (1.9 miles) to the access on the right. **42° 10.452′ N, 71° 19.397′ W**

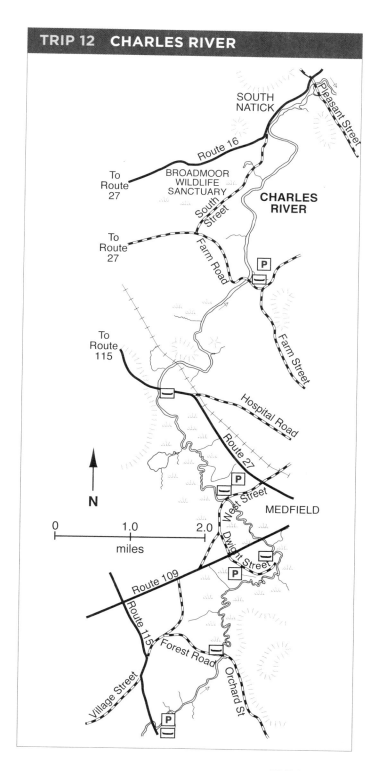

SOUTH
NATICK

Pleasant Street

Route 16

To
Route
27

BROADMOOR
WILDLIFE
SANCTUARY

South Street

CHARLES
RIVER

To
Route
27

Farm Road

P

To
Route
115

Farm Street

Hospital Road

Route 27

N

P

West Street

MEDFIELD

0   1.0   2.0
miles

Dwight Street

P

Route 109

P

Route 115

Forest Road

Village Street

Orchard St

P

West Street From the junction of Routes 109 and 115, go 1.0 mile east on Route 109, and turn left on Dover Road (turns into West Street). Go 1.1 miles (2.1 miles) to the access on the left, just over the bridge. **42° 11.347′ N, 71° 20.004′ W**

Route 27 From the junction of Routes 27 and 115, go 0.3 mile south on Route 27 to the access on the right, just over the bridge. **42° 12.591′ N, 71° 21.063′ W**

Farm Road From Sherborn, go south on Routes 16 and 27, and bear left onto Route 27 at the Y. From the Y, go 0.3 mile and turn left on Farm Road. Go 2.4 miles (2.7 miles) to the access on the left, just across the bridge. **42° 13.965′ N, 71° 19.788′ W**

Broadmoor Wildlife Sanctuary From the junction of Routes 16 and 27 in Sherborn, go 1.6 miles northeast on Route 16 to the visitor center on the right. **42° 15.379′ N, 71° 20.361′ W**

WHAT YOU'LL SEE

If you think of boating on the Charles River as sailing or rowing through Cambridge, prepare to be surprised when you try the upper Charles, one of the finest paddling destinations in the Northeast. It begins its 80-mile meander from Echo Lake in Hopkinton, flowing down to Boston Harbor, dropping an average of only about 4 feet per mile. We cover, more or less, the river's middle section.

When we paddled here in late June, wild grapes clung to the streamside vegetation, swamp rose bloomed in profusion, and the sweet scent of swamp azalea wafted along on the slightest breeze. Red maple dominates the shores in marshy areas, but you may also spot some stately elms and swamp white oaks, along with a variety of other trees.

In the Charles's north-flowing upper reaches, the boat compass needle swung back and forth endlessly as the river meandered through low-lying red maple swamps and wet meadows. As a muskrat swam before us, towing a clump of grass, and a great horned owl eyed us from an overhead perch, we marveled at this truly wild place that lies a stone's throw from Boston suburbs.

Two very large snapping turtles dove for cover in deeper water as we glided by, and we watched a green heron and a great blue heron stalk the shallows for fish and other prey. A red-tailed hawk wheeled overhead while a variety of songbirds sang from hidden perches. We listened to the beautiful, flutelike notes of a hermit thrush—normally a deep-woods resident—and thought of the area's similarities to northern New England. No road noise disturbed nature's sounds.

Medfield State Forest, Sherborn Town Forest, The Trustees of Reservations, Massachusetts Audubon Society, and private landowners protect much of the land in this section from development. The Forest Road access marks the beginning of a river section navigable even during periods of low water. We recommend paddling upstream to start, especially in spring, and letting the light current help carry you back down. Our favorite paddle starts at Dwight Street and heads upstream (south) to Route 115, a round-trip distance of 7.5 miles through the most pristine areas.

Hiking trails abound. About a mile downstream from Farm Road, The Trustees of Reservations maintains a landing on the left bank. From there, you can hike uphill for nearly a mile to King Philip's Lookout in the contiguous Sherborn Town Forest. Foot trails wind through Peters Reservation on the right bank, just downstream from Farm Road. Also, visit Broadmoor Wildlife Sanctuary (owned by Mass Audubon; see previous page for directions) with its elevated boardwalk and 9 miles of trails.

TRIP 13

NEPONSET RIVER

The Neponset River, which forms Boston's southern boundary, flows lazily for about 8 miles through extensive wetlands with very limited development. Streamside trees, shrubs, and vines form an overarching canopy in many areas, making it an inviting place to paddle on hot, sunny days. You can find wood duck, great blue heron, beaver, and deer here.

LOCATION Boston, Canton, Dedham, Milton, Norwood, MA

MAPS *Massachusetts Atlas & Gazetteer*, Map 52: A3, Map 53: A4; USGS Blue Hills, Norwood

LENGTH 8 miles one way; shorter trips possible

TIME All day

HABITAT TYPE Meandering, slow-flowing river through mostly preserved land; marshlands

FISH Largemouth bass, pickerel (see fish advisory, Appendix A)

INFORMATION The Trustees of Reservations, thetrustees.org; Neponset River Reservation, mass.gov/locations/neponset-river-reservation

TAKE NOTE Limited development; no motors

GETTING THERE

Brush Hill Road From I-93, Exit 2B, go 1.3 miles north on Route 138, and veer right onto Canton Avenue. Go 0.1 mile (1.4 miles), and turn left onto the connector to Brush Hill Road. Drive 0.9 mile (2.3 miles) to the access on the left, just before Neponset Valley Parkway. **42° 14.013′ N, 71° 7.34′ W**

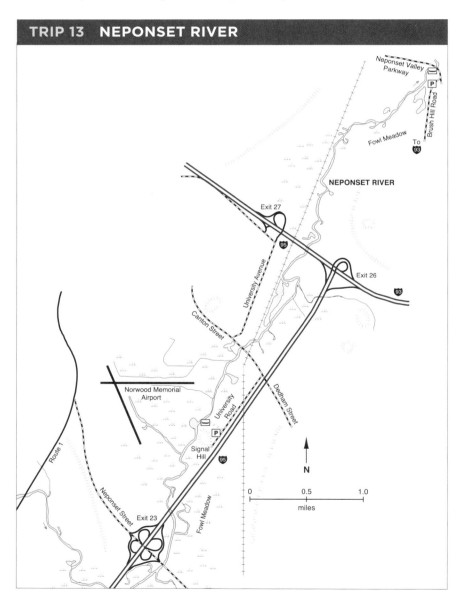

TRIP 13   NEPONSET RIVER

University Road From I-95, Exit 27, go 0.1 mile, and turn right on University Avenue. Go 1.0 mile (1.1 miles), and turn left on Canton Street. Continue 0.2 mile (1.3 miles), and turn right on University Road. Go 0.8 mile (2.1 miles) to the Signal Hill (The Trustees of Reservations) access on the right. 42° 11.115′ N, 71° 9.576′ W

WHAT YOU'LL SEE

The Neponset River offers a fabulous paddling resource, especially given its location on the very edge of metropolitan Boston. It actually forms Boston's southern and Quincy's northern boundaries. This section flows for 8 leisurely miles through the Fowl Meadow section of Neponset River Reservation, from Route 1 down to Paul's Bridge (Brush Hill access). We prefer putting in at Paul's Bridge, paddling upstream, and letting the slow-flowing river help carry us back to the access. This strategy allows a day trip of any length; going all the way to Route 1 and back would take most of a day. You could spend even more time if you explored the many side channels that flow into the river.

Trees and shrubs line the length of the river, providing relatively shady paddling, ideal for hot, sunny days. Impressive amounts of wild grapevine drape trees and shrubs, hanging out over the river, making it seem narrower than it is. Look for royal fern tucked under the canopy along the shore. When we paddled here in mid-August, large numbers of birds fed on the abundant fruits of shrubs and trees. We noted buttonbush, red osier dogwood, and many others.

Red maple; red, scarlet, white, and swamp white oaks; chokecherry; and quaking aspen provide much of the shade. Swifts cruise above for insects, while wood ducks try to hide along the shore. Beavers and storms occasionally topple a tree, but you should be able to negotiate most of these without having to portage around. Look for deer in the evening or early morning.

From Paul's Bridge, you can also hike 2.5-mile Burma Road, viewing the marshes from another angle. If you are at the University Road access, be sure to climb Signal Hill to view Fowl Meadow and the Blue Hills. Maintained by The Trustees of Reservations, this site also offers a place to rent canoes on weekends and holidays from April through October.

The Neponset River salt marshes were the first in Massachusetts to be publicly owned. Since purchasing the marshes in the late 1880s, the state has acquired, protected, and rehabilitated 750 acres along the river, which now make up Neponset River Reservation.

TRIP 14

WEYMOUTH BACK RIVER

This is a great place to paddle at or near high tide; watch out for extensive mud flats as tides recede. You should see osprey against a wooded shore backdrop; osprey pairs nest here successfully nearly every year, sometimes fledging as many as three young. Huge numbers of fish that the locals call herring spawn here.

LOCATION Hingham and Weymouth, MA

MAPS *Massachusetts Atlas & Gazetteer*, Map 41: C6, Map 53: A6; USGS Hull, Weymouth

LENGTH 3.6 miles one way

TIME 4 hours round trip

HABITAT TYPE Tidal estuary, wooded shores

FISH Striped bass, alewife, herring, rainbow smelt (see fish advisory, Appendix A)

INFORMATION Tide charts, usharbors.com

CAMPING Wompatuck State Park

TAKE NOTE No water-skiing or personal watercraft south of Route 3A bridge; no development; visit at or near high tide—exposed mud banks at low tide dramatically reduce paddling area

GETTING THERE

From I-93, Exit 12 southbound, go 6.8 miles southeast on Route 3A (follow signs carefully) to the stoplight at the junction of Route 3A (Bridge Street) with Green Street (right/south) and Neck Street (left/north). Directions to the three access points are given from this junction.

Abigail Adams Park is the preferred access; carry over the bank to the water. Weymouth Public Launch is the easiest access but is not free. Great Esker Park does not have a developed boat launch but is recommended for launching in windy conditions. It's very muddy at low tide.

Abigail Adams Park From the junction, go 0.3 mile (7.1 miles) east on Route 3A, and turn right to cross Route 3A into the park, just before the bridge. **42° 14.846′ N, 70° 54.019′ W**

Weymouth Public Launch From the junction, go 0.6 mile (7.4 miles) north on Neck Street to the access on the right. Launch fee. **42° 15.116′ N, 70° 56.18′ W**

Great Esker Park From the junction, go 1.1 miles (7.9 miles) south on Green Street, and turn left on East Street. Go 0.8 mile (8.7 miles), and turn left on Puritan Road. Drive 0.5 mile (9.2 miles) to the end, and park by the gate. **42° 13.785′ N, 70° 55.65′ W**

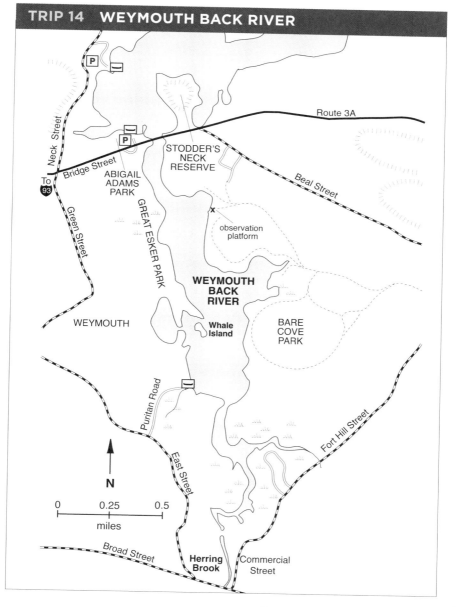

TRIP 14 WEYMOUTH BACK RIVER

WHAT YOU'LL SEE

Bounded by wildlife preserves, Weymouth Back River presents an outstanding paddling resource within the Greater Boston metropolitan area. Harbormasters from Hingham and Weymouth established the river as a no-wake zone, with no water-skiing and no personal watercraft allowed south of the Route 3A bridge. The wooded shores—the longest in the Boston Harbor area—enclose modest sections of salt marsh, standing in stark contrast to the seas of cordgrass encountered in other estuaries.

The 469 acres of Bare Cove Park host many species of plants, including scrub or bear oak and pitch pine growing on tree-covered dunes. Look for coyote, fox, and deer here; an observation platform provides views of the river and the surrounding woods. Hiking trails course through the park and also through 1.5-mile-long, 237-acre Great Esker Park across the way. The esker, which reaches 90 feet in height, appears as a long, snakelike ridge of stratified sand and gravel and was formed during the last glacial epoch about 12,000 years ago. Subglacial streams laid the deposits as they tunneled beneath the melting glacier. Also in this area, valuable archaeological finds dating back as far as 9,000 years indicate a long presence of native people along the river.

Alewives, locally known as herring, make a famous annual spring pilgrimage here, up the river to Whitman's Pond. From eggs laid in spring, young fish grow up to 4 inches long by fall when they migrate to the sea. As adults, the silvery fish, now 12 inches long, return the following spring to begin the cycle anew. As Henry Beston wrote in his book *The Outermost House*:

> Somewhere in the depths of the ocean each Weymouth-born fish remembers Whitman's Pond, and comes to it through the directionless leagues of the sea. What stirs in each cold brain? What call quivers, as the new sun strikes down into the river of ocean? How do the creatures find their way? Whatever the reason, the herring are "in" at Weymouth, breasting the brook's overflow to the ancestral pond.

The Hingham Land Conservation Trust reported in 2017 that four pairs of ospreys typically nest in this area, a dramatic rebound from the years when DDT resulted in nesting failures and drastically depleted the population. Researchers annually band as many as 24 young along the South Shore.

SECTION 2

SOUTHEASTERN MASSACHUSETTS AND CAPE COD

This section includes nine entries, extending from the Rhode Island border out onto Cape Cod. Hock-omock Swamp provides the most unusual features; the swamp, rivers, and associated wetlands compose a 17,000-acre Area of Critical Environmental Concern. Not infrequently, people paddle into and get lost in this vast swamp that also  forms the headwater of the Town River. In contrast, we include the short, narrow Bungay River. Hockomock Swamp hosts the largest Atlantic white cedar swamp in New England, but the most important red maple swamp in Massachusetts surrounds the Bungay River.

East Head Pond lies within Myles Standish State Forest. Look here for the extremely rare Plymouth redbelly turtle (*Pseudemys rubriventris bangsi*) amid the extensive, but rare, pitch-pine and scrub oak forest that thrives only on ancient sand dunes. You may find other rare species here, as well. To the south, we include two tidal rivers: Westport River East Branch and Slocums River. Besides geography, the underlying sand strata ties together the rivers and East Head Pond, although the rivers offer radically different paddling. Instead of turtles and pine-oak forest, look for shorebirds, long-legged waders, ospreys, and other aquatic birds at the rivers.

A more extensive salt marsh habitat awaits at protected Nauset Marsh. Paddling here can be a challenge because of exposed mud flats at low tide, difficult currents, and wind, but we really enjoy visiting this spot, especially during shorebird migrations. Nearby tidal Herring River offers a real treat, partly because it's away from typical Cape Cod tourist attractions, but mostly because it's a bird-filled refuge. In this area, you will find Nickerson State Park, one of the few public camping areas in southeast Massachusetts.

BUNGAY RIVER

The narrow Bungay River undulates through what is reputed to be the most important red maple swamp in Massachusetts. Look for Atlantic white cedar, royal fern, buttonbush, and painted turtles. Beware of poison ivy.

LOCATION Attleboro and North Attleborough, MA

MAPS *Massachusetts Atlas & Gazetteer*, Map 56: A2; USGS Providence

LENGTH 2 miles one way

TIME 3 hours round trip

HABITAT TYPE Narrow, meandering river

FISH Brook and rainbow trout, largemouth and smallmouth bass, pickerel (see fish advisory, Appendix A)

TAKE NOTE Large stands of poison ivy along the shore

GETTING THERE

From I-95, Exit 7, go east on Toner Boulevard, and turn right on Route 152/ Main Street. Go 1.0 mile, and turn left on Holden Street. The access is on the left in 0.5 mile (1.5 miles). **41° 57.244′ N, 71° 16.821′ W**

WHAT YOU'LL SEE

The Bungay River offers a pleasant morning or afternoon of paddling. When we visited on a beautiful mid-June afternoon, we saw just two kayakers during the 3-hour up-and-back trip. Leaving the hand-carry access, you initially pass a few houses on the east bank, but after that, no houses impinge on the water, and only road noise from I-95—which is about a mile to the west when you start out but gets closer as you paddle north—reminds you of nearby civilization.

Tannins stain the water of this gently flowing river a deep brown. Its sinewy bends will test your paddling skills, especially if you're in a longer canoe, requiring lots of draw strokes by the bow paddler to make the tight turns. If paddling a kayak and wanting to push as far upstream as possible, you might want to bring a single paddle or a break-down double paddle for greater maneuverability.

Heavy vegetation straddles the river's shoreline. Shrubs include silky dogwood, sweetgale, buttonbush, alder, highbush blueberry, a wild azalea that blooms in early June, and invasive buckthorn. Unfortunately, lush poison ivy vines also populate the banks—often reaching out into the water.

Red maples dominate the tree species; in fact, the area surrounding Bungay River is considered the most important red maple swamp in Massachusetts. Other trees include Atlantic white cedars and a few white pines and white oaks. Lots of royal fern, pickerelweed, yellow pondlily, and various grasses and sedges grow where the overhanging trees and shrubs afford them light.

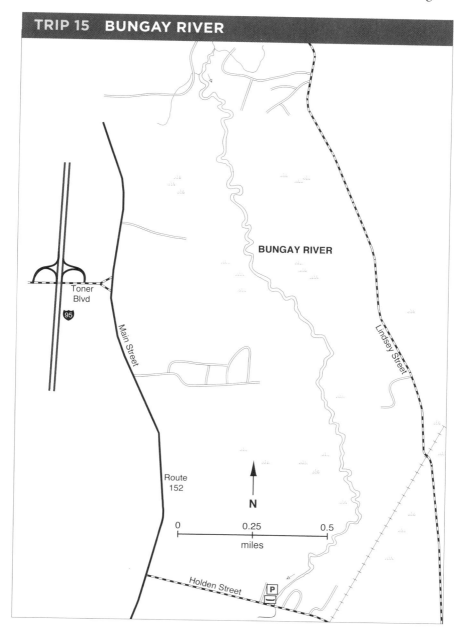

TRIP 15   BUNGAY RIVER

BUNGAY RIVER

Toner Blvd

95

Main Street

Lindsey Street

Route 152

N

0   0.25   0.5
miles

Holden Street

P

The aromatic flowers of swamp azalea make paddling the Bungay River in late summer a real pleasure.

A few logs occur along the shore, and where you see them, you are likely to spot painted turtles sunning. We saw about twenty on our up-and-back trip. These skittish creatures rarely let you get close before plopping into the water. Large snapping turtles live here as well. You will see lots of nest boxes along the river's lower stretch. (We saw one that was clearly a wood duck nest box but were not sure about target species for the others.)

As you paddle north, the river gradually narrows; if you travel far enough, you'll have to push the brush aside as you squeeze through. Be on the lookout for poison ivy; in some places we had to be very careful to avoid contact.

We paddled upstream for about an hour and a half, perhaps 2 miles, until several large logs across the river blocked our way. We could have pulled our boat across, but the channel had narrowed to the point that we frequently had to hold branches back as we pushed through, and we probably could not have made it much farther.

LAKE NIPPENICKET, HOCKOMOCK SWAMP, AND TOWN RIVER

Hockomock Swamp is an extraordinary paddling resource with huge biodiversity. Take care not to get lost in the swamp's depths. Lake Nippenicket may experience significant boat traffic at times, but on a quiet morning it can be pleasant—and offers access to the swamp. You can paddle the Town River within the swamp or a separate downstream section, where you can't get lost.

LOCATION Bridgewater and West Bridgewater, MA

MAPS *Massachusetts Atlas & Gazetteer*, Map 53: C5, C6, Map 57: A5; USGS Abington, Taunton

AREA/LENGTH Hockomock Swamp, 16,950 acres; Lake Nippenicket, 354 acres; Town River, 2 miles one way

TIME All day (unless you get lost in the depths of the swamp); shorter trips possible

HABITAT TYPE Extensive undeveloped Atlantic white cedar swamp

FISH Largemouth and calico bass, white and yellow perch, pickerel (see fish advisory, Appendix A)

INFORMATION Hockomock Swamp, mass.gov/service-details /hockomock-swamp-acec

TAKE NOTE Heavy motorboat traffic on Lake Nippenicket on summer weekends

GETTING THERE

Lake Nippenicket From Route 24, Exit 24, go 0.2 mile west on Route 104, and turn right on Lakeside Drive. Turn immediately left into the access. **41° 57.866′ N, 71° 2.02′ W**

Town River From Route 24, Exit 28, go east on Route 106 to the junction of Routes 106 and 28 in West Bridgewater, and turn right on Route 28. Drive 0.4 mile, and turn left on Ash Street. Go 0.6 mile (1.0 mile), and turn left into the Reynolds Landing access. **42° 0.758′ N, 70° 59.612′ W**

WHAT YOU'LL SEE

LAKE NIPPENICKET

Lake Nippenicket, locally known as "The Nip," is a modest-sized, shallow lake between Brockton and Taunton. While the lake offers pleasant paddling, don't expect peace and solitude on the water, as motorboats and personal

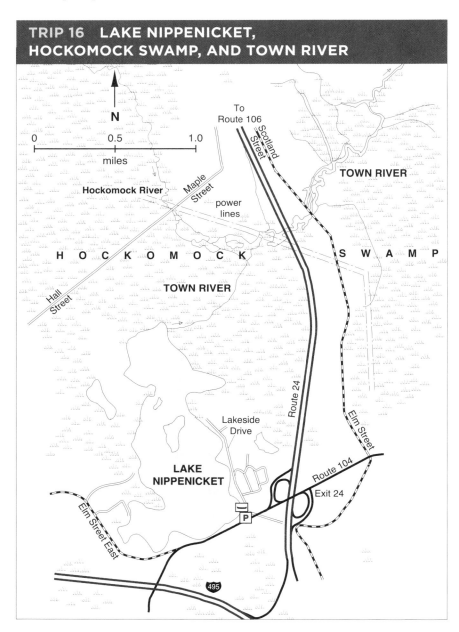

TRIP 16   LAKE NIPPENICKET, HOCKOMOCK SWAMP, AND TOWN RIVER

N

0   0.5   1.0
miles

To
Route 106

Scotland Street

TOWN RIVER

Hockomock River   Maple Street

power lines

H O C K O M O C K   S W A M P

Hall Street

TOWN RIVER

Route 24

Lakeside Drive

Elm Street

LAKE NIPPENICKET

Route 104

Exit 24

Elm Street East

P

495

watercraft dominate on summer weekends, and you hear a lot of road noise from Route 24 and I-495, both of which come within a half-mile of the lake.

We paddled here twice, once in late September with a fairly low water level and accompanying heavy vegetation, which limited passage. We also paddled in mid-June, following a period of heavy rain. With the load of tannins in the water limiting visibility, you may not appreciate the lake's shallowness—a maximum depth of 6 feet and an average depth of just 3 feet.

Significant residential and some commercial development impinges on the southwestern cove, and houses along the eastern shore extend north to the island, but most of the shoreline is either swampy or marshy, especially along the northern half of the lake that abuts Hockomock Swamp.

HOCKOMOCK SWAMP

Hockomock Swamp, spanning parts of six towns, is the largest vegetated freshwater wetlands in Massachusetts. The swamp and associated wetlands compose a 16,950-acre Area of Critical Environmental Concern (ACEC) and form the headwater of the Town River, which drains into the Taunton River.

In the right conditions, you can paddle into the swamp from Lake Nippenicket—but doing so is hard and potentially dangerous. Every year people get lost in the swamp. This even includes rescuers getting stuck trying to reach lost visitors.

We visited in mid-June after a wet several weeks caused significant regional flooding; at normal water levels, most of the swamp would likely be inaccessible by boat. If you can get in, it is an extraordinary place, the largest Atlantic white cedar swamp in New England—but we were as much struck by the large number of swamp white oaks scattered throughout.

We entered the swamp from the northeastern tip of Lake Nippenicket. Paddling back and forth along the shoreline, looking for a way in, we wove among the flooded trees and shrubs but were ultimately blocked. Eventually, at the far eastern tip of the north end, we found a hidden channel amid a stand of 20-foot-tall willow trees that offered access. Look for a modest channel in the center of that willow stand.

As we paddled generally eastward and then northeastward, the channel became somewhat easier to follow, although still a challenge, making it very clear how people get lost. You might do well here with a Global Positioning System (GPS) that offers a detailed map database to be able to pinpoint your location—or a guide who knows the area intimately.

As the channel turned northward, huge power lines that cross the swamp came into view. Here, we picked up flow from the Hockomock River that merges with the slow swamp flow to become the Town River. Paddling downstream, we passed under the power lines and then under Route 24—having to duck slightly with the elevated water level. We continued a short way across some broader expanses of open water to the Elm Street/Scotland Street bridge, where high water did not allow us to paddle beneath it when we visited.

When we entered the Town River, we carefully tried to mark our return visually so that we could find the channel that would take us back to Lake Nippenicket. We did make some turns into the wrong cove of open water, but after exploring a bit we would find the proper channel. At one place, we had to proceed cautiously to avoid a lush growth of poison ivy extending out into the channel.

Despite the struggle to navigate the swamp—or perhaps because of it—our efforts were richly rewarded. No other place like this exists in New England. In fact, nowhere in the Northeast have we seen swamp white oak in such numbers. We also saw Atlantic white cedar, black gum, silver maple, red maple, ash, and myriad shrubs, as well as both floating and emergent wetlands plants.

TOWN RIVER EAST OF ROUTE 28

We also enjoyed several miles of wonderful paddling and exploring on the Town River, putting in at the well-maintained Reynolds Landing on Ash Street in West Bridgewater. During high-water conditions, we had no trouble getting our boats into the river from the landing; later in summer or during a dry spring, the access could be more challenging.

Leaving the access, watch for a golf course immediately opposite. Paddling downstream (to the right), follow a wide, grassy channel with lots of

Co-author Alex and his wife, Jerelyn, do their best not to get themselves and their dog lost while wending their way through Hockomock Swamp.

arrowhead amid the grasses and sedges. We saw one mute swan here and a few painted turtles, along with lots of red-winged blackbirds, tree swallows, and eastern kingbirds. Earlier in the season, we would expect to see more waterfowl.

We paddled downstream to the village of Stanley, reaching a small dam, and then paddled back upstream, past the access, to Route 28. With the water level as high as it was, there was no way to paddle under the bridge, but doing so might be possible at a lower water level. If passage weren't hampered by high water, you could travel into Hockomock Swamp and Lake Nippenicket from the access point on the Town River.

We saw a few black gum trees along here, as well as Atlantic white cedar, red and silver maples, ash, a few white pines, and pin cherry. Closer to shore grow thick stands of swamp loosestrife, silky dogwood, alder, and other shrubs.

TRIP 17

SNAKE RIVER

The Snake River flows, barely, from Winnecunnet Pond to Lake Sabbatia, passing through portions of Hockomock Swamp and under I-495. Though road noise is audible, the river seems quite wild. Expect to see wood duck, great blue heron, painted turtles, beaver, muskrat, and loads of streamside vegetation, some of it making paddling challenging.

LOCATION Taunton, MA

MAPS *Massachusetts Atlas & Gazetteer*, Map 57: A4; USGS Taunton

LENGTH 7 miles round trip

TIME All day; shorter trips possible

HABITAT TYPE Tightly winding river through thick vegetation

FISH Largemouth bass, chain pickerel, white and yellow perch, black crappie (see fish advisory, Appendix A)

INFORMATION Hockomock Swamp, mass.gov/service-details /hockomock-swamp-acec

TAKE NOTE Significant road noise in some places from I-495; parking fee

GETTING THERE

From I-495, Exit 25, go 1.2 miles south on Bay Road to the Lake Sabbatia access on the left. **41° 56.783′ N, 71° 6.881′ W**

WHAT YOU'LL SEE

Snake River is a hidden gem at the edge of Hockomock Swamp (Trip 16). On a windy day, this secluded, tightly twisting waterway provides an ideal destination. You can have an all-day adventure, leisurely exploring nearly up to the bridge over the outlet from Winnecunnet Pond, or turn around at any point.

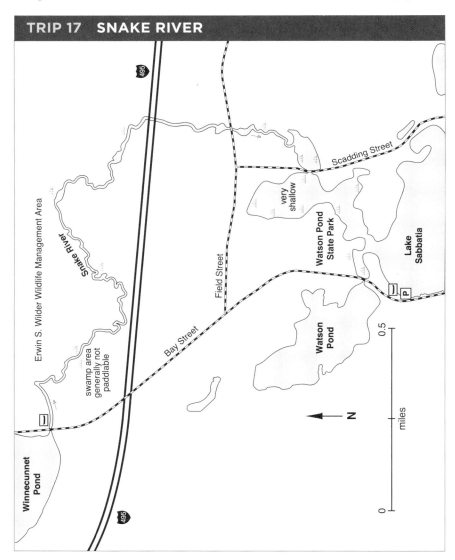

TRIP 17   SNAKE RIVER

To get into the river from the Lake Sabbatia access, paddle to the left—northeast—through shallow water, thick with floating and submerged vegetation, including yellow pondlily, American white waterlily, and pondweed. Unfortunately, there is also significant Eurasian watermilfoil and water chestnut—two problematic invasive plants. As we paddled, we observed a muskrat, along with several families of Canada geese, kingfishers, red-winged blackbirds, great blue herons, and mute swans (an introduced species).

Watch for the Scadding Street bridge; paddle under it into the Snake River, the primary inlet into the lake. The concrete bridge rests on wooden piers, which looks quite unusual. Following the Snake River's serpentine path, you are likely to leave behind any fishers who might be plying the shallows of Lake Sabbatia.

Despite the drone of vehicles on I-495, the Snake River has a very wild feel to it. The dark, tannin-laden water flows deep, and the channel—at least for the lower reaches—is easy to paddle. The channel's narrowness could make using a standard kayak paddle challenging. We traveled in a canoe with shorter paddles. In a kayak, we would want a paddle that could break down to use just half.

Emergent vegetation—arrowhead, pickerelweed, bullrushes, bur-reed, royal and sensitive ferns, cattail, and large tufts of native grasses—dominates the shoreline. Trees include white pine, red maple, black gum, and sassafras, to mention a few. Shrubs include buttonbush, silky dogwood, sweet pepperbush, swamp rose (in bloom with delicate pink flowers in July), and highbush blueberry.

Not far into the trip, pass under the Field Street bridge, followed by the I-495 bridges. Note the thick stands of highly invasive common reed (*Phragmites*). Debate swirls around whether this is an introduced species or a native that becomes invasive on disturbed land. Past the I-495 bridges, the channel narrows, with mostly silky dogwood, buttonbush, alder, and some willow reaching nearly across in places. Where there are suitable logs for sunning, painted turtles may be seen here—but they are skittish, so you'll have to be quiet if you want to catch more than a glimpse. In a few places, we noticed beaver lodges just off the channel and mostly hidden by thick vegetation.

Bends in the river seem to get tighter as you get farther upstream. Eventually, after passing very close to I-495 again, the channel largely disappears as the river spreads out through Hockomock Swamp. We managed to navigate this final stretch, but we had to drag our canoe through thick vegetation in places (think Humphrey Bogart in *The African Queen*), trying to dodge stinging nettles and poison ivy! We recommend that you turn around when the river channel passes along I-495. It may take some effort to find a spot where the river is wide enough to turn your boat around; you might have to paddle backward for a little ways.

LAKE RICO AND BIG BEARHOLE POND

In this excellent location for a leisurely paddle away from motorboats, expect to see mute swans, ducks, geese, herons, and egrets. It can get crowded on busy summer weekends, and fishing pressure can get a little heavy at times, but this is still a great place to explore wooded shorelines.

LOCATION Taunton, MA

MAPS *Massachusetts Atlas & Gazetteer*, Map 57: B6; USGS Assawompset Pond, Bridgewater, Somerset, Taunton

AREA Lake Rico, 250 acres; Big Bearhole Pond, 37 acres

TIME 4 hours

HABITAT TYPE Wooded reservoir in a state park

FISH Largemouth and calico bass, yellow perch, pickerel (see fish advisory, Appendix A)

INFORMATION Massasoit State Park, mass.gov/locations/massasoit-state -park, 508-828-4231

CAMPING Myles Standish State Forest

TAKE NOTE No motors; limited development

GETTING THERE

From I-495, Exit 14 southbound, go 0.4 mile south on Route 18, and turn right on Taunton Street/Middleboro Avenue, following signs to Massasoit State Park. Go 2.4 miles (2.8 miles) to the Lake Rico access on the left. **41° 52.941′ N, 70° 59.941′ W**

To reach Big Bearhole Pond, turn in to the state park (0.2 mile before Lake Rico), and follow signs to the access; the pond can also be reached off Turner Street. **41° 51.928′ N, 80° 50.222′ W**

WHAT YOU'LL SEE

Lake Rico and the other small ponds in Massasoit State Park provide superb quietwater paddling—some of the best in this part of the state. Though some maps show six bodies of water (Lake Rico, Kings Pond, Furnace Pond, Middle

Pond, and Little and Big Bearhole ponds), Lake Rico, Kings Pond, and Furnace Pond are connected. Formerly used by cranberry growers, these separate ponds merged when the state raised the water level after acquiring the property. Some development intrudes on the western side of Furnace Pond and Lake Rico and on the eastern end of Big Bearhole Pond, but the rest of these ponds lie fully within the 1,500-acre Massasoit State Park, so only recreational development occurs there.

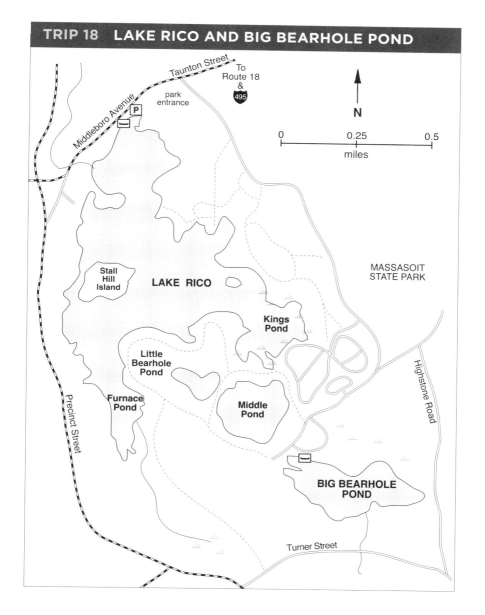

In the early morning light, mist rising off still waters makes Lake Rico look almost mystical.

Lake Rico offers several miles of shoreline, enough to provide an enjoyable half-day paddle. From the access on Middleboro Avenue, you can see only Lake Rico's northern cove. Paddling to the south, leave the road noise, passing some large stands of white pine with open forest floor—quite accessible if you want to get out for a picnic lunch or a short walk. Marshy Kings Pond presents a challenge, but you can pick your way through the abundant vegetation, paddling carefully around the bulrushes, pickerelweed, stands of cattail, and waterlilies. Near the tip of this cove, listen for the small waterfall inlet from Middle Pond (you can carry into Middle Pond). Expect to see waterfowl species, especially great blue heron, green heron, wood duck, teal, and pied-billed grebe, here.

We saw two pairs of mute swans, each with two cygnets, on the more open sections of the pond. While much open water remains, invasive watermilfoil and Carolina fanwort seemed to be crowding out the bladderwort, pondweed, and other native aquatic vegetation on our visit. Other invasive plants—purple loosestrife and phragmites—also seemed to be taking hold.

Big Bearhole Pond, a lot smaller than Lake Rico and with some houses on the eastern tip, still rates a visit. White pine dominates the shoreline vegetation, mixed with red maple, black gum, scarlet oak, gray birch, sweet pepperbush, blueberry, winterberry, and alder. Patches of swamp loosestrife grow along the shore, and some shallow coves sport patches of yellow pondlily and American white waterlily. Underwater vegetation includes Carolina fanwort and bladderwort.

TRIP 19

EAST HEAD POND

This pristine pond nestles within the 14,635-acre Myles Standish State Forest. Look for endangered Plymouth redbelly turtles. Besides paddling this beautiful body of water, you can also take advantage of camping and extensive hiking and mountain-bike trails. The backdrop includes numerous kettle-hole ponds and trees adapted to sand barrens—pitch pine and scrub oak.

LOCATION Carver and Plymouth, MA

MAPS *Massachusetts Atlas & Gazetteer*, Map 58: B3; USGS Wareham

AREA 92 acres

TIME 2 hours

HABITAT TYPE Glaciated kettle hole surrounded by sand barrens

FISH Largemouth bass, yellow perch, pickerel (see fish advisory, Appendix A)

INFORMATION New England Herpetological Society (Plymouth redbelly turtles), neherp.com/plymouth-redbelly-turtle; Myles Standish State Forest, mass.gov/locations/myles-standish-state-forest, 508-866-2526

CAMPING Myles Standish State Forest

TAKE NOTE No gasoline motors; no development

GETTING THERE

From I-495, Exit 2 southbound, go 2.5 miles north on Route 58, and continue straight on Tremont Street when Route 58 goes left. Go 0.8 mile (3.3 miles), and turn right on Cranberry Road. Continue 2.7 miles (6.0 miles) to Myles Standish State Forest. Park left of the gate, and carry your boat about 100 yards, crossing the bridge over the outlet, to the access on the left. **41° 50.348′ N, 70° 41.446′ W**

WHAT YOU'LL SEE

Myles Standish State Forest—one of the largest publicly owned tracts of land in Massachusetts at 14,635 acres—harbors many rare and endangered plants and animals and contains many ecologically rich kettle-hole ponds. When the glaciers receded 12,000 years ago, they left a few large chunks of glacial ice behind, usually buried in debris. As these ice blocks melted, they left depressions in the surrounding sand that formed ponds.

Compared with most of New England, a quite different species set surrounds East Head Pond and the other, smaller ponds of the state forest. Dominant species include pitch pine (*Pinus rigida*) and bear or scrub oak (*Quercus ilicifolia*) in a pine barrens ecosystem. This forest community develops on acidic, sandy soil and requires frequent fires for pitch pine seed release.

Along with the dominant species, red maple, gray birch, white pine, black gum, scarlet oak, and bigtooth aspen grow along the shores of East Head Pond. A rich diversity of shrubs also lines the shore: two species of blueberries (highbush and black highbush), sweet pepperbush, leatherleaf, sweetgale, mountain laurel, wild raisin or withe rod (*Viburnum cassinoides*), and inkberry, a type of swamp-loving holly (*Ilex glabra*). Pond vegetation includes watershield, American white waterlily, and bladderwort. Freshwater mussels inhabit

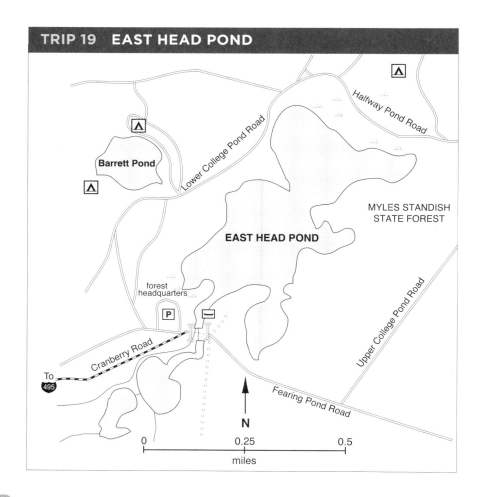

TRIP 19 EAST HEAD POND

Halfway Pond Road

Barrett Pond

Lower College Pond Road

MYLES STANDISH
STATE FOREST

EAST HEAD POND

forest
headquarters

P

Upper College Pond Road

Cranberry Road

To
495

Fearing Pond Road

N

0   0.25   0.5
miles

the sandy bottom. Anglers fish for largemouth bass, pickerel, and yellow perch, and you may be lucky enough to see an osprey join the human anglers, as we did on an early September morning. If you are extraordinarily lucky, you might see one of the approximately 300 remaining endangered Plymouth redbelly turtles (*Pseudemys rubriventris*) in one of these coastal ponds. Redbelly adults are much larger than the ubiquitous painted turtle (*Chrysemys picta*), also found here, along with the common snapping turtle and the rare spotted turtle.

With no gasoline-powered motors, East Head Pond offers an inviting spot for a morning or evening of relaxed paddling. The extremely popular campground (reservations required) provides a base for hiking on one of the many trails of the state forest. In all, the state forest boasts 90 miles of hiking, horse, and bicycle trails that crisscross the pine barrens.

Myles Standish State Forest and surrounding areas contain the largest community of pitch pine and scrub oak remaining in New England and, along with those on Long Island and in New Jersey, one of only three major pine barrens ecosystems remaining in the Northeast. Unfortunately, more economically valuable white and red pines have replaced much of the pitch pine; agriculture and development have pared away the surrounding barrens; and destructive off-road vehicles have threatened other rare and endangered plants of the community. Although off-road vehicles have been banned for many years, rogue riders continue to degrade portions of this fragile ecosystem.

During the eighteenth century, settlers mined the ponds in this area for bog iron. After this industry petered out, cranberry production took over; many commercial cranberry bogs still dot the area.

TRIP 20

WESTPORT RIVER EAST BRANCH

The Westport River East Branch provides an excellent spot to paddle along a salinity gradient into a salt marsh estuary. A modest amount of development occurs along the shore. Many ospreys nest here, along with a bald eagle pair. In addition to osprey and bald eagle, expect to see great blue heron, marsh wren, herring gull, red-winged blackbird, cormorant, and more.

LOCATION Westport, MA

MAPS *Massachusetts Atlas & Gazetteer*, Map 63: B5, C5; USGS Head of Westport

LENGTH 8 miles round trip to Hix Bridge

TIME Half a day; longer trips possible if paddling south of Hix Bridge

HABITAT TYPE Tidal river with salt marsh ecosystem; limited development

FISH Striped bass, bluefish (see fish advisory, Appendix A)

INFORMATION Westport River Watershed Alliance, wrwa.com; tide charts, usharbors.com

TAKE NOTE Wind from the south-southwest may be stronger than tidal current; best to paddle near high tide

GETTING THERE

Head of Westport From I-195, Exit 16, go 3.5 miles south on Route 88, and turn left on Old County Road. The access is on the right in 1.0 mile (4.5 miles). **41° 37.233′ N, 71° 3.567′ W**

Hix Bridge From the Head of Westport landing, cross the river, and turn left on Drift Road. Go 3.8 miles, and turn left on Hixbridge Road. The access is on the right, just over Hix Bridge. (Note: Nonresidents cannot park here.) The access offers a put-in or take-out location for dropoffs. **41° 34.19′ N, 71° 4.246′ W**

WHAT YOU'LL SEE

The Westport River East Branch offers a very pleasant morning or afternoon of paddling—or an all-day trip if you choose to explore south of Hix Bridge toward the river's mouth. The access at Head of Westport is picturesque, with an easy access to the narrow river channel contained in masterfully built stone walls across from a town park. Osprey Sea & Surf Adventures provides convenient kayak, canoe, and paddleboard rentals. The office of the Westport River Watershed Alliance, an organization doing excellent work to ensure the health of the watershed and to educate the public, is also here; if the office is open, stop in to view some interesting displays.

As you paddle south, a few houses appear, most set well back or architecturally interesting. Narrow-leaved cattail and common reed (*Phragmites*) dominate the heavily vegetated shoreline along the river's upper reaches. Farther south, as the salinity gradient increases, salt marsh cordgrass (*Spartina*), adapted to the widely varying salinity and fluctuating water level, becomes more common. Along the banks are a wide variety of mostly deciduous trees, including red maple, black gum, sassafras, black cherry, and various species of

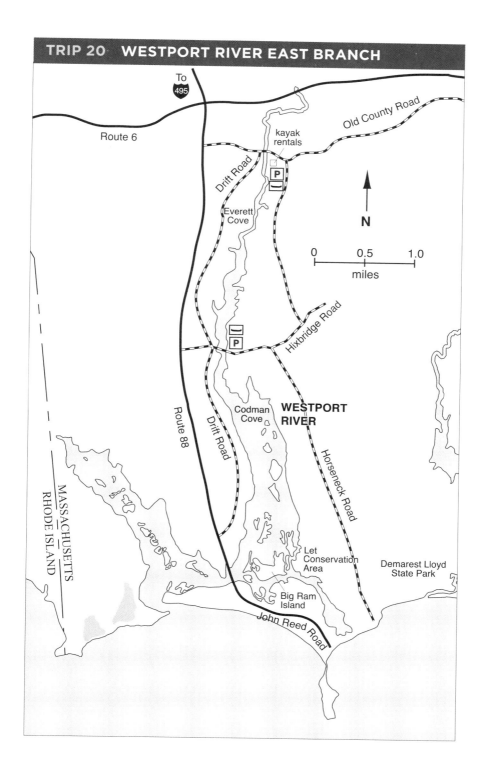

To 495

Old County Road

Route 6

kayak
rentals

Drift Road

P

Everett
Cove

N

0   0.5   1.0
miles

Hixbridge Road

P

Route 88

Drift Road

Codman
Cove

WESTPORT
RIVER

Horseneck Road

MASSACHUSETTS
RHODE ISLAND

Let
Conservation
Area

Demarest Lloyd
State Park

Big Ram
Island

John Reed Road

oak, including white and pin. At one point, we were surprised to see unusual stands of American beech; we suspect these are root-cloned trees that spread vegetatively from planted specimens.

Continuing south, explore the shallow reaches of several inlet creeks on both sides, including Everett Cove and Coleman Hill Creek on the left (east), and Snell Creek on the right (west). In an afternoon paddle, we saw Canada geese, great blue herons, great egrets, mute swans, herring gulls, red-winged blackbirds, and a bald eagle. Eagles had been nesting in a dead tree along here, but that came down in a storm, and we assume they have a new nesting location along the river. Numerous osprey nests occur south of Hix Bridge, making it likely to see those birds here. Marsh wrens sang to us from the salt marsh, though we only caught glimpses of them.

It makes sense to time your paddling with the tides—ideally, close to high tide. With a 3- to 3.5-foot tidal differential, water can be quite shallow at low tide, making it tricky to stay in the channel. We started out just at high tide and had an easy 4-mile paddle to Hix Bridge. Although our return was against the outgoing tide, a south wind (common in the afternoons) counteracted the current and made for easy paddling.

You can also continue upstream a short distance, passing under the Old County Road bridge. At high tide, you can paddle several hundred yards north until shallow water and rocks eventually block your way.

South of Hix Bridge, watch out for motorboat traffic in the channel and strong tidal currents near the Route 88 bridge. Enjoy excellent quietwater paddling along the eastern side, exploring the shallow islands, some with well-used osprey nesting platforms, and the Let Conservation Area. Be careful not to get stuck in the mud at low tide!

Visitors to Horseneck Beach State Reservation, at the river's mouth, bring congestion on pleasant days during summer. But in a kayak or canoe at high tide, you can find plenty of room to explore virtually alone.

TRIP 21

SLOCUMS RIVER

Expect to see herons, egrets, and nesting ospreys when you visit this delightful estuary. The upper reach is well protected, but due to winds in the more open lower bay, especially in the afternoon, it's best to paddle here in the morning. Look for fiddler crabs along the shore at lower tides.

LOCATION Dartmouth, MA

MAPS *Massachusetts Atlas & Gazetteer*, Map 63: C5, C6; USGS New Bedford South, Westport

LENGTH 4 miles one way

TIME 4 hours round trip

HABITAT TYPE Tidal estuary, salt marsh

FISH Striped bass, bluefish (see fish advisory, Appendix A)

INFORMATION Demarest Lloyd State Park, mass.gov/locations/demarest-lloyd-state-park, 508-636-3298 (summer), 508-363-8816 (winter); Lloyd Center for the Environment, lloydcenter.org, 508-990-0505; tide charts, usharbors.com

CAMPING Horseneck Beach State Reservation

TAKE NOTE Little development; motors allowed

GETTING THERE

Slocums River From I-195, Exit 22 southbound, go 5.0 miles south on Faunce Corner Road and then Old Westport Road; veer left on Chase Road, and turn right on Russells Mills Road at the T. Go 1.0 mile (6.0 miles), and stay straight onto Horseneck Road. Continue 0.2 mile (6.2 miles) to the access on the left at Russells Mills Town Park. **41° 34.105′ N, 71° 0.304′ W**

Demarest Lloyd State Park From above, continue south on Horseneck Road, turn left onto Barneys Joy Road, and follow it to the park. **41° 31.538′ N, 70° 59.423′ W**

Lloyd Center for the Environment From the junction of Horseneck and Russells Mills roads, go 2.5 miles (8.5 miles) southeast on Rock O'Dundee and Potomska roads to the entrance on the right. **41° 32.534′ N, 70° 58.665′ W**

WHAT YOU'LL SEE

Slocums River represents one of the best tidal rivers in New England for quiet paddling, birds, and salt marsh plants. You could easily spend a day or two exploring the waterway, getting to know its different personalities at high and low tide. The few houses nearby do not detract from the peace.

The Slocum family originally settled this isolated corner of Dartmouth Township. Joshua Slocum, a distant relative, sailed a small ketch out of nearby Fairhaven and around the world in the early 1900s in the first solo circumnavigation of the Earth in a small craft. The feat perhaps epitomizes the rigor and determination of the early Slocums: Anthony, who first cleared the land,

and Giles, who founded the Society of Friends Apponegansett Meeting in 1638. The society is still active not far from Russells Mills.

The 8-mile round trip from Russells Mills Town Park to Demarest Lloyd State Park at the entrance to Buzzards Bay can be paddled in half a day, but

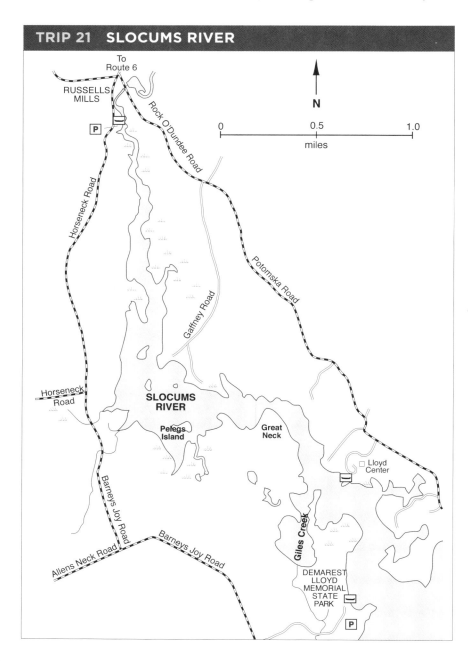

TRIP 21 SLOCUMS RIVER

SECTION 2: SOUTHEASTERN MASSACHUSETTS AND CAPE COD

Slocums River, one of New England's most beautiful tidal estuaries, provides wonderful wildlife-watching opportunities.

we recommend that you spend more time and explore the islands, inlets, and coves. We particularly enjoyed paddling up Giles Creek and the various inlets near Pelegs Island.

Giles Creek often fills with egrets, herons, and gulls that feed amid the salt marsh grass (*Spartina spp.*). At low tide, you may see only the egrets' heads extending above the grasses. An unnamed creek to the west of Pelegs Island offers a superb spot to learn about the salt marsh ecosystem. Paddling up this creek in early September at just about low tide, we saw literally thousands of fiddler crabs along the banks (one claw grows much larger than the other, making the critter look as if it's holding a fiddle). The exposed mud flats seemed to move as we came close and the startled crabs scurried to safety—with the clickety-clack of thousands of tiny legs on the pebbles and mud.

When we visited in early July, some large patches of fragrant swamp azalea diverted our attention from the legions of fiddler crabs. We also imagine that many migrating waterfowl join the resident black ducks in fall. Out on Buzzards Bay, watch for gulls and terns. Though the bay has swells, barrier islands usually keep the water fairly calm.

While here, you may want to visit the Lloyd Center for the Environment, across the mouth of the river from Demarest Lloyd State Park. This highly regarded nature center, on 55 acres, offers exhibits and a wide range of educational programs, nature walks, lectures, and canoe trips. You can reach the center either by boat or by car.

TRIP 22
HERRING RIVER AND WEST RESERVOIR

Birds abound along the Herring River and West Reservoir. Look for osprey, ducks, geese, mute swan, herons, egrets, kingfisher, and treetop warblers. The river's protected upper portion is a gorgeous place to paddle among cattails and streamside grasses.

LOCATION Harwich, MA

MAPS *Massachusetts Atlas & Gazetteer*, Map 67: A4; USGS Harwich

AREA/LENGTH Herring River, 4.5 miles one way; West Reservoir, 47 acres

TIME 4 hours round trip

HABITAT TYPE Freshwater and saltwater estuary; wooded reservoir

FISH Striped bass, bluefish (see fish advisory, Appendix A)

INFORMATION Tide charts, usharbors.com

CAMPING Nickerson State Park

TAKE NOTE Limited development; motors allowed

GETTING THERE

Herring River From the junction of Routes 28 and 134, go 2.1 miles east on Route 28 to the access on the right, just over the bridge. From the junction of Routes 28 and 39, go 0.9 mile west on Route 28 to the access on the left, just before the bridge. **41° 40.108′ N, 70° 6.535′ W**

West Reservoir From the Route 28 bridge over the Herring River, go 0.5 mile west on Route 28, and turn right on Depot Road. Go 0.8 mile (1.3 miles), and bear right on Depot Street. Drive 0.2 mile (1.5 miles), and turn right on an unmarked dirt road. In 0.2 mile (1.7 miles) reach the access by the Harwich Conservation Lands sign. The gate was locked when we last visited; you may have to reach the access by carrying up from the river. **41° 40.95′ N, 0° 7.589′ W**

WHAT YOU'LL SEE
HERRING RIVER

Well away from usual Cape Cod recreation destinations, the Herring River provides superb quietwater paddling through bird-filled saltwater and freshwater marshes. The best paddling occurs from Route 28 up to West Reservoir. You can also travel south to Nantucket Sound, but houses interrupt the solitude below Route 28.

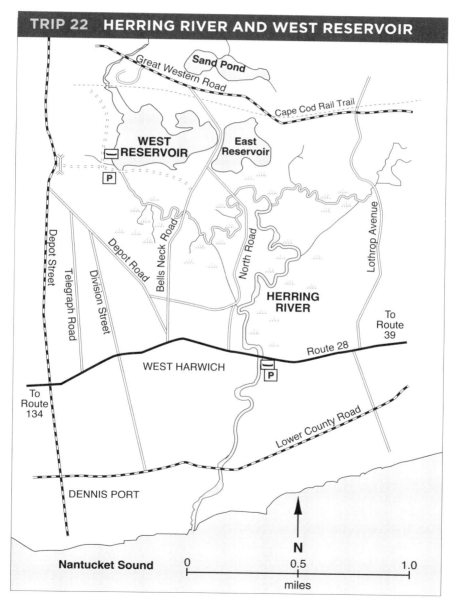

TRIP 22   HERRING RIVER AND WEST RESERVOIR

Great Western Road

Sand Pond

Cape Cod Rail Trail

WEST RESERVOIR

East Reservoir

P

Depot Street

Telegraph Road

Division Street

Depot Road

Bells Neck Road

North Road

Lothrop Avenue

HERRING RIVER

To Route 39

Route 28

WEST HARWICH

P

To Route 134

Lower County Road

DENNIS PORT

N

Nantucket Sound

0   0.5   1.0

miles

Paddling upriver from the Route 28 bridge, you will quickly leave the few houses behind and wind through a wild, broad salt marsh, a tremendous spot for birding. You might see gulls, snowy egrets, great blue and green herons, yellowlegs, Canada geese, cormorants, mallards, black ducks, mute swans, red-winged blackbirds, kingfishers, and various hawks. The salt marsh environment grows thick with grasses and cattails that provide nesting habitat for species of birds that you hear but rarely see: marsh wren, swamp sparrow, Virginia rail, and least bittern. Trees along the marsh's edge contain many woodland species, including northern parula, a warbler that uses the beard moss hanging from many trees here to make its nest.

The Herring River, although tidal for its entire length, has an increasing saltwater gradient as it flows downstream. Heading upriver on an incoming tide makes for easier paddling, although the river flows gently enough that wind—a common Cape companion—usually presents a bigger obstacle than current. Near high tide you can explore numerous little canals and inlets along the river. At the West Reservoir outlet, carry up over the dike on the left by the herring fish ladder to get onto the reservoir. During the herring (alewife) spawning season, you can watch the fish swimming up the fish ladder.

WEST RESERVOIR

West Reservoir provides an excellent location for studying freshwater aquatic plants, birds, and other wildlife. We saw a dozen black-crowned night herons, but the turtle life excited us even more, including literally hundreds of painted turtles sunning on logs. We also saw a good-sized snapper and two far less common stinkpot turtles (*Sternotherus odoratus*). This latter species sports a steeply humped carapace that seems undersized, has a pointed "beak," and emits a musky smell you will probably notice if you pick one up (a defensive secretion released from glands on both sides of the body). The odor that emanates from the stinkpot and other musk turtles gives them their names. Generally, you see these turtles underwater, but on occasion they sun on protruding logs or rocks, even in trees—and unlike painted turtles, they may allow you to paddle quietly right up to them for close observation. Rare spotted and box turtles also occur here, although we've not seen any on our trips.

Groves of black and white oaks and pitch pine surround this fairly deep reservoir. Black gum (also called black or swamp tupelo)—with brilliant crimson fall foliage—grows by the water's edge. The Town of Harwich Conservation Lands protects much of the land surrounding the reservoir and the Herring River. A pleasant trail and several dirt roads begin at the reservoir. Also, the Cape Cod Rail Trail passes the reservoir's north end. This wonderful biking and hiking trail extends for 25 miles along an abandoned railway bed through the towns of Dennis, Harwich, Brewster, Orleans, Eastham, and Wellfleet.

NAUSET MARSH AND SALT POND BAY

Nauset Marsh provides hours of paddling through hundreds of salt marsh acres. Shorebirds and other birds occur in profusion. Not many people paddle here, and navigating can be a bit tricky. Low tide can leave you stranded, and wind often howls across the marsh unimpeded.

LOCATION Eastham, MA

MAPS *Massachusetts Atlas & Gazetteer*, Map 61: B6, C6; USGS Orleans

AREA 1,300 acres

TIME 4 hours or more

HABITAT TYPE Tidal estuary, salt marsh

FISH Striped bass, bluefish (see fish advisory, Appendix A)

INFORMATION Cape Cod National Seashore, nps.gov/caco, Salt Pond Visitor Center, 508-255-3421; tide charts, usharbors.com

CAMPING Nickerson State Park

TAKE NOTE Little development; too shallow for motors in most places; check with rangers at Salt Pond Visitor Center about tide and wind conditions before venturing out; novice paddlers should avoid this area; red tide has closed the marsh to shellfishing in recent years

GETTING THERE

Salt Pond From Route 6 eastbound at the rotary where the limited-access highway ends, continue 2.7 miles east on Route 6, and turn right on Salt Pond Landing. **41° 50.106′ N, 69° 58.407′ W**

Salt Pond Visitor Center From Salt Pond Landing, go 0.2 mile north on Route 6, turn right on Nauset Road, and continue 100 feet to the visitor center on the right. **41° 50.278′ N, 69° 58.360′ W**

WHAT YOU'LL SEE

Salt Pond Bay in Nauset Marsh provides enjoyable paddling in a fascinating salt marsh ecosystem, at least at high tide. Low tide exposes vast areas of mud flats that could leave you stranded. We paddled here twice on falling tides and both times had to drag our boats through rapidly retreating waters. Fortunately, the mud underfoot was quite solid. At high tide you can paddle around quite easily, but watch out for strong tidal currents in some channels. Also, wind can cause problems as it blows unimpeded over vast expanses of salt marsh and low-lying islands.

Cape Cod National Seashore—a 40-mile-long preserve of dunes, beach, and estuary between Chatham and Provincetown—includes Nauset Marsh.

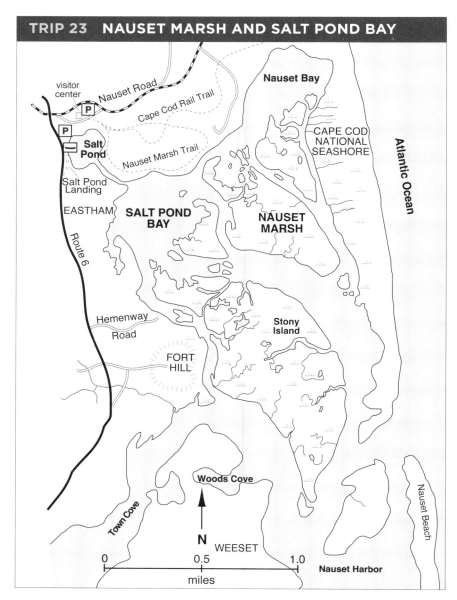

TRIP 23   NAUSET MARSH AND SALT POND BAY

visitor center

Nauset Road

Cape Cod Rail Trail

Nauset Marsh Trail

Salt Pond

Salt Pond Landing

EASTHAM

Route 6

SALT POND BAY

Nauset Bay

CAPE COD NATIONAL SEASHORE

Atlantic Ocean

NAUSET MARSH

Hemenway Road

FORT HILL

Stony Island

Woods Cove

Town Cove

N

WEESET

Nauset Beach

Nauset Harbor

0   0.5   1.0

miles

Established in 1961, the national seashore provides superb hiking, bicycling, swimming, and fishing opportunities for tens of thousands of visitors each year, though few people think of paddling here. Salt Pond, where you launch, was once a freshwater kettle-hole pond, but the ocean broke through, and tides now feed the pond twice daily through a narrow channel connecting it to Salt Pond Bay and the large Nauset Marsh estuary.

Nauset Marsh, a classic tidal estuary, is rich in birdlife, woodland mammals, marine animals (including quahogs, oysters, mussels, and various fish), and the unusual plants that compose this ecosystem. As you get out into the bay, note the thick masses of peat that gulls and sandpipers scour for food on the many islands that dot this huge marsh. On one early trip, we watched 50 harbor seals near the break between Coast Guard and Nauset beaches (harbor seals winter in this area, but most head to Maine to raise their young). Today, gray seal populations have mushroomed, making them much more common and also drawing in more great white sharks. (As of this writing, the increased shark presence has not dampened beachgoer enthusiasm.)

We spent many hours looking with binoculars at myriad birdlife, including skeins of cormorants and several gull species. Black duck, kingfisher, great blue heron, snowy egret, semipalmated plover, black-bellied plover, lesser yellowlegs, and sanderling also frequent this location. Alas, we did not see the threatened piping plover that nests on the beach, of which Thoreau had this to say:

> But if I were required to name a sound, the remembrance of which most perfectly revives the impression which the beach has made, it would be the dreary peep of the piping plover (*Charadrius melodus*) which haunts there. Their voices, too, are heard as a fugacious part in the dirge which is ever played along the shore for those mariners who have been lost in the deep since first it was created. But through all this dreariness we seemed to have a pure and unqualified strain of eternal melody, for always the same strain which is a dirge to one household is a morning song of rejoicing to another.
>
> —*Cape Cod* (1865)

If you are here at low tide, you can enjoy wonderful hiking near the Salt Pond Visitor Center or, farther north, within Cape Cod National Seashore. Nauset Marsh Trail leads from the Salt Pond Visitor Center along the east side of Salt Pond and then along the edge of Salt Pond Bay. This mile-long trail provides a great way to learn to identify some of the more common flora here: black oak, pitch pine, black locust, eastern red cedar (juniper), beach plum, winterberry, saltmeadow cordgrass, and smooth cordgrass. Get a trail map at the visitor center.

A lesser yellowlegs scurries along the shore of Nauset Marsh.

Also, you can bicycle the scenic 25-mile Cape Cod Rail Trail that connects the visitor center with Nickerson State Park. Occupying the bed of an abandoned railway, this ideal biking trail covers generally flat terrain with minimal road crossings and interruptions. You can pick up a map of the trail and rent bicycles at Nickerson State Park.

SECTION 3

MARTHA'S VINEYARD

Long known as a destination for sailing, beachcombing, bed-and-breakfast hopping, gift shopping, and general vacationing, Martha's Vineyard also offers truly spectacular paddling. We include descriptions of six bodies of water in this guide. Most have permanent or periodic access to the sea, which renews their nutrients and fish species.

Many people come here to fish for striped bass and bluefish. Most visitors reach Martha's Vineyard via ferry out of Woods Hole. Summer rates for the ferry in 2023 ranged from $202 to $270 round-trip for a car, depending on vehicle length and day of the week, plus $20 per passenger and driver; reservations are highly recommended.

Anyone wishing to paddle on Martha's Vineyard should think about timing. The population increases from about 16,000 in winter to more than 100,000 during peak summer periods. Unless you reserve early, the ferry, inns, and campsites will be full. Many visitors scoot around on mopeds when not shopping, contributing to traffic problems. A possible solution: Schedule your visit before mid-June or after Labor Day (ferry rates drop after November 1). You might not get warm sun during off-season visits, but you will compete less for space.

The island's great salt ponds offer fabulous paddling, but we do not recommend the Vineyard to novice paddlers. Sailboarders love the Vineyard for its windy conditions, and sudden weather changes crop up often. Ponds open to the sea can suffer from extremely strong tidal currents—in some places the tidal current moves faster than you can paddle. Combined with a strong breeze, this can engender very hazardous paddling conditions. A paddleboarder fatality in 2023 on Edgartown Great Pond brought these risks to light. Use caution and good sense when paddling here so that you can fully enjoy what the Vineyard offers. Wear PFDs, especially with children—simply having PFDs onboard is not sufficient.

The information below pertains to all trips in this section.

INFORMATION For ferry reservations: steamshipauthority.com. For tide charts: usharbors.com.

BOOKS *Discover Martha's Vineyard* (see Appendix B).

CAMPING AND ACCOMMODATIONS One private campground: Martha's Vineyard Family Campground—in Vineyard Haven, campmv.com/staying-with-us. Accommodations: American Youth Hostel, hiusa.org/find-hostels; Martha's Vineyard Chamber of Commerce, mvy.com.

TAKE NOTE Motors are allowed on most ponds, though limited access and the island location mean that motorboating disturbance is relatively modest; minimal development; wind and tide can create hazardous conditions—novice paddlers should avoid this area on windy days; wear PFD; respect private property.

TRIP 24

EDGARTOWN GREAT POND

Edgartown Great Pond is one of our favorite paddling spots in Massachusetts. Wildlife abounds. Look for osprey, herons, egrets, and tree-top warblers. You might see otters and least terns and piping plovers on the dunes. Salt-tolerant plants inhabit most of the shoreline, with occasional salt-intolerant plants in some coves, leading to high plant species diversity.

LOCATION Edgartown, MA

MAPS *Massachusetts Atlas & Gazetteer*, Map 69: B5; USGS Edgartown

AREA 890 acres

TIME All day; shorter trips possible

HABITAT TYPE Saltwater pond, salinity depends on how long the pond has been cut off from the ocean

FISH Striped bass, bluefish, white perch (see fish advisory, Appendix A)

GETTING THERE

From Main Street in Edgartown, go 1.8 miles west on Edgartown–West Tisbury Road, and turn left on Meeting House Way. Go 1.4 miles (3.2 miles) on a rough, sandy road, and then turn sharply right onto a less traveled, unmarked sand road. The access is in 0.8 mile (4.0 miles). Be careful not to block the access points used for loading by commercial shellfish harvesters.
41° 22.006' N, 70° 33.027' W

WHAT YOU'LL SEE

One of our favorite paddling spots in all of Massachusetts, Edgartown Great Pond has very little development, lots of wildlife, a 10 HP limit, and more than 15 miles of shoreline to explore. The pond's south edge backs up against a barrier beach, separating it from the Atlantic Ocean, and you can hear waves crash just across the low dunes. The beach isolates the pond from the ocean, freeing it from tidal currents.

Edgartown Great Pond and Tisbury Great Pond (Trip 25) stand among the best remaining examples anywhere of great salt ponds, a geological feature

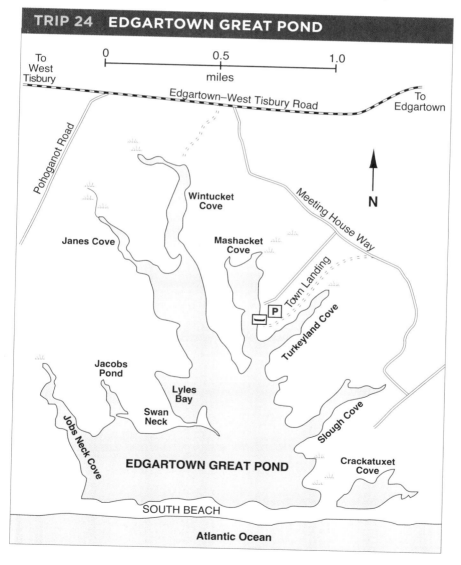

TRIP 24 EDGARTOWN GREAT POND

of coastal outwash plains. The rippling topography on Martha's Vineyard resulted from glacial streams depositing till as they flowed. As glaciers receded northward, meltwater flowed south off them, creating streams carrying silt and sand, which eventually deposited their burden to form the outwash plains found here and on Nantucket, Cape Cod, and Long Island. Moving coastal sands then sealed off the south end of these ponds with barrier beaches.

The great salt ponds' varying salinity results in considerable plant and animal diversity. Periodically, storms open and close channels between pond and ocean, causing freshwater and salt water to mix. Hurricane Bob in 1991, for example, swept ocean water over the barrier beach, thoroughly mixing Edgartown Great Pond's water with sea water in a few hours. In recent decades, an artificial channel has been cut four times a year to maintain adequate salinity for shellfish and to allow alewives to enter, followed by the great angling prize, striped bass. But major storms can make that work difficult. In 2012, both Hurricane Sandy and a following nor'easter deposited huge amounts of sand, closing off the pond.

At the tips of some Edgartown Great Pond coves, freshwater ecosystems harbor salt-intolerant plants, such as cranberry, wool grass, and grass pink (a type of orchid). Salt-tolerant species, such as salt marsh grasses (*Spartina spp.*), glasswort, and saline saltbush, grow along the main pond.

Piping plover, a threatened species, and least tern, a species of special concern, nest on the dunes here. Ospreys nest on several platforms around the

Edgartown Great Pond, a rare great salt pond, boasts more than 15 miles of shoreline, filled with wildlife.

pond, and numerous warblers and other songbirds nest in the surrounding area. Paddling here in September, we saw many great blue herons, snowy and great egrets, black-crowned night herons, black-backed and herring gulls, and various sandpipers and plovers. We also had the good fortune to see a family of five otters. Otter density on the Vineyard is probably the highest in Massachusetts. Look for otters early in the morning or toward dusk.

Janes Cove seems the most remote of the Edgartown Great Pond coves. We saw the otters and a pair of large snapping turtles here. Note the thick moss draped over some of the old red maples and beetlebung trees (a local name for black gum). Jobs Neck Cove, with just one house on it, also looks great. As you paddle along the shore, watch for blue crabs scurrying away. Specimens up to 8 inches across occur here (note the bright blue claws of some individuals).

Historically, the Wampanoag settled here and periodically opened the pond to the sea to maintain their fishery. Later, settlers fished here as early as 1660, primarily for alewife. A school of alewives feeding at the surface of calm water looks like a mass of bubbles breaking the surface. They enter the pond through the South Beach opening in spring to spawn, leaving in fall when the barrier beach breaches. Anglers also catch yellow and white perch, eel, and occasional trapped oceanic fish such as striped bass, flounder, and bluefish. Today, the primary commercial fishery in Edgartown Great Pond is shellfish: oysters and steamer clams.

During the COVID pandemic, The Nature Conservancy entered into a unique partnership with commercial oyster producers to buy, at a discounted price, oversized oysters that could not be sold commercially and to use those oysters to restore oyster beds in the Slough Cove area of Edgartown Great Pond. This kept oyster producers in business while restoring ecosystems.

Paddling the full perimeter of Edgartown Great Pond could easily take a full day, especially if you spend time studying its varied plants and wildlife. Remember to respect private property. Except for the public landing on Mashacket Neck, the entire shoreline is privately owned: no camping and no strolling along South Beach allowed.

TRIP 25

TISBURY GREAT POND

Tisbury Great Pond is very similar to Edgartown Great Pond. Look here for the same species: osprey, herons and egrets, warblers, otter, least tern, and piping plover, along with high plant species diversity.

LOCATION Chilmark and West Tisbury, MA

MAPS *Massachusetts Atlas & Gazetteer*, Map 69: B4; USGS Tisbury Great Pond, Vineyard Haven

AREA 790 acres

TIME All day; shorter trips possible

HABITAT TYPE Saltwater pond, brackish water

FISH Striped bass, bluefish, white perch (see fish advisory, Appendix A)

GETTING THERE

From Main Street in Edgartown, go 7.7 miles west on Edgartown–West Tisbury Road, and turn left on New Lane (coming from West Tisbury, New Lane is 0.3 mile past Old Country Road). New Lane quickly becomes Tiah Cove Road. Go 1.2 miles (8.9 miles), and turn right on Clam Point Road. Park on

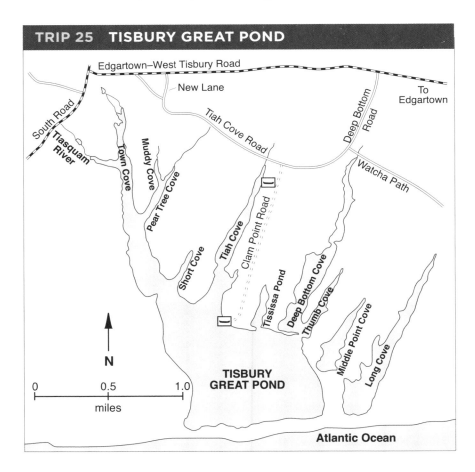

the left; carry your boat about 200 feet down to the water. **41° 22.340′ N, 70° 38.954′ W**

An access at the end of Clam Point Road allows a shorter carry. **41° 21.623′N, 70° 39.291′ W**

WHAT YOU'LL SEE

With long, fingerlike coves that head away from the barrier beach, Tisbury Great Pond closely resembles Edgartown Great Pond (Trip 24), with one important difference: Tisbury suffers more from development. To get a feel for what it would be like to paddle on Tisbury, see the Edgartown Great Pond trip. Martha's Vineyard Land Bank owns property along Tiah Cove, which contains the public access. In 2013, The Nature Conservancy, along with the towns of Chilmark and West Tisbury, were in the process of developing an oyster sanctuary in the middle of the pond.

All the Vineyard's great ponds suffer from nitrogen eutrophication, mostly from septic tanks and leach fields, but also from sewage treatment plants and fertilizer runoff. In an effort to reduce harmful algal blooms resulting from too much nitrogen, the towns have taken significant steps to reduce nitrogen pollution.

TRIP 26

POCHA POND

Perched on the northwest corner of the Vineyard, Pocha Pond offers the most remote paddling, along scenic dunes. Look for herons and egrets and all the other birds that populate the Vineyard's ponds. For an extended trip, paddle up into Cape Poge Bay, at least under less windy conditions.

LOCATION Edgartown, MA

MAPS *Massachusetts Atlas & Gazetteer*, Map 69: B6; USGS Edgartown

AREA 210 acres

TIME 2 hours, more if you paddle Cape Poge Bay

HABITAT TYPE Saltwater pond and marsh

FISH Striped bass, bluefish (see fish advisory, Appendix A)

INFORMATION Long Cove, Cape Poge Wildlife Refuge, Wasque Reservation, or Mytoi Japanese-style garden: The Trustees of Reservations, thetrustees.org; Chappaquiddick Ferry, chappyferry.com

TAKE NOTE Cape Poge Bay not recommended for novice paddlers

GETTING THERE
From Edgartown, take the ferry to Chappaquiddick Island ($15 plus $5 per passenger in 2023). From the ferry, go 2.4 miles east on Chappaquiddick Road, and continue straight on dirt Dike Road when the paved road curves sharply right. Go 0.6 mile (3.0 miles) to the access at Dike Bridge. **41° 22.416′ N, 70° 27.235′ W**

WHAT YOU'LL SEE
This pond and the connecting channel into Cape Poge Bay provide wonderful paddling and public access across the Cape Poge dunes to several miles of beautiful, remote ocean beach. From the access, you can paddle south into Pocha Pond. A couple of houses near the end of Dike Road and a few at the pond's south end represent the only signs of development amid acres of marvelous salt marsh.

Paddling here on a September morning, we saw dozens of great blue herons, great and snowy egrets, gulls, and cormorants, plus a few black scoters and kingfishers. Salt marsh plants include Carolina sea lavender (*Limonium carolinianum*), glasswort (*Salicornia depressa*), and salt marsh cordgrasses (*Spartina*

Pocha Pond offers some of the most remote paddling on Martha's Vineyard ponds.

patens and *S. alterniflora*). Pocha Pond links to the sea via the Cape Poge Gut, so only plants that withstand saltwater flooding survive here. On the exposed peat at low tide, beneath the salt marsh grass, grow diverse seaweeds and mussels, and in the water, sponge colonies, various crabs, and mollusks (we found some very large whelk shells). Past the open marsh, you will see pitch pine, scrub and swamp white oaks, and black gum.

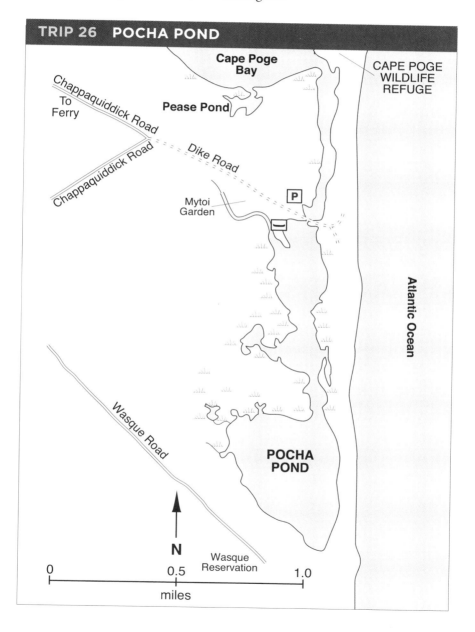

Just southwest of Dike Bridge, a narrow inlet creek invites exploration. Watch out for mollusk-encrusted rocks and shell conglomerates here, particularly near low tide. A phragmites marsh inhabits the end of this little creek, along with a dense grove of black gum, whose leaves turn brilliant crimson in early fall.

North of Dike Bridge, the channel narrows along Toms Neck (an area called the Lagoon) but opens up into Cape Poge Bay. In a strong breeze, the bay gets quite rough. With winds from the south, you can reach Pease Pond without too much difficulty (at low tide, exposed sand banks present obstacles). You can also land on the Atlantic side of the Lagoon or Cape Poge Bay and hike the 14 miles of trails in the wildlife refuge along the beach, although four-wheeler trails preclude having a true wilderness experience. Also, note that poison ivy grows profusely amid the dunes. Waves crash the sandy shores of this beautiful beach. Surf fishing for striped bass and bluefish is considered to be among the best on the Atlantic Coast—and you may find some interesting things washed up on the beach; on a visit many years ago, we came across the remains of a whale.

TRIP 27

MENEMSHA POND AND QUITSA POND

We prefer to paddle here late in the day to take advantage of gorgeous sunsets, with light playing on the buildings of a classic New England fishing village. Because of treacherous currents at the put-in on Menemsha Pond, we prefer starting out at Quitsa Pond (Nashaquitsa Pond).

LOCATION Chilmark and Gay Head, MA

MAPS *Massachusetts Atlas & Gazetteer*, Map 68: B3, C3; USGS Squibnocket

AREA Menemsha Pond, 665 acres

TIME 4 hours

HABITAT TYPE Saltwater pond, open to ocean

FISH Striped bass, bluefish (see fish advisory, Appendix A)

TAKE NOTE Strong rip current at jetty, north end of Menemsha Pond; area not recommended for novice paddlers; significant road noise

GETTING THERE

Quitsa Pond From the junction of Menemsha Cross Road and State Road in Chilmark, go 1.3 miles southwest on State Road to the access at the bridge. **41° 19.722′ N, 70° 45.598′ W**

Menemsha Pond From the junction of Menemsha Cross Road and North Road northwest of Chilmark, go 0.5 mile southwest on North Road, and turn right on Basin Road. Go 0.3 mile (0.8 mile) to the parking lot at Dutcher Dock. Hand launch just before the jetty. **41° 21.268′ N, 70° 46.004′ W**

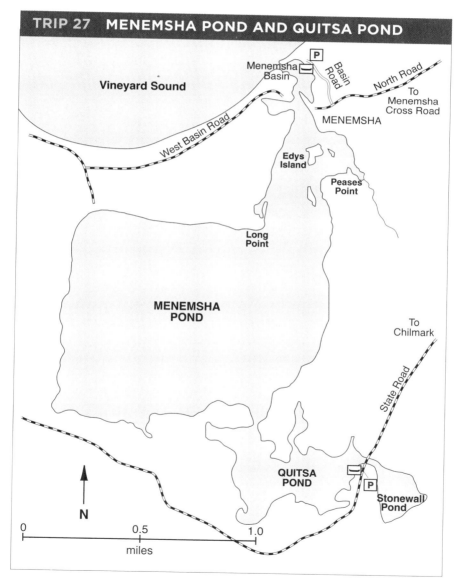

TRIP 27 MENEMSHA POND AND QUITSA POND

Vineyard Sound

Menemsha Basin

Basin Road

North Road

To Menemsha Cross Road

MENEMSHA

West Basin Road

Edys Island

Peases Point

Long Point

MENEMSHA POND

To Chilmark

State Road

N

QUITSA POND

Stonewall Pond

0   0.5   1.0

miles

Quitsa (or Nashquitsa) Pond is smaller and more protected from wind and currents than Menemsha Pond to the north; a channel connects the two.

WHAT YOU'LL SEE

From the water at the north end of Menemsha Pond, you can admire a quintessential New England fishing village, known outside the region as the backdrop for the movie *Jaws*. Some fishing boats that dock here run very large. Smaller fishing and sailing boats moor along the perimeter of both Menemsha and Quitsa ponds. Despite the development, we recommend paddling here for the scenic beauty, especially the renowned sunsets. You could use the access at the end of Dutcher Dock near the large public beach area at the north end of Menemsha Pond, but because of strong tidal currents on Menemsha Creek leading into the pond, we recommend the access on Quitsa Pond. If you paddle up to Menemsha's north end, use caution there to avoid strong tides.

The northern shore and an area near the southwest tip of Menemsha Pond are part of the Wampanoag-Aquinnah Land Trust, owned by the Wampanoag Tribe of Gay Head, a federally recognized Native American Tribe. Near the southwest tip of Menemsha Pond is a culvert connecting Menemsha and Squibnocket ponds.

SENGEKONTACKET POND

Although this pond suffers from development and road noise, it's well worth exploring the numerous marshy coves and islands along the western shore. Look for the typical plants and birds of the Vineyard here.

LOCATION Edgartown and Oak Bluffs, MA

MAPS *Massachusetts Atlas & Gazetteer*, Map 69: A5, B5; USGS Edgartown

AREA 726 acres

TIME 5 hours

HABITAT TYPE Saltwater pond

FISH Striped bass, bluefish (see fish advisory, Appendix A)

INFORMATION Felix Neck Wildlife Sanctuary, Massachusetts Audubon Society, massaudubon.org/places-to-explore/wildlife-sanctuaries/felix-neck

TAKE NOTE Significant road noise; much of the shoreline is conserved; wind and tide can create hazardous conditions—novice paddlers should use great care

GETTING THERE

From the junction of Edgartown and Vineyard Haven roads in Edgartown, go 2.0 miles north on Edgartown–Oak Bluffs (Beach) Road to the access on the left. You could also hand-launch from several other locations along the road. **41° 25.914′ N, 70° 33.397′ W**

WHAT YOU'LL SEE

Located between Oak Bluffs and Edgartown, this large pond suffers from a fair amount of development and road noise but offers pleasant paddling nonetheless. Numerous marshy coves and islands along the western shore beg to be explored. On Felix Neck near the pond's midpoint (reachable from Vineyard Haven Road), the Massachusetts Audubon Society maintains Felix Neck Wildlife Sanctuary, which offers a trail network, various educational programs, and research programs, including osprey monitoring.

Several other natural areas around Sengekontacket Pond, including Pecoy Point Preserve and Caroline Tuthill Wildlife Preserve, along with the Farm Neck Golf Club, near the north end, limit residential development and result in a wilder feel to the shoreline. Funding provided by the Martha's Vineyard

Land Bank and the general appreciation of open space by residents of the Vineyard have contributed to these and other natural areas on the island, and paddlers can benefit from that.

Fortunately, you don't have to be able to pronounce the pond's name to paddle on it.

TRIP 28 SENGEKONTACKET POND

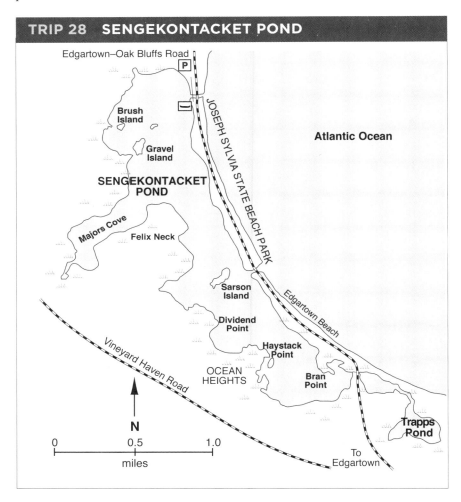

SECTION 4

CENTRAL MASSACHUSETTS

Seventeen entries compose this section of Massachusetts and include several within fabulous wildlife refuges. The bodies of water extend from the New Hampshire border to the Connecticut border and lie between I-91 and I-495.

Many wilderness and semiwilderness areas occur in the region. We love paddling Tully Lake and East Branch Tully River, where you're virtually guaranteed to see beaver on an evening outing. Wildlife refuges, wildlife management areas, and state forests encompass sections of additional rivers, including the Nashua, Squannacook, Quaboag, East Brookfield, Quinebaug, Millers, Otter, and Ware rivers, making them wildlife-rich locations. Most of these waterways flow lazily through extensive wetlands, backed by unbroken forest. Compared with eastern Massachusetts rivers, they exude a wilder feel. We see lots of muskrats when paddling here, along with the occasional river otter. On one trip on the Ware River, we saw a great horned owl and a coyote, both close up. Sometimes we see mink. Birdlife abounds.

Two of these rivers, the Quaboag and the Ware, meet the Swift River in Three Rivers, there forming the Chicopee River. We describe the downstream section of the Chicopee River, backed up behind a dam.

We include Pottapaug Pond, the one part of giant Quabbin Reservoir that's open to paddlers. Adjacent Muddy Brook, which flows into Hardwick Pond, possibly attracts the fewest paddlers, particularly in its upper reaches that traverse some serious beaver swamps; we spotted a beaver in the middle of the day, indicating that it probably sees few human intruders. Though not protected by federal or state lands, Beaver Brook offers a great place to paddle through an extensive swamp. It's marshier than most other rivers and an excellent location to look for beaver and muskrat.

We also mention some small ponds that you can paddle, which we sometimes visit to study aquatic plants. We've seen huge blooms of eastern purple bladderwort on Eames Pond. In June, we like to travel to Paradise Pond for its spectacular mountain laurel bloom. If you want to paddle through abundant floating aquatic vegetation, then by all means visit Lake Rohunta.

TRIP 29

NASHUA RIVER AND PEPPERELL POND

We include two sections of the Nashua River, with this, the northern section, backed up behind a dam in Pepperell. Numerous channels and coves provide habitat for a variety of wildlife and hours of paddling. Look for muskrat, beaver, mink, otter, and many bird species.

LOCATION Groton and Pepperell, MA

MAPS *Massachusetts Atlas & Gazetteer*, Map 27: B4, B5; USGS Pepperell

LENGTH 5 miles one way

TIME 6 hours

HABITAT TYPE Dammed-up meandering river; shrubby marshlands; many islands and protected bays

FISH Largemouth, smallmouth, and calico bass; yellow perch; pickerel (see fish advisory, Appendix A)

CAMPING Willard Brook State Forest, Pearl Hill State Park

INFORMATION J. Harry Rich State Forest, stateparks.com/j_harry_rich _state_forest_in_massachusetts.html

TAKE NOTE Little development; motors allowed; take care to avoid getting lost

GETTING THERE
From Groton at the junction of Routes 111, 119, and 225, go 1.4 miles north on Routes 111 and 119 to the access on the right, just before the bridge. **42° 37.62′ N, 71° 35.571′ W**

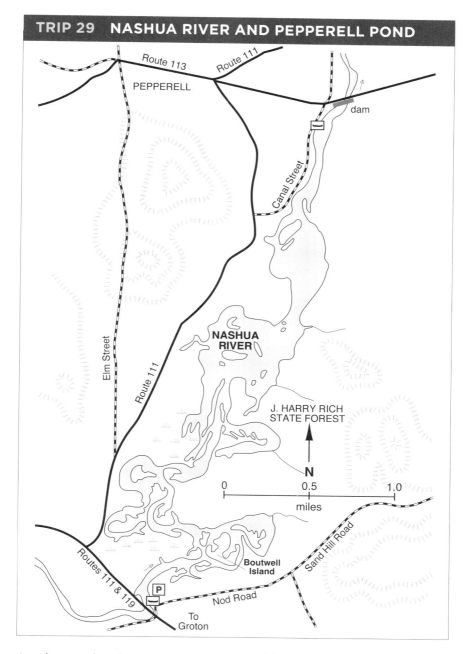

TRIP 29 NASHUA RIVER AND PEPPERELL POND

An alternate hand-carry access, maintained by the Pepperell Conservation Commission, is on Canal Street, 0.1 mile south of Route 113 in Pepperell.
42° 39.832′ N, 71° 34.693′ W

WHAT YOU'LL SEE

Pepperell Pond, a dammed-up section of the Nashua River, lying halfway between Fitchburg and Lowell, would take an entire day to explore fully. Twists and turns among the many islands, coupled with adjacent oxbows and side channels, turn this inundated marshland into a giant 5-mile-long maze. Be careful not to become disoriented. If you have limited time and want to avoid getting lost, take along a compass and a photocopy of this book's map.

A shrubby, marshy shoreline provides cover for numerous ducks, geese, and other birds. We observed lots of beaver activity and several muskrats. As we paddled along, we thought we saw a beaver swimming. When it hustled out onto a 25-foot-long, horizontal dead tree and ran toward the shore, we realized it was a gorgeous reddish gray mink, which dove for cover into the dead tree's stump. If you sit patiently, chances are a mink will pop back into view after a few minutes to check you out, as this one did. Confirming that we were interlopers, it slipped back into the stump.

Though shrubs and cattails cover much of the marshy shoreline, a large number of majestic white pines tower overhead, especially along the eastern shore in the J. Harry Rich State Forest, giving the entire area a substantial wilderness feel. The state allows motors but limits their speed to 22 MPH.

We love paddling here in spring, listening to the returning songbirds staking out their nesting territories and the choruses of spring peepers. This location's gorgeous setting, large size, and plentiful wildlife make it one of the best places to paddle in central Massachusetts.

TRIP 30

SQUANNACOOK RIVER

The Squannacook provides a peaceful paddling resource away from civilization and road noise. Anglers ply the water for trout, and birds fill the trees. Look for wood duck, beaver, and muskrat.

LOCATION Groton and Shirley, MA

MAPS *Massachusetts Atlas & Gazetteer*, Map 27: B4; USGS Ayer, Townsend

LENGTH 3 miles one way

TIME 3 hours round trip

HABITAT TYPE Dammed-up meandering river; extensive marshlands

FISH Brook, brown, and rainbow trout (see fish advisory, Appendix A)

CAMPING Willard Brook State Forest, Pearl Hill State Park

TAKE NOTE No development; too shallow for motors

GETTING THERE

From the junction of Routes 13 and 119 in Townsend, go 2.8 miles east on Route 119, and turn right on Townsend Road. Go 2.5 miles (5.3 miles), and turn right by the yellow fire hydrant at the West Groton Water Supply plant on the right. **42° 36.893′ N, 71° 38.332′ W**

From Route 225 in West Groton, go 1.1 miles north on Townsend Road to the access on the left.

WHAT YOU'LL SEE

Paddling through Squannacook River Wildlife Management Area, away from the bustle of everyday life, you may become entranced with the peacefulness.

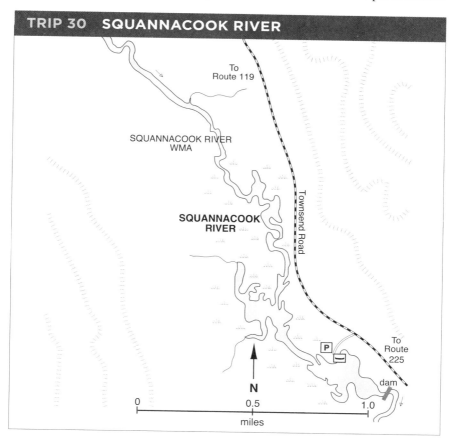

TRIP 30   SQUANNACOOK RIVER

Marshlands spread out like fingers in the lower reaches, providing ample opportunity for exploration. Birdlife abounds, and—judging by the number of anglers—trout fill the waters. The side channels flourish with American white waterlily, along with lesser amounts of yellow pondlily, watershield, pondweed, and pickerelweed.

We found an enormous beaver lodge with winter stores of freshly cut boughs jammed butt-first into the mud. Beaver swim out under the winter ice, retrieving branches to gnaw the bark that sustains them. We watched the occasional musk-rat harvest streamside grasses for winter. Great blue herons patrolled the coves, and we scared up a few flocks of wood ducks as we intruded on their territories.

As you paddle upstream away from the dam, side channels disappear, and the canopy closes in over the narrow, twisting river. Besides the occasional white pine, deciduous trees hold sway. We paddled the Squannacook on a truly gorgeous, misty but balmy autumn day. Fall colors filled the air, and migrating sparrows filled the streamside vegetation. We navigated upstream through the slow current until a ledgy rapids blocked our way. We lingered there, soaking in the golden hues of the streamside ferns and regretting our need to turn around.

TRIP 31

BEAVER BROOK

Beaver Brook is a heavily vegetated haven for wildlife, surrounded by suburban Westford. Expect to see cattail, pickerelweed, smartweed, and the usual assemblage of marshland birds. We saw an otter here, and beaver often appear at dusk.

LOCATION Littleton and Westford, MA

MAPS *Massachusetts Atlas & Gazetteer*, Map 27: C6; USGS Westford

LENGTH 3 miles one way

TIME 4 hours round trip

HABITAT TYPE Meandering, slow-flowing, cattail-lined brook

FISH Trout, largemouth bass, yellow perch, pickerel (see fish advisory, Appendix A)

CAMPING Willard Brook State Forest, Pearl Hill State Park

TAKE NOTE Little development; too shallow for motors

GETTING THERE

From I-495, Exit 80, go 0.7 mile west on Route 119, and turn right on Beaver Brook Road. Go 1.2 miles (1.9 miles) to the access on the right, just over the bridge. **42° 34.355′ N, 71° 28.71′ W**

WHAT YOU'LL SEE

You can paddle downstream from the unimproved boat ramp (other side of the road from the access) on Beaver Brook Road a few hundred feet to the

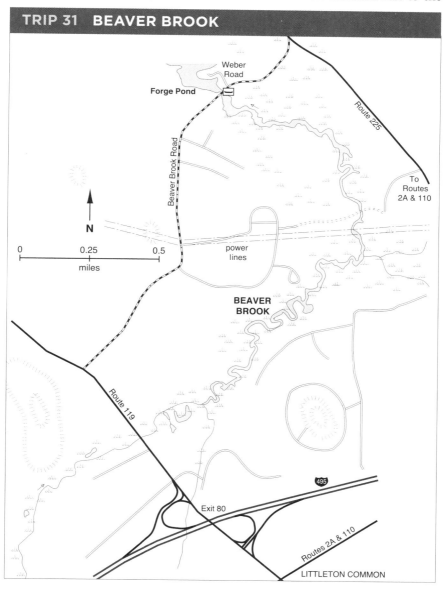

TRIP 31   BEAVER BROOK

Weber Road

Forge Pond

Route 225

Beaver Brook Road

To Routes 2A & 110

N

0   0.25   0.5

miles

power lines

BEAVER BROOK

Route 119

495

Exit 80

Routes 2A & 110

LITTLETON COMMON

Forge Pond inlet, but we wouldn't bother paddling the pond itself because of development and because of numerous high-powered motorboats that populate these waters. Going back upstream from Forge Pond, we contemplated paddling through one of the twin culverts under Beaver Brook Road but decided against it. Debris clogged the upstream ends of both culverts, and dragging the boat over the accumulated debris while crouched—trying to dodge the dozens of spiderwebs hanging from the culvert ceilings—did not seem appealing.

Instead, we portaged up over the road and put in at the easy access on the northeast side of the bridge. You can avoid carrying over the road by parking at this access. Even though we paddled here in mid-September, we immediately started seeing wildlife. Look for red-winged blackbird, great blue heron, black duck, green heron, Canada goose, common yellowthroat, yellow warbler, and other marshland species. We saw dozens of painted turtles, including a surprisingly large number of young ones.

While we did not see any of the eponymous beaver on our visit, we did see quite a bit of evidence of them. (You should be able to see beaver here in the evening.) Just south of Beaver Brook Road on our way back to the access, with the afternoon trending toward dusk, we glimpsed a river otter that quickly disappeared into the marsh.

Cattails line the shore of this section of Beaver Brook. Beaver often keep channels open on narrow streams, making paddling easier.

Although cattails dominate this brook, we also observed plenty of American white waterlily, yellow pondlily, pickerelweed, bulrush, sensitive fern, marsh fern, buttonbush, and a reddish-stemmed aquatic smartweed in bloom—extensive smartweed stands gave the shoreline a pinkish blush in places. Some shoreline red maples had begun to turn red. Farther from shore, white pine dominates, interspersed with sugar maple, ash, and other northern hardwoods.

We paddled a little more than a mile upstream from the access until thick vegetation blocked our way. In early spring, before cattails fill the channel, you should be able to push farther upstream—although probably not all the way to Route 119.

TRIP 32

NASHUA RIVER AND OXBOW NATIONAL WILDLIFE REFUGE

This protected section of river is a wonderful paddling resource, filled with ducks and other birdlife. Look for deer, muskrat, and painted and snapping turtles under the branches of silver maple that extend out over the water.

LOCATION Bolton, Harvard, Lancaster, and Shirley, MA

MAPS *Massachusetts Atlas & Gazetteer*, Map 27: C4, Map 39: A4; USGS Ayer, Hudson

LENGTH 9.5 miles one way

TIME 7 hours round trip

HABITAT TYPE Meandering, slow-flowing river

FISH Largemouth, smallmouth, and calico bass; yellow perch; pickerel (see fish advisory, Appendix A)

INFORMATION Oxbow National Wildlife Refuge, fws.gov/refuge/oxbow

CAMPING Willard Brook State Forest, Pearl Hill State Park

TAKE NOTE A little development north of Route 2; too shallow for motors

GETTING THERE

From Route 2, Exit 109, go 1.6 miles south on Routes 110/111, and turn right on Route 110 when they split. Go 2.0 miles (3.6 miles) to the sign for Oxbow

National Wildlife Refuge, and turn right on Still River Depot Road. Drive 0.5 mile (4.1 miles) to the access (after crossing the tracks, jog left, then right). **42° 29.758′ N, 71° 37.568′ W**

WHAT YOU'LL SEE

This Nashua River section flows from Bolton Flats Wildlife Management Area (WMA) north through Oxbow National Wildlife Refuge (NWR) and the site of the former Fort Devens Military Reservation and passes under the Route 2 bridge. The refuge and wildlife area, along with the Fort Devens site, have protected the waterway from development. The river has three distinct segments. Upstream from the access—up through Bolton Flats WMA—the narrow, shallow, sandy-bottomed river has many overhanging branches, lots of downed timber to negotiate, and moderate current in a few places. During times of high water, you may have to paddle the upper segment in one direction. (We enjoyed paddling the upper segment in late summer because of reduced current and boat traffic.)

The middle segment between the Oxbow NWR access and Route 2 flows between the Fort Devens site on the west and Oxbow NWR on the east. A wooded shoreline encloses the narrow, winding river, with multiple-stemmed silver maple branches draped over the water, making it difficult to get by in a few spots. Although silver maple dominates, we also saw many sycamore and gray birch. A couple dozen migrating wood ducks took off from a tree as we drew near, and we also came upon a large flock of mallards. Deer approached the water to drink; several muskrats harvested pickerelweed and streamside grasses, seemingly

Dead trees populate the marsh, providing great habitat for cavity-nesting birds.

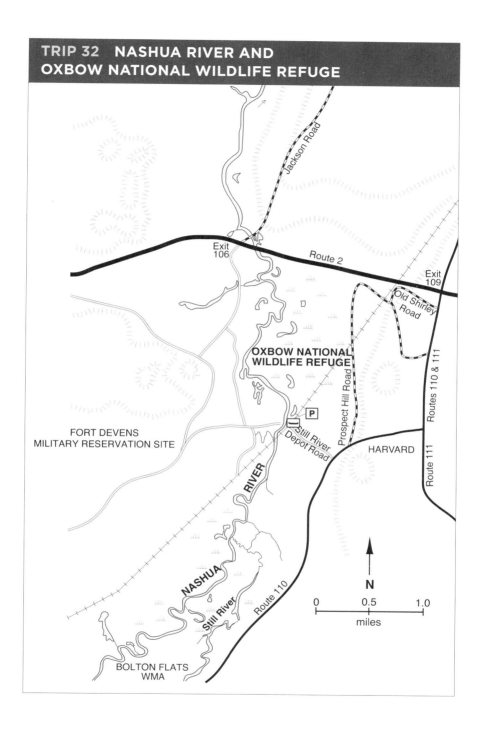

oblivious to passing boats. We watched a large snapping turtle feed on underwater vegetation, while dozens of painted turtles basked on branches and logs.

The segment farthest downstream—north of Route 2—runs much wider and deeper than the previous segments. The banks boast greater tree-species diversity. With the sky unobscured by overhanging branches, we observed a beautiful red-tailed hawk circle overhead. A Cooper's hawk chased songbirds through the woods, and we looked in vain for cuckoos that might be feeding on the abundant tent caterpillars on gray birches. On the way back to the access, we checked out a beaver dam on a bay off to the Fort Devens side that featured huge patches of pickerelweed.

TRIP 33

ASSABET RIVER RESERVOIR (MILL POND, A-1 SITE)

This is a satisfying location for anglers and for paddlers who don't mind weaving their way through a stump-filled reservoir. The wooded hillsides and scattered islands lend a scenic beauty. Look for great blue heron prowling the west end marshes.

LOCATION Westborough, MA

MAPS *Massachusetts Atlas & Gazetteer*, Map 39: C4; USGS Marlborough

AREA 333 acres

TIME 3 hours

HABITAT TYPE Wooded, marshy reservoir

FISH Largemouth and calico bass, yellow perch, northern pike, muskellunge (see fish advisory, Appendix A)

INFORMATION Westborough Community Land Trust, westboroughlandtrust.org

TAKE NOTE Many submerged and partially submerged stumps keep motors away; limited development

GETTING THERE

From I-495, Exit 59 southbound, go west on Route 9 for 3.2 miles, and exit on Route 135 east. Drive 0.7 mile (3.9 miles), and turn right on Maynard

Street. Go 0.6 mile (4.5 miles), passing under the railroad tracks, then bear right on Fisher Street. Turn left almost immediately on Mill Street, and go 0.4 mile (4.9 miles) to the access on the right. **42° 15.944' N, 71° 38.034' W**

WHAT YOU'LL SEE

Assabet River Reservoir, locally known as Mill Pond (also called the A-1 Site) provides a wonderful location to paddle just a few miles from busy Route 9 in Westborough. Thousands of closely spaced tree stumps, left over from the creation of this flood-control reservoir in 1969, keep out most motorboats and make paddling here somewhat of a challenge.

Great blue herons, ospreys, and tree swallows used to nest in profusion here. Unfortunately, most of the dead trees have fallen, eliminating the great blue heron rookery and the holes used by tree swallows. When we paddled here in 1992, nearly two dozen heron nests perched precariously among the spindly tops; in 2002 only nine nests remained, along with a wonderful addition, an osprey nest. By 2013, the dead trees had disappeared.

The reservoir's fairly open eastern end gives way to a forest of protruding and submerged stumps once you round the point of land extending down from the

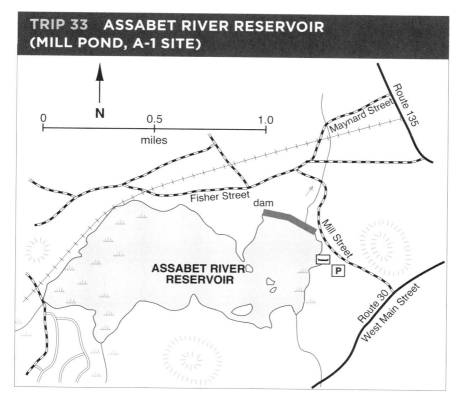

TRIP 33   ASSABET RIVER RESERVOIR (MILL POND, A-1 SITE)

Shallow, marshy, stump-filled Assabet River Reservoir is popular with anglers and bird-watchers.

north. In places, you literally have to weave your boat around these stumps to get through. The once-abundant tree swallows kept the mosquito population somewhat in check, though that is unfortunately no longer the case.

The shallow, stump-filled waters of Assabet River Reservoir—15 feet at the deepest—provide plenty of cover for fish. Someone caught a 6-pound largemouth bass during our first trip here. Cattails and bulrushes line most of the marshy perimeter, with watershield floating on open water. Looking at the reservoir, you might guess that thick muck covers the bottom; somewhat surprisingly, sand coats much of the bottom instead. Piles of freshwater mussel shells are evidence of many raccoon meals. Willow, alder, red maple, red oak, and aspen surround the reservoir. Several scattered islands add scenic beauty but offer little in the way of access for rest or a picnic. Along with watching for swallows, great blue herons, and ospreys, keep an eye out for green herons, cedar waxwings, wood ducks, and lots of painted turtles.

PARADISE POND

Islands increase the amount of shoreline to explore on this small, scenic pond. Shrubs bloom throughout spring and summer, but nothing beats the spectacular mountain laurel display in June, when the entire shoreline seems lit up with pale pink blossoms.

LOCATION Princeton, MA

MAPS *Massachusetts Atlas & Gazetteer*, Map 26: C1; USGS Fitchburg, Sterling

AREA 61 acres

TIME 2 hours

HABITAT TYPE Wooded pond

FISH Largemouth, smallmouth, and calico bass; yellow perch; pickerel (see fish advisory, Appendix A)

CAMPING Willard Brook State Forest, Pearl Hill State Park, Lake Denison State Recreation Area, Otter River State Forest

INFORMATION MassWildlife, mass.gov/doc/paradise-pond/download

TAKE NOTE No development; no internal combustion motors

GETTING THERE

From Route 2, Exit 92, go 4.0 miles south on Route 140, and turn sharply back left on Fitchburg Road (Route 31 north). In 0.2 mile (4.2 miles) and for the next 0.5 mile (4.7 miles) after that, several access points are on the right. **42° 30.014′ N, 71° 51.464′ W**

From Route 2, Exit 95, go 3.1 miles south on Route 31 to the first of several access points on the left. **42° 30.38′ N, 71° 51.498′ W**

WHAT YOU'LL SEE

Bordering Leominster State Forest, undeveloped, and free of gasoline motors, Paradise Pond provides an idyllic place to paddle. With an undulating shoreline and several islands and coves to explore, you could spend a few hours on this small pond, especially in mid-June when the abundant mountain laurel puts on a spectacular display. Noise from Route 31 occasionally intrudes on the peace and quiet.

Vegetation includes a number of species rarely seen this far north: swamp honeysuckle, a fairly late-blooming azalea with tubular, sticky white flowers; sweet pepperbush, a late-blooming shrub with clusters of small, fragrant white flowers that you can still find in bloom at the end of August; and sassafras.

The islands on Paradise Pond are quite interesting and well worth visiting. Instead of white pine and the various deciduous trees that compose most of the woods around the pond, pitch pine—a three-needled pine with large plates of bark on older trees—dominates the islands. A thick bed of needles and the open understory provide ideal locations for a picnic lunch.

In some sections, watershield covers the surface; you can easily distinguish this from other aquatic plants because the stem extends down from the center of the oval leaves. Feel the slippery stems and the undersides of the leaves. Carnivorous plants occur here as well. Lots of bladderwort is in the water, and if you look

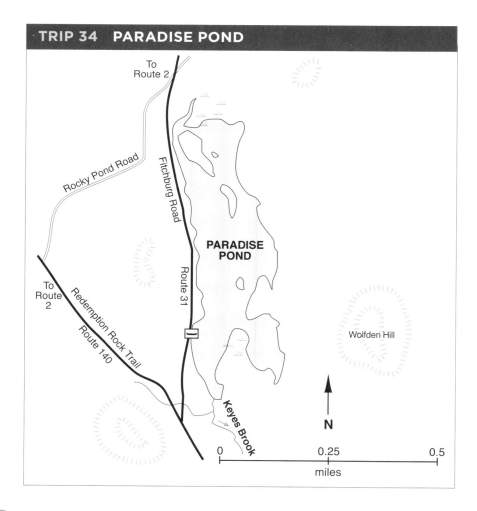

TRIP 34 PARADISE POND

SECTION 4: CENTRAL MASSACHUSETTS

carefully, you will find sundews on floating logs and sphagnum hummocks. We also saw a water snake here, entwined on a branch over the water.

The ruins of an old mill building stand at the southern tip of the pond; an 1870 map shows this as the E. B. Walker Saw Mill. Earlier maps show other sawmills to the northwest on the Keyes Brook branch of the Stillwater River. An old country road ran closer to this river route than the present Route 140, which is also known as Redemption Rock Trail. Early colonial negotiators chose Princeton as the site for a prisoner redemption at "Redemption Rock," off Route 140, less than a mile north of the junction with Route 31, deep in the woods. It was here in 1675 that Mary Rowlandson, who had been captured during the midwinter massacre at Lancaster and held in Quebec, Canada, for eight weeks, was freed for twenty pounds sterling and some whiskey.

On the east side of Paradise Pond, Leominster State Forest provides some worthwhile hiking on old logging roads and trails that wind through needle-carpeted open woodland. Wildflowers flourish here in spring.

TRIP 35

EAMES POND

This heavily vegetated pond harbors acres of waterlilies, but the real treat is the enormous amount of eastern purple bladderwort abloom in August. Look for beaver here in the evening or early morning.

LOCATION Paxton, MA

MAPS *Massachusetts Atlas & Gazetteer*, Map 37: C6; USGS Worcester North

AREA 74 acres

TIME 2 hours

HABITAT TYPE Shallow, marshy pond

FISH Largemouth and calico bass, yellow perch, pickerel (see fish advisory, Appendix A)

INFORMATION Moore State Park, mass.gov/locations/moore-state-park

CAMPING Wells State Park

TAKE NOTE Limited development; hand launch, shallowness, and vegetation keep motors out

GETTING THERE

From the junction of Routes 31, 56, and 122 in Paxton, go 1.4 miles north on Route 122 to the access on the left, just before the culvert. **42° 19.541′ N, 71° 56.840′ W**

WHAT YOU'LL SEE

With much of the shoreline protected by Moore State Park, Eames Pond offers a wonderful paddling opportunity, especially if you don't mind making your way through endless seas of lily pads. Beaver maintain something of a channel—guarded by pickerelweed and arrowhead—that wends its way through

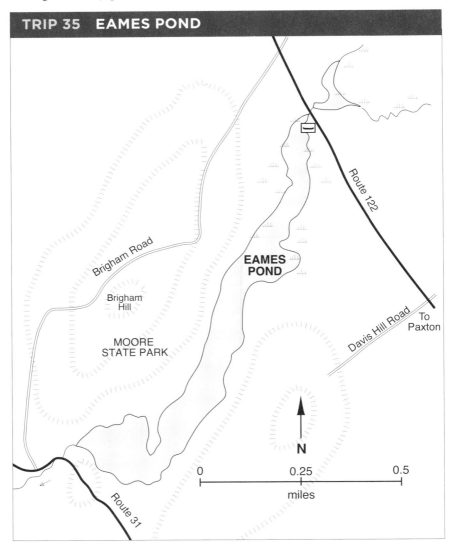

TRIP 35 EAMES POND

EAMES POND

Route 122

Brigham Road

Brigham Hill

To Paxton

Davis Hill Road

MOORE STATE PARK

N

0   0.25   0.5

miles

Route 31

what is truly a carpet of American white waterlily. As we paddled down the pond, we noticed what looked like a small island near the eastern shore; upon closer inspection, it turned out to be a massive beaver lodge at least 25 feet long, with abundant branches stored underwater as a winter larder.

In contrast to most of the American white waterlily seen on many ponds in Massachusetts, the *tuberosa* subspecies grows here. The plant has huge green leaves, some spanning a foot. American white waterlily occurs as two subspecies: *Nymphaea odorata odorata* and *N. o. tuberosa*. Most guidebooks list these as separate species, but taxonomists have recently lumped them into one. The more common subspecies, *odorata*, bears much smaller leaves, with both the leaves and the flower sepals tinged with purple. *Tuberosa* produces large green leaves and green sepals.

As you paddle into the pond's southern reaches, American white waterlily gives way to watershield and pondweed. Most striking by far, though, when we visited in mid-August, was a truly stupendous amount of eastern purple bladderwort (*Utricularia purpurea*) in bloom, more than we had seen on all other ponds combined. The entire south end radiated a purple glow that could be seen for hundreds of yards. As we paddled closer, an incredibly sweet aroma wafted toward us on a gentle breeze. Floating yellow-brown pondweed leaves provided an interesting contrast to the sea of tiny purple flowers on slender 4-inch stalks. We reveled in this gorgeous setting, not wanting to paddle back to the access. We also wondered if the *N. o. tuberosa* would eventually take over the southern end as well, crowding out the huge mats of eastern purple bladderwort.

Though few people paddle this wonderful pond, many hikers use the several trails that course through Moore State Park. We prefer the paddling, especially when we see goldfinches and great blue herons among the bur-reed, joe-pye weed, sweetgale, buttonbush, wild rice, and dwarf red maple in this broad marsh. But we will never get over the sight of the purple-flowered bladderwort.

TRIP 36

QUABOAG POND, QUABOAG RIVER, AND EAST BROOKFIELD RIVER

The rivers, connected by Quaboag Pond, are extraordinary paddling resources, passing through largely undisturbed habitat. Look for deer, beaver, muskrat, painted and stinkpot turtles, osprey, wood duck, and great blue heron.

LOCATION Brookfield, East Brookfield, Warren, and West Brookfield, MA

MAPS *Massachusetts Atlas & Gazetteer*, Map 48: A3, Map 49: A4, A5; USGS Warren

AREA/LENGTH Quaboag Pond, 541 acres; Quaboag River, 9 miles one way; East Brookfield River, 2 miles one way

TIME All day; shorter trips possible

HABITAT TYPE Shallow pond and marshy rivers

FISH Brook, brown, and rainbow trout; largemouth and calico bass; white and yellow perch; pickerel; northern pike (see fish advisory, Appendix A)

CAMPING Wells State Park

TAKE NOTE Development and motors on pond; little development on rivers

GETTING THERE

Access points are given in order, starting upstream.

Quaboag Pond (north end) and East Brookfield River From the junction of Routes 9 and 148 in Brookfield, go 1.0 mile east on Route 9, and turn right on Quaboag Street. Go 1.4 miles (2.4 miles) to the access on the right. Because of development and water-skiers, avoid Quaboag Pond on summer weekends, except as access to the East Brookfield (or Sevenmile) River. **42° 12.209′ N, 72° 3.777′ W**

Route 148 From the junction of Routes 9 and 148 in Brookfield, go 0.6 mile south on Route 148 to the access on the left, between the two bridges. **42° 12.462′ N, 72° 6.124′ W**

Route 67 From Route 9 in West Brookfield, go less than 0.1 mile south on Routes 19 and 67 to the access and picnic area on the left. **42° 14.108′ N, 71° 9.717′ W**

Warren From Route 67 in Warren, go 0.4 mile north on Old West Brookfield Road to Lucy Stone Park on the left. This is a take-out point only (for when you have two vehicles); going downstream from here will take you into dangerous whitewater. **42° 13.042′ N, 72° 11.585′ W**

WHAT YOU'LL SEE
EAST BROOKFIELD RIVER

We love paddling the inlet and outlet rivers, both of which provide an extraordinary undeveloped, wildlife-rich paddling resource. East Brookfield River flows into Quaboag Pond at the northeastern tip. Traveling upstream from the Quaboag Street bridge, the slow-flowing East Brookfield hugs the road for a few hundred yards and then turns north and east. Initially, the wide channel winds through Allen Marsh, the sides thick with pickerelweed, grasses, sedges, and buttonbush. American white waterlily, yellow pondlily, and pondweed leaves float on the water's surface. Bladderwort and watermilfoil flow in the current beneath. Though rarely visible, freshwater mussels thrive in the sandy bottom. Look for painted turtles and the less common stinkpot turtle—we saw a stinkpot perched on a protruding branch well above the water. Wood ducks raise their broods here, and great blue herons patrol the shorelines. You may see muskrats harvesting streamside grasses as you paddle along.

Farther north, the channel narrows and becomes more defined, with fewer backwater ponds to explore. About 2 miles upriver, after reaching a fork, fallen trees and beaver dams impede your progress, though with perseverance you

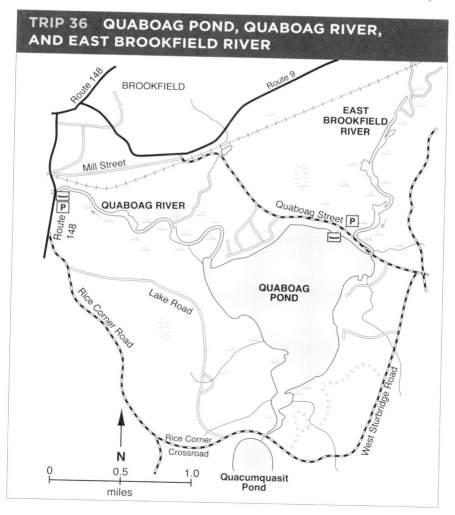

might make it to Lake Lashaway (left fork) or to the town of East Brookfield (right fork); still, portaging over the numerous deadfalls would likely be quite an ordeal. In the upper stretches, we saw a beaver swimming midday and an osprey with a fish.

QUABOAG RIVER

At Quaboag Pond's northwestern tip, the Quaboag River rises, beginning the westward journey to its confluence with the Ware and Swift rivers, where they form the Chicopee River. Quiet, meandering flat water, through wide marshlands teeming with wildlife, marks this 9-mile section of river. Paddling down and back takes at least a full day, especially if you stop to revel in the gorgeous scenery and to watch the ubiquitous wildlife. For more than the first half of the journey, the Quaboag River winds through marshy Quaboag Wildlife Management Area. Thick shrubs line the banks, and underwater vegetation forms thick mats. Clumps of swamp loosestrife, some extending for hundreds of yards along the shore, arch gracefully out over the water. Along this stretch of river, trees line the higher ground a few hundred yards across the marsh.

Paddling farther downstream one evening, where trees and taller shrubs encroach on the shores, we saw seven beavers beginning their nightly branch-gathering forays. We listened to hermit thrushes, catbirds, towhees, song sparrows, and cardinals call from the dense undergrowth and heard a veery singing in the woods. We watched muskrats swim about and a deer come down for a drink. Swamp rose grows in profusion, and some huge swamp white oaks occur along the banks in the downstream sections.

After the expansive marshes, the river narrows and trees line the banks. When you reach the section with several large rocks jutting above the surface in succession, the current picks up. Turn around here, especially during times of high water. If you have two cars, you can paddle down to the take-out at Lucy Stone Park in Warren.

In years long past, the Quaboag River served as a major thoroughfare for the region's native people. A short portage connected Quaboag Pond to the nearby Quinebaug River, which runs south through Nipmuk and eastern Niantic lands to meet other tributaries of the Pawcatuck River system, which meanders from southern Rhode Island through Narragansett lands. In this way, native people of this south coastal region could communicate and trade with one another, journey north to Quaboag Pond, and then turn west and down the Chicopee River to Connecticut country.

In the uprising known as King Philip's War, native nations along this route ravaged the more isolated English settlements. Old Brookfield, a frontier village about 8 miles to the northwest on Foster Hill, became an easy target. On August 2, 1675, Quaboag warriors ambushed an armed team of English negotiators from Boston intending to extract a pledge of neutrality amid

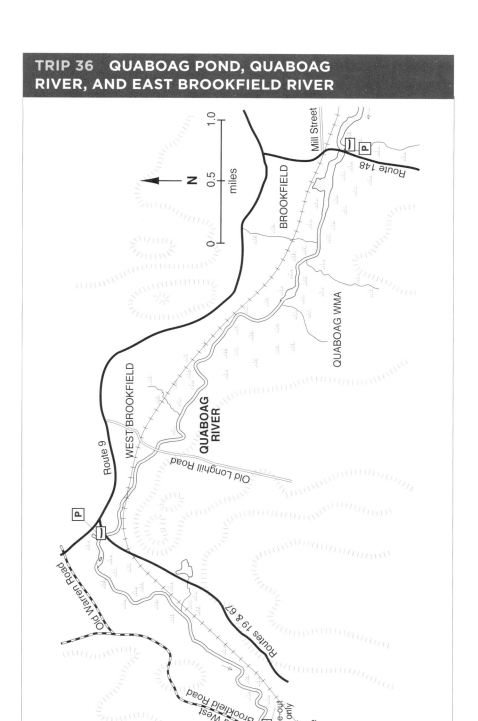

growing warfare in southeastern New England. The retreating English took hasty refuge with Brookfield's families in the town's largest building, Ayres' Tavern. Ephraim Curtis, a scout of that party, finally crept through a determined siege in which all other structures were burned, to bring about eventual rescue from Marlborough. Fifty women and children and 32 men held the tavern, while two sets of twin babies were born within. The settlers soon abandoned the town for safer and more central Hadley, in today's "Pioneer Valley" near Amherst.

TRIP 37

EAST BRIMFIELD LAKE, QUINEBAUG RIVER, HOLLAND POND, AND LONG POND

Quinebaug River Water Trail represents one of the finest quietwater resources in Massachusetts. With virtually no current, it wends for more than 4 miles through wildlife-filled swampland. Look for deer, muskrat, beaver, otter, turtles, ducks, geese, and songbirds.

LOCATION Brimfield, Holland, and Sturbridge, MA

MAPS *Massachusetts Atlas & Gazetteer*, Map 49: B4, C4; USGS Brimfield, Holland, Sturbridge

AREA/LENGTH Holland Pond, 85 acres; East Brimfield Lake and Long Pond, 420 acres; Quinebaug River, 4.5 miles one way (5.5 miles one way to the East Brimfield Lake access)

TIME Quinebaug River, 5 hours; continue through East Brimfield Lake and Long Pond, all-day round trip

HABITAT TYPE Slow, marshy, peaceful river; ponds with wooded shores

FISH Brook, brown, and rainbow trout; largemouth and smallmouth bass; white and yellow perch; pickerel; northern pike (see fish advisory, Appendix A)

INFORMATION Quinebaug River Water Trail, thelastgreenvalley.org /wp-content/uploads/2014/10/QuinebaugRiverTrailEBrimfieldLake.pdf; U.S. Army Corps of Engineers, nae.usace.army.mil/Missions/Recreation /East-Brimfield-Lake

CAMPING Wells State Park

TAKE NOTE No motors on river; lakes congested with motorboats, 10 MPH limit

GETTING THERE

Holland Pond/Canoe Trail From the junction of Routes 20 and 148 in Fisk-dale, go 1.6 miles west on Route 20, and turn left on Holland–East Brimfield Road. Go 2.0 miles (3.6 miles), and turn right on Morse Road. After 0.2 mile (3.8 miles), turn left on the access road. Go 0.3 mile (4.1 miles) to Canoe Trail around to the right, skirting the Holland Pond north shore. **42° 4.938′ N, 72° 9.817′ W**

Long Pond From the junction of Routes 20 and 148, go 0.7 mile west on Route 20 to the access on the right, just across from the entrance to Streeter Road Beach. **42° 6.779′ N, 72° 7.901′ W**

East Brimfield Lake Continue 0.4 mile (1.1 miles) beyond the Long Pond access to the access on the left. **42° 6.622′ N, 71° 8.355′ W**

WHAT YOU'LL SEE

Near historic Old Sturbridge Village you can enjoy a full day of paddling on the various bodies of water that collectively compose East Brimfield Lake. This section of the slow-flowing Quinebaug River—part of the Quinebaug River Water Trail, a designated National Recreational Trail—connects Holland Pond to the south with Long Pond to the north. If you have limited time, you could paddle the quieter and less congested Quinebaug River, putting in at the Holland Pond access. With more time, you could paddle the 12-mile round trip up to the north end of Long Pond and back to Holland Pond.

Small but very attractive Holland Pond has just a few houses on the west side, well away from and above the water. Two sandy beaches—a small one near the outlet and a larger one across the pond at the Holland Pond Recreation Area—offer a respite from the summer heat.

From Holland Pond, depending on water level, you may have to carry over the road into the Quinebaug River. The river passes some farmland near the north end but mostly winds through thick marshes filled with birdlife. Ferns grow thickly along sections of the bank, and in the few places where wooded slopes rise steeply from the water, you will see mountain laurel beneath the canopy of red and white oaks. Underwater vegetation fills the shallows. When we paddled here in July, swamp rose bloomed in profusion along the banks, while pickerelweed and waterlilies bloomed on the water. You will scarcely notice the current, because the water level drops only about 3 feet over 3 miles.

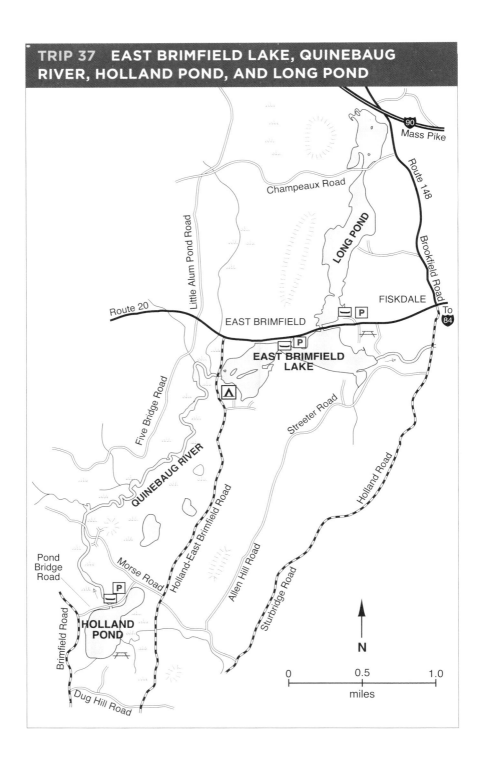

Those interested in open-water paddling can explore East Brimfield Lake south of Route 20; though a dam looms over the east end, detracting from the shoreline, the lake includes a public beach and picnic area, a large and well-used boat ramp, and a popular private campground. For solitude, stick to the river or head immediately up to Long Pond, north of Route 20.

Long Pond extends about 1.5 miles north from the Route 20 access, almost to I-90. White pine, red and white oaks, and sugar and red maples dominate the heavily wooded shoreline. Unfortunately, invasive watermilfoil has crowded out some of the native vegetation; some development has also sprouted along the east shore. Two-thirds of the way up, you have to paddle under the very low Champeaux Road bridge. From there, marshy coves, floating pond vegetation, ferns along the banks, and lots of birds abound along the more interesting northern shoreline. A red oak and white pine grove juts into the water, making a convenient picnic area on the northwestern side of Long Pond. Though shielded pretty well by trees, I-90 vehicle noise intrudes on the northern end of the pond.

While in the area, you can visit historic Old Sturbridge Village, a living museum portraying New England life in the 1830s.

TRIP 38

MILLERS RIVER, OTTER RIVER, AND LAKE DENISON

It's rare to see other paddlers on these spectacular rivers, which can be traveled both directions except during times of high water. Look for beaver, muskrat, otter, mink, snapping and painted turtles, great blue heron, ducks, geese, and lots of songbirds.

LOCATION Templeton and Winchendon, MA

MAPS *Massachusetts Atlas & Gazetteer*, Map 25: A4, B4, B5; USGS Athol, Royalston, Winchendon

AREA/LENGTH Lake Denison, 82 acres; Millers River, 7.5 miles one way; Otter River, 3 miles one way

TIME All day; shorter trips possible

HABITAT TYPE Meandering unspoiled rivers; shrubby marshlands

FISH Brook, brown, and rainbow trout; largemouth, smallmouth, and calico bass (see fish advisory, Appendix A)

CAMPING Lake Denison State Recreation Area, Otter River State Forest, Tully Lake

INFORMATION Lake Denison Recreation Area, mass.gov/locations /lake-dennison-recreation-area

TAKE NOTE No motors; no development

GETTING THERE
Lake Denison From the junction of Routes 68 and 202 in Baldwinville, go 2.2 miles north on Route 202, and turn left into the recreation area. **42° 38.802′ N, 72° 5.547′ W**

Millers and Otter Rivers After turning in to the recreation area, go 0.7 mile (2.9 miles), and veer left on New Boston Road. Go 0.4 mile (3.3 miles) to the access on the left, just past the bridge. **42° 38.731′ N, 72° 5.941′ W**

Alternate Route From the junction of Routes 12 and 202 in Winchendon, go 1.8 miles south on Route 202, and turn right on Main Street. Go 1.7 miles (3.5 miles) to the Lake Denison access on the left. For the river access, continue 0.1 mile (3.6 miles) south, and turn right on New Boston Road. Go 0.4 mile (4.0 miles) to the access on the left, just past the bridge.

WHAT YOU'LL SEE
Bounded by Birch Hill Wildlife Management Area and Otter River State Forest, these two rivers offer an unspoiled paddle through red maple, alder, red osier

Except during times of high water, you can paddle this section of Millers River in both directions.

dogwood, and buttonbush swamps. Because we love the seclusion, we have paddled here many times. In spring, the current can flow swiftly enough to make traveling upstream difficult in some places. On one trip, we paddled nearly 3 miles up the Millers River until a massive logjam blocked our way. Logjams, left over from floods, can occur anywhere on rivers. On our return

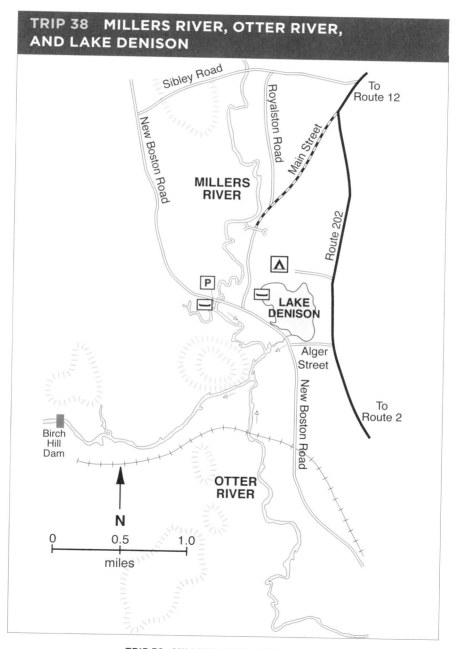

TRIP 38 MILLERS RIVER, OTTER RIVER, AND LAKE DENISON

trips with low water in summer and fall, several beaver dams filled the channels. Spring floods wash out the dams, followed by rebuilding in summer.

Beaver have also impounded the north-flowing Otter River, necessitating portages to reach broad upstream meadows. Many species of fern grow along the banks, including cinnamon, interrupted, royal, and marsh ferns. Marsh birds are profuse here. In mid-June, wood ducks, Canada geese, and mallards herded broods of young away from approaching boats. Great blue herons fed in the shallows, and killdeer nested on mud flats on the river's upper reaches. Crows mobbed a great horned owl, several snapping turtles fed just below the clear water's surface, and muskrats harvested streamside vegetation as we paddled by.

These rivers go up with rains and come back down relatively quickly. Stay out of the river if you cannot paddle upstream easily. At times of high water, steer clear of trees—they could cause you to capsize. Better yet, paddle Lake Denison instead. Receding glaciers formed this kettle-hole lake; a large chunk of glacier submerged in glacial till gradually melted, leaving a shallow lake with sandy shores and bottom, ideal for swimming.

In 2013, a camera crew filmed a sequence on East Branch Tully River for New Hampshire Public Television's *Windows to the Wild*.

TULLY LAKE AND EAST BRANCH TULLY RIVER

If you paddle the East Branch of the Tully River in the evening, you are guaranteed to see beaver in this marvelous marshland. Tully Lake, with its numerous islands, offers hours of exploration amid a wooded backdrop.

LOCATION Athol and Royalston, MA

MAPS *Massachusetts Atlas & Gazetteer*, Map 24: A3, B3; USGS Royalston

AREA/LENGTH Tully Lake, 243 acres; East Branch Tully River, 3 miles one way

TIME Tully Lake, 4 hours; East Branch Tully River, 3 hours round trip

HABITAT TYPE Tully Lake, dammed-up river, shrubby marshlands, many islands, protected bays; East Branch Tully River, marshlands and beaver swamps

FISH Brook and rainbow trout, largemouth and calico bass, yellow perch, pickerel, northern pike (see fish advisory, Appendix A)

CAMPING Tully Lake, Lake Denison State Recreation Area, Otter River State Forest

INFORMATION Tully Lake Recreation Area, nae.usace.army.mil /Missions/Recreation/Tully-Lake/

TAKE NOTE No development; motors allowed (10 HP limit) on Tully Lake; no motors on Tully River

GETTING THERE

Tully Lake From Route 2, Exit 75, go 5.8 miles north on Route 32 to the access on the right. **42° 38.597′ N, 72° 13.341′ W**

Tully River From the Tully Lake access, continue north on Route 32 for 0.4 mile (6.2 miles), and turn right on Doane Hill Road. Go 1.0 mile (7.2 miles) to the access on the left, just over the bridge. **42° 39.054′ N, 72° 12.498′ W**

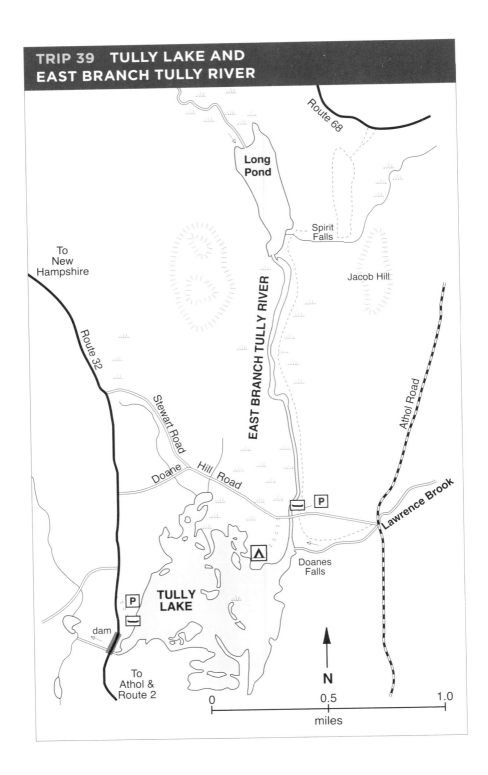

Route 68

**Long
Pond**

Spirit
Falls

To
New
Hampshire

Jacob Hill

EAST BRANCH TULLY RIVER

Route 32

Stewart Road

Athol Road

Doane Hill Road

P

Lawrence Brook

△

Doanes
Falls

**TULLY
LAKE**

P

dam

To
Athol &
Route 2

N

0   0.5   1.0
miles

WHAT YOU'LL SEE

TULLY LAKE

Tully Lake, in north-central Massachusetts, not far from the New Hampshire border, is known to few people outside the immediate area. A highly varied shoreline provides an interesting paddling experience, with dozens of islands and deep winding coves to explore. A primitive walk-in camping area at the north end provides an added bonus.

Along the shore, white pine predominates, mixed with red maple, hemlock, red and white oaks, some quaking aspen, and white birch, along with a fairly dense border of shrubs, including buttonbush, various heaths, alder, blueberry, and—in places—cranberry with tiny oval leaves that are dwarfed by large cranberries in late summer and fall. Farther from shore, the woods open up, providing great picnicking and hiking opportunities on 18 miles of trails. On the large island near the lake's south end, we found a few highbush blueberries absolutely covered with berries during a visit in early August. Scrub oak—a species more common on dry, sandy hills—grows near the south end of the lake, along with the more common white pine.

EAST BRANCH TULLY RIVER

Underwater vegetation sways in the current, but otherwise you would hardly know which way the East Branch of the Tully River flows. Sweetgale, grasses, royal fern, buttonbush, and other shrubs grow thickly along the banks of this wide, gorgeous marsh. Look for American white waterlily, yellow pondlily, pondweed, and watershield along the edges and for pitcher plant on the sphagnum hummocks.

On our paddle up and back in early June, we noticed that muskrats had uprooted many of the tender shoots of pickerelweed. As hermit thrushes called from the woodlands, we saw several beavers; they had also girdled a number of the streamside hemlocks, killing them, which eventually will make way for more palatable species. Beaver are especially visible here in the evening. We've seen beaver on every one of several trips here.

As you round the last bend, paddling north, the river opens up into serene Long Pond, surrounded by thick woodland. The pond marks the end of open water. You can continue on beyond the power line at the pond's north end, portaging over repeated beaver dams, or you can pull up your boat near the south end of Long Pond on the east side and hike to Spirit Falls along Spirit Brook Trail. You can also hike along another trail that starts from the Tully River access that leads both to Doanes Falls on Lawrence Brook and to Spirit Falls.

TRIP 40

WARE RIVER AND EAST BRANCH WARE RIVER

Three sections of the Ware River offer varied paddling opportunities, with lots of wildlife. We've seen beaver, muskrat, coyote, mink, deer, great horned owl, great blue heron, bittern, ducks, geese, turtles, and many more.

LOCATION Barre and Rutland, MA

MAPS *Massachusetts Atlas & Gazetteer*, Map 37: A5, A6, B5; USGS Barre, Sterling

LENGTH East Branch, North Rutland, 2 miles one way; East Branch, upstream from Barre Falls Dam, 2.3 miles one way; Ware River, downstream from Barre Falls Dam, 3 miles one way

TIME About 3 hours for each section, round trip

HABITAT TYPE Marshy, slow-flowing rivers

FISH Brook, brown, and rainbow trout (see fish advisory, Appendix A)

CAMPING Willard Brook State Forest, Pearl Hill State Park, Lake Denison State Recreation Area, Otter River State Forest, Tully Lake

TAKE NOTE Minor development on East Branch, North Rutland; no development on other sections; no motors

GETTING THERE

East Branch, North Rutland From Route 2, Exit 86, go south on Route 68. From the junction of Routes 62 and 68, continue 1.4 miles on Route 68, and turn left on River Road. Go 0.6 mile (2.0 miles) to the unmarked access on the right, just before Pout and Trout Campground. **42° 26.274′ N, 71° 58.257′ W**

East Branch, Upstream from Barre Falls Dam From the junction of Routes 62 and 68, go 2.2 miles west on Route 62 to the Barre Falls Dam access road on the left. Go 1.1 miles (3.3 miles) to the access at the picnic area parking lot, just after crossing the dam. **42° 25.426′ N, 72° 1.428′ W**

From the downstream access described below, turn left on Route 122, go 0.3 mile, and turn left on Coldbrook Road. Drive 3.0 miles (3.3 miles) to the picnic area parking lot.

Ware River, Downstream from Barre Falls Dam From the junction of Routes 32, 62, and 122 in Barre, go south on Routes 32 and 122 for 1.2 miles to the Y, and turn left on Route 122. Head 3.2 miles (4.4 miles) to the access on the left, just before the bridge. **42° 23.698′ N, 72° 3.038′ W**

WHAT YOU'LL SEE

The Ware River presents several opportunities for quietwater paddling in areas where current allows travel in both directions. We include three nearby sections here, including one downstream of Barre Falls Dam on the Ware River and two upstream of the dam on the East Branch. We found these sections to be thick with wildlife, with very few other boaters in evidence. We cover them in order from upstream to downstream.

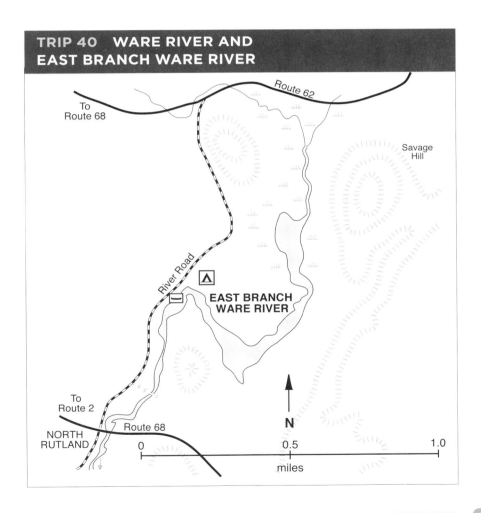

EAST BRANCH, NORTH RUTLAND

From the access, you can paddle a short way downstream, past a few back-yards, until you come to a small falls and a covered bridge. We enjoyed watching the phoebes and other birds that congregate just above the bridge, but the far more interesting section lies upstream from the access. You will encounter negligible current here as you work your way through extensive marshes, their banks thick with grasses and shrubs. Red maple, white pine, and other trees line the faraway shoreline, which leads to scenic hillsides in the background.

Paddling here in the morning, you will see muskrats rooting up the ubiquitous pickerelweed. In the evening, watch for beaver dragging branches to make dam repairs, to increase the size of their already huge lodges, or to store them, stuck butt-first into the river-bottom mud outside their lodges. You can paddle up

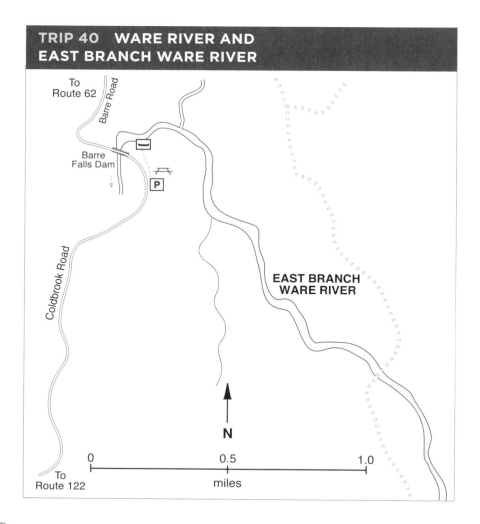

TRIP 40 WARE RIVER AND
EAST BRANCH WARE RIVER

beyond a series of beaver dams, but only the adventuresome will want to go very far—the streambed narrows and logjams occur with frequency.

We observed a large snapping turtle hanging lazily, fishing in the open channel, as dozens of yellow warblers sang from the streamside shrubbery. Painted turtles scrambled out onto logs to sun as red-winged blackbirds squabbled over breeding territories. We found nesting Canada geese and mallards and watched a red-tailed hawk circle overhead. Amazingly, we saw three bitterns, which usually stay well hidden.

EAST BRANCH, UPSTREAM FROM BARRE FALLS DAM

Do not attempt to paddle upstream from the dam unless you crave adventure. A 100-plus-yard carry down to the water from the picnic area awaits you; moreover, you have to carry back up when you may be tired from paddling. The river above the dam also can have a fair amount of current. Though we could paddle against it fairly easily, some tight, narrow turns presented a real challenge when the current pushed the bow away from our intended direction. After paddling slightly less than a mile upstream, we had to carry over a beaver dam, which gave us access to about another mile of river. By the time we finished paddling here, we knew that we had done some work.

You undoubtedly will not have much company if you choose to paddle this wide, shrubby, treeless marsh. Expect to see the same marsh birds as on other sections. You will also see red and white pine plantations, sometimes red on one side of the river and white on the other.

A great horned owl casts a wary eye in our direction as we paddle by.

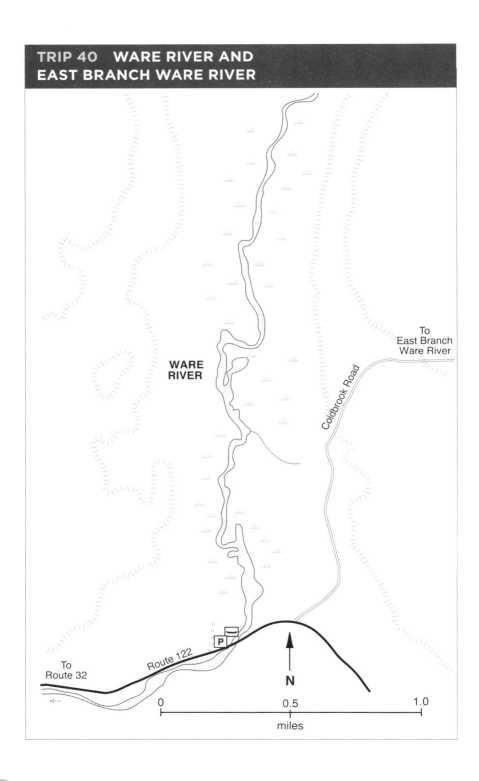

TRIP 40   WARE RIVER AND
EAST BRANCH WARE RIVER

To
East Branch
Ware River

WARE
RIVER

Coldbrook Road

P

Route 122

To
Route 32

N

0   0.5   1.0
miles

WARE RIVER, DOWNSTREAM FROM BARRE FALLS DAM

As we paddled through this wildlife paradise, a sphinx-type moth hover-fed on arrowwood flowers, and we studied iridescent green damselflies, tiger swallowtails, and several species of dragonflies. A great horned owl eyed us warily from a streamside perch as we paddled by, and we watched a coyote burst forth from cover to chase a duck that had hidden in the pickerelweed along the shore. The Ware River also boasts the largest fish species diversity in central Massachusetts.

The pondweed and pickerelweed, with yellow pondlily in protected coves, seem to withstand spring runoff, and we could paddle against the current, but we visited when the river was low enough that we often scraped our paddle blades on the bottom in the shallow areas. At times of high water, the current would make paddling here too much of a chore. The beaver that prune back the streamside alders here burrow into the banks rather than build the typical lodge that would wash away in a flood.

OSPREY: FISH HAWK BACK FROM THE BRINK

The osprey, or fish hawk, lives near dozens of the lakes, ponds, and estuaries covered in this guide. Though we often see osprey on inland waterways perching or diving for fish, we find them in much larger numbers along the coast, where you may also observe them nesting.

The osprey, *Pandion haliaetus*, the sole species in the family Pandionidae, occurs on all continents except Antarctica. The bird, dark brown to almost black above and white below, soars with a characteristic M-like shape on a nearly 6-foot wingspread.

Osprey feed exclusively on fish. They soar or hover at a height of about 150 feet, using their keen eyesight to locate fish near the water's surface, and then dive, crashing into the water feet first. There, they catch and grasp fish with their specially adapted feet, which have sharp, spiny projections.

These birds generally mate for life and return to the same nesting site each year. Males arrive first from the Gulf states or Latin American wintering grounds, followed a week later by the females. Returning males sometimes engage in a sky dance, repeatedly flying steeply up, hovering with tail fanned and talons extended, and then diving down. This may be courtship behavior, a territorial display, or both.

Traditionally, osprey have nested in tall, dead trees, but more recently in southern New England they have taken to hundreds of artificial nesting platforms that have been erected since the early 1970s. Their stick nests typically measure about 5 feet in diameter and 2 to 7 feet thick, depending on age. To collect sticks, the male uses an interesting technique: he alights near the end of a dead branch and breaks it off. The female collects most of the nest lining material (moss, bark, twigs, grass, and seaweed).

The female lays two or three eggs—whitish with reddish brown blotches—over a period of several days. The chicks hatch after a 34- to 40-day incubation period, during which the female does most of the sitting. Because the young hatch over the course of several days, they vary in size. Though osprey often fledge two or three young, in a year of food shortages the largest chick will outcompete its smaller siblings and may be

the sole survivor. The male osprey does virtually all the fishing during the incubation and nestling stage. Young osprey take to flight after seven or eight weeks, but they do not become fully independent for another month or two. After migrating south, the young spend two winters and the summer between in the wintering ground. Returning to the vicinity of their natal haunts the following year, they may pair up and begin nest building, but they do not breed until their third year.

The bald eagle, far less adept at fishing, frequently tries to steal an osprey's fish. We often spot gulls in hot pursuit as well. A far more significant enemy, however, has been humankind and its chemical warfare against insect pests.

Introduced in 1947, the "miracle" insecticide DDT was widely used on coastal salt marshes to control mosquitoes. Over the years, DDT, an extremely long-lived chlorinated hydrocarbon, accumulated in the fatty tissue of animals. Small fish ate sprayed insects, larger fish ate the small fish, and so on, gradually moving up the food chain to osprey. At each step, ingested DDT and its metabolites were stored in fatty tissue rather than excreted. At the top of the food chain, osprey ate many DDT-laced fish over a long life span and suffered from very high DDT concentrations. Those levels resulted in eggshell thinning and, as a result, extremely high rates of nesting failure. Osprey populations plummeted. Along the Connecticut River delta, for example, the osprey population dropped from 200 nesting pairs in 1938 to 12 by 1965. By the end of the 1960s, the birds had nearly disappeared from the eastern United States. The realization that DDT caused this decline led to its ban in the early 1970s. Since that time, osprey populations have gradually recovered.

Though osprey seem to be thriving, they still face threats from dwindling habitat, high-speed boating, water pollution, and ever-increasing use of pesticides. Some evidence exists of increased competition from gulls because local landfills have closed. In addition to pesticide exposure in the United States, osprey also ingest pesticides at their wintering quarters, where environmentally dangerous chemicals such as DDT are still applied. With international efforts to eliminate use of such chemicals worldwide, and with better controls on water pollution in the United States, we will be able to enjoy watching osprey hover over our waterways for many years to come.

LAKE ROHUNTA

Lake Rohunta's shallow waters host legions of aquatic plants, sometimes making paddling slow going, especially on the southern reaches. Look for osprey, ducks, geese, and other waterfowl here, along with deer. Blueberries grow in profusion in some places, and this is an excellent site to study trees, shrubs, and aquatic plants.

LOCATION Athol, New Salem, and Orange, MA

MAPS *Massachusetts Atlas & Gazetteer*, Map 24: C2; USGS Orange

AREA: 383 acres

TIME 4 hours

HABITAT TYPE Shallow pond, wooded shores

FISH Largemouth bass, yellow perch, pickerel, northern pike (see fish advisory, Appendix A)

CAMPING Lake Denison State Recreation Area, Otter River State Forest, Tully Lake

INFORMATION MassWildlife, mass.gov/doc/rohunta-lake/download

TAKE NOTE Shallow water and abundant aquatic vegetation limit motors; limited development

GETTING THERE
Northern Access From Route 2, Exit 71, head 0.2 mile south on Route 202, and turn left on Eagleville Road. Go 0.7 mile (0.9 mile) to the access. **42° 33.65′ N, 72° 16.489′ W**

Southern Access From Route 2, Exit 71, go 1.0 mile south on Route 202, and turn left on Old South Road/Blackinton Road. Follow it for 1.5 miles (2.5 miles), and turn left on Branch Bridge Road. Go 0.4 mile (2.9 miles) to the access before the culvert. Note the huge solar photovoltaic array across from the turn to Old South Road. **42° 32.09′ N, 72° 16.354′ W**

WHAT YOU'LL SEE
Anyone who drives across central Massachusetts on Route 2 has probably wondered about Lake Rohunta. We drove by it many times before taking the time to check it out thoroughly. From the highway, the main lake appears

to extend north from Route 2, but far more water actually lies to the south. While some houses occur along the lake at its widest sections, few motorboats ply these shallow, weedy waters. The surrounding woods may entice you to spread out a picnic lunch—particularly on the east side of the lake north of Route 2. The open pine and hemlock woods harbor dense carpets of needles and acid-loving laurels and blueberry bushes along the shore.

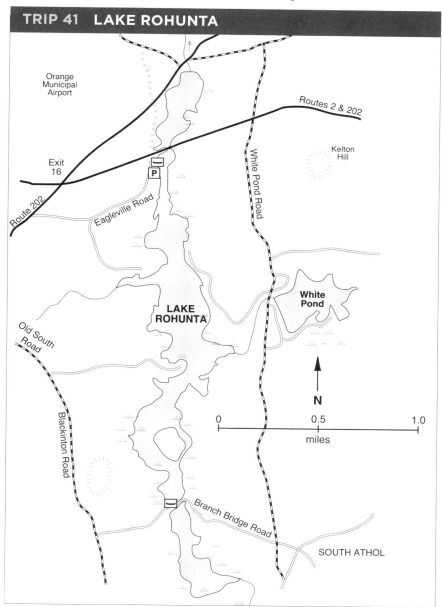

TRIP 41   LAKE ROHUNTA

Highbush blueberries, which ripen in late summer along Lake Rohunta's shores, can seriously slow down the paddling.

Our first time here, we spent a wonderful half day paddling the north end of the lake and the southern section down as far as Branch Bridge Road (where a small culvert blocks passage to the lake's southernmost section), exploring the diverse aquatic vegetation, watching painted turtles bask in the sun, and gorging ourselves on plentiful blueberries in July's waning days. We paddled through acres of American white waterlily, yellow pondlily, watershield, pickerelweed, pondweed, and two types of bladderwort, with buttonbush along the shores. In the most protected coves, the remains of trees killed by rising water after construction of the dam at the pond's north end jutted above the water's surface. On the mossy tussocks around these stumps, we found two species of sundews, round-leaved and spatulate-leaved. On the upper side of their leaves, these tiny carnivorous plants sport sticky hairs that catch small insects. Enzymes in the leaves digest the insects to help nourish the plant.

The farther south you paddle, the shallower and weedier it gets. When we visited in late April, an osprey fished the clear water as aquatic vegetation just began to emerge, and we paddled unfettered. But by midsummer, floating vegetation covers more than 90 percent of the water's surface and impedes paddling. Near the south end, we worked our way around a large, heavily wooded island. Though staying right presents an easier path, thicker stands of blueberry are on the left.

Plowing through the pickerelweed and yellow pondlilies requires some work but offers the chance to see some exciting wildlife. We observed black ducks, Canada geese, and a pair of broad-winged hawks (which may nest on the island); a few wood ducks flew to safety as we paddled near. Early in the morning, look for mink or even a river otter.

Local historians believe that the name Rohunta comes from one Rodney Hunt, who operated a hydropower facility at the waterway's south end in the late 1800s. The area also has a bit of post-Colonial history: In 1787, Daniel Shays led a straggling band of rebellious farmers along this way in retreat from Springfield. It marked the last desperate hurrah of "Shays' Rebellion," when farmers in western Massachusetts, suffering under post-Revolution economic depression, protested the imprisoning of debtors by occupying the Springfield courthouse—an action that alarmed even President Washington. The uprising was quickly quelled, and Shays, a reluctant leader, escaped to Vermont, where he was eventually pardoned.

TRIP 42

MUDDY BROOK AND HARDWICK POND

Muddy Brook and Hardwick Pond offer a great place for intrepid explorers to paddle. Fully investigating Muddy Brook requires portaging over beaver dams, but it's worth the effort to reach pristine beaver meadows filled with wildlife.

LOCATION Hardwick, MA

MAPS *Massachusetts Atlas & Gazetteer*, Map 36: B3, C3; USGS North Brookfield

AREA/LENGTH Hardwick Pond, 66 acres; Muddy Brook, 1.6 miles one way

TIME 3 hours round trip

HABITAT TYPE Reservoir and slow-flowing, marshy river through beaver swamp

FISH Rainbow trout, largemouth and calico bass, yellow perch, pickerel (see fish advisory, Appendix A)

INFORMATION Muddy Brook Wildlife Management Area, mass.gov /info-details/muddy-brook-wma

TAKE NOTE Limited development and some motors on Hardwick Pond; no personal watercraft

GETTING THERE

From the North From the junction of Routes 32 and 32A in Petersham, go 9.6 miles south on Route 32A, and turn right on Greenwich Road. Drive 0.3 mile (9.9 miles), and turn left on Patrill Hollow Road for 3.2 miles (13.1 miles), then turn left on Greenwich Road. Go 1.2 miles (14.3 miles), and turn sharply left on Hardwick Pond Road. Continue 0.3 mile (14.6 miles) to the access on the left. **42° 18.011' N, 72° 14.495' W**

From the South From Route 9 in Ware, go 1.3 miles north on North Street (traffic light). At the T, turn right on Greenwich Road. Go 2.4 miles (3.7 miles), and turn right on the second Hardwick Pond Road. The access is 0.3 mile (4.0 miles) on the left.

WHAT YOU'LL SEE

After exploring Hardwick Pond, paddle north through Muddy Brook Wildlife Management Area, up the slow-flowing, picturesque brook through a broad beaver marsh, a valley filled with shrubs and songbirds. Cardinals, catbirds, yellowthroats, and yellow warblers call from dense undergrowth, and scores of red-winged blackbirds sing from the marsh in early June. Shrubs line the banks and cover the islands and hummocks along the side channels of the marsh, with an occasional red maple sprouting up.

At high water, you can paddle over drowned-out beaver dams, but be prepared to portage over some dams. One dam had a thick growth of swamp rose on and around it. Another had a beaver working on it at 4:15 in the afternoon. The beaver climbed off the dam, swam over and gave us the hairy eyeball,

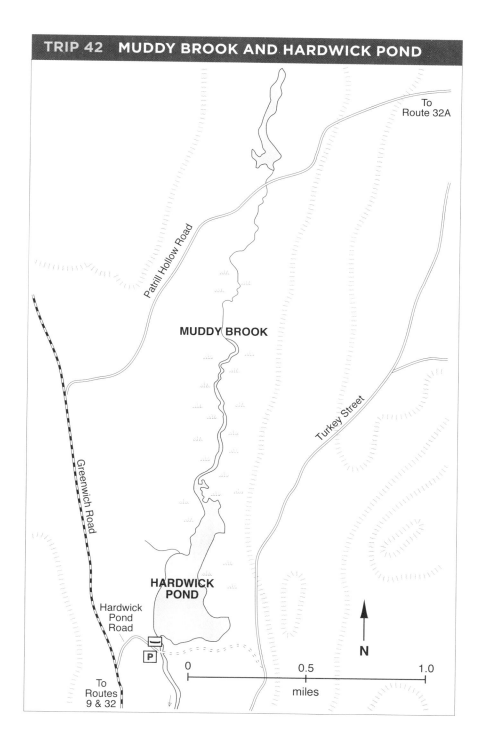

TRIP 42   MUDDY BROOK AND HARDWICK POND

To
Route 32A

Patrill Hollow Road

MUDDY BROOK

Turkey Street

Greenwich Road

HARDWICK POND

Hardwick
Pond
Road

P

To
Routes
9 & 32

N

0   0.5   1.0
miles

slapped its tail on the water, and dove for cover—strong evidence that the brook's upper reaches receive few visitors.

After we had paddled a mile or more up the brook, we came to a 5-foot-high beaver dam. We portaged through open woods around the right side of the dam onto a shrub-filled lagoon with standing dead trees, nesting wood ducks, great blue herons, snapping turtles, red-tailed hawks, and cedar waxwings. We also saw a relatively rare yellow-billed cuckoo. We found the main channel above the lagoon with some difficulty and had to bushwhack through shrubs as we paddled and pulled ourselves along, noting the beauty of fern-clad banks, with patches of royal, interrupted, cinnamon, and hay-scented ferns. Though you can paddle up to Patrill Hollow Road, most folks will get tired of portaging over logjams and beaver dams and pulling their way through shrubs long before reaching the road.

From the pond, you can also paddle down the outlet. You will undoubtedly have to lie down in your boat to make it under the bridge. (Try not to disturb the phoebe nesting there.)

TRIP 43

POTTAPAUG POND

Protected, undeveloped woods surround Pottapaug Pond, part of the Quabbin Reservoir complex. The pond represents the sole paddling opportunity on the huge, wild Quabbin reserve. Look for wood duck, great blue heron, bald eagle, deer, and beaver.

LOCATION Hardwick and Petersham, MA

MAPS *Massachusetts Atlas & Gazetteer*, Map 36: A3, B3; USGS Petersham

AREA 570 acres

TIME Half day or more

HABITAT TYPE Reservoir with shallow coves; protected, wooded shores

FISH Largemouth and smallmouth bass, chain pickerel, northern pike, white and yellow perch (see fish advisory, Appendix A)

TAKE NOTE Restricted to anglers; boat restrictions (see below)

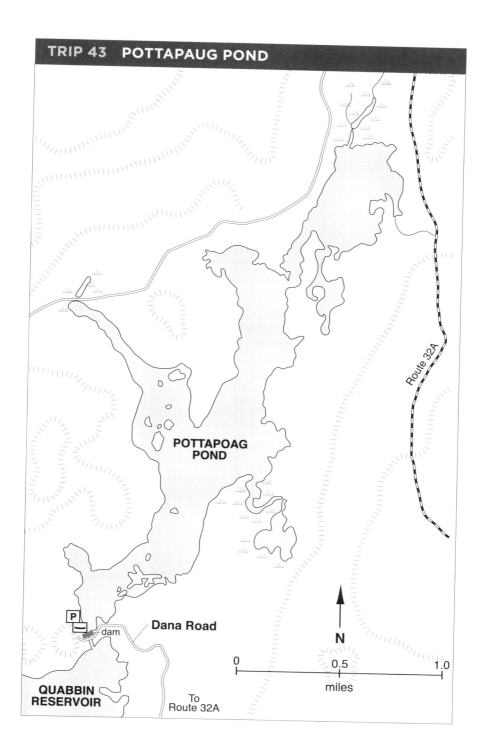

Route 32A

POTTAPOAG POND

P

dam

Dana Road

N

QUABBIN
RESERVOIR

To
Route 32A

0   0.5   1.0
miles

GETTING THERE

From Route 2, Exit 75, drive 6.3 miles south on Route 32, and turn right on Routes 122/32A. Go 0.5 mile (6.8 miles), and turn left on Route 32A for 9.1 miles (15.9 miles), then turn right on Session Road. Continue 0.5 mile (16.4 miles), and turn right on Greenwich Road. Go 1.8 miles (18.2 miles), and turn right for Gate 43. In 1.7 miles (19.9 miles), reach a small bridge and Fishing Access 3 gatehouse, where you register to paddle (and fish). **42° 23.567′ N, 72° 14.367′ W**

WHAT YOU'LL SEE

Because of public access rules established in the 1950s, Pottapaug Pond is open only for fishing; visitors must have a valid Massachusetts fishing license and fishing gear—even if they are not actively fishing. At the access, you can buy a one-day Massachusetts license for $5 (in 2023). Private boats, inspected for invasive plants, were allowed until June 2023, but after officials found an invasive bladderwort, only on-site rental boats may be used. A few canoes and kayaks are available for a modest rental fee.

Undeveloped Pottapaug Pond, rich with wildlife and native flora, is one of the best paddling and fishing destinations in southern New England. Shallow, protected coves provide hours of paddling among carpets of ferns under towering, lichen-covered pines—uncut, we suspect, since the reservoir's creation in the 1930s. Beaver have removed most deciduous trees along the shoreline, and we could see their new work farther up the hillsides. We observed at least twenty beaver lodges along the shore, wood ducks and great blue herons in the shallow coves, and a bald eagle at the northern tip.

On a late June visit, the fragrance of swamp azalea (*Rhododendron viscosum*) filled the air. The white-flowered shrubs are scattered along much of the shoreline, interspersed with highbush blueberry, leatherleaf, sweetgale, and other common wetlands shrubs. Red maples reach out over the water, with white pines forming a backdrop. Floating vegetation fills the shallow fingers: American white waterlily, yellow pondlily, watershield, floating heart (with tiny heart-shaped leaves), water celery, bur-reed, and pondweed (*Potamogeton spp.*). Unfortunately, we found lots of submerged, highly invasive Eurasian watermilfoil, which is choking many bodies of water in the region.

At the north end, we saw a stand of narrow-leaved cattail (*Typha angustifolia*)—with narrower leaves than the more typical common cattail (*Typha latifolia*). We also found a few small island hillocks thick with rose pogonia orchid (*Pogonia ophioglossoides*), a beautiful wetlands plant about a foot tall with distinctive pink flowers, including a fringed, spoon-shaped, yellow-and-pink lower petal. Hillocks also contained the carnivorous northern pitcher plant (*Sarracenia purpurea*) and round-leaved sundew (*Drosera rotundifolia*).

Paddlers can access Pottapaug Pond only by the dam and have to bring fishing gear with them; in 2023, the only option for paddling here was to use one of Quabbin Reservoir's rental canoes or kayaks, such as the one pictured here.

As the largest undeveloped tract in Massachusetts, Quabbin Reservoir hosts rich and diverse wildlife, including black bear, coyote, deer, moose, bobcat, fisher, mink, and otter. Sporadically, people claim sightings of cougars and wolves, including genetically confirmed scat from a cougar in April 1997 (possibly from a released animal) and confirmed photographs of cougar tracks in March 2011. A move to reintroduce rattlesnakes to Mount Zion, the reservoir's largest island, was abandoned in 2017 because of local opposition.

HISTORY OF QUABBIN RESERVOIR AND POTTAPAUG POND

In the 1930s, damming the Swift River's three branches created Quabbin Reservoir to satisfy growing water needs in eastern Massachusetts. After the state acquired land through direct acquisition and eminent domain—despite significant local opposition—2,500 residents were evacuated and large parts of four towns (650 homes) were flooded. On April 28, 1938, the towns of Dana, Enfield, Greenwich, and Prescott were disincorporated—that is, they ceased to exist.

Completed in 1939, the reservoir took seven years to fill. With a surface area of 38.6 square miles (nearly 25,000 acres) holding 412 billion gallons of water,

Quabbin Reservoir is the largest body of water in Massachusetts and is believed to be the largest human-made reservoir in the world that is used solely as a water supply. Most of its water flows through the 25-mile-long Quabbin Aqueduct to Wachusett Reservoir and from there to Boston and about 40 other towns. A separate, more recent, aqueduct serves several western towns. Through watershed and water management, the reservoir is one of just a handful of public water supplies in the United States where filtration is not required.

Pottapaug is one of two "regulating ponds" that feed into Quabbin Reservoir. Controlled by a small dam at the access, the pond regulates the flow of the East Branch of the Swift River. Before the flooding, a smaller Pottapaug Pond existed in the town of Dana. Look for stone wall remnants while paddling here, and try to imagine the valley before flooding. Today, the pond feels wild and natural, and paddling here is wonderful. Fishing is pretty good too!

TRIP 44
SWIFT RIVER

The outlet of Quabbin Reservoir, the Swift River provides a wildlife-filled paddling experience. Look for muskrat, beaver, deer, wild turkey, ducks and geese, and songbirds galore.

LOCATION Belchertown and Ware, MA

MAPS *Massachusetts Atlas & Gazetteer*, Map 36: C1, C2, Map 48: A1, A2; USGS Palmer, Winsor Dam

LENGTH 4.5 miles one way

TIME 4 hours round trip

HABITAT TYPE Slow-flowing wooded river

FISH Brook, brown, and rainbow trout; smallmouth bass (see fish advisory, Appendix A)

INFORMATION Herman Covey Wildlife Management Area, mass.gov/info-details/herman-covey-wma

CAMPING Swift River lean-tos, Wells State Park, Tully Lake

TAKE NOTE Some development; shallow water and hand launch limit motors; no personal watercraft

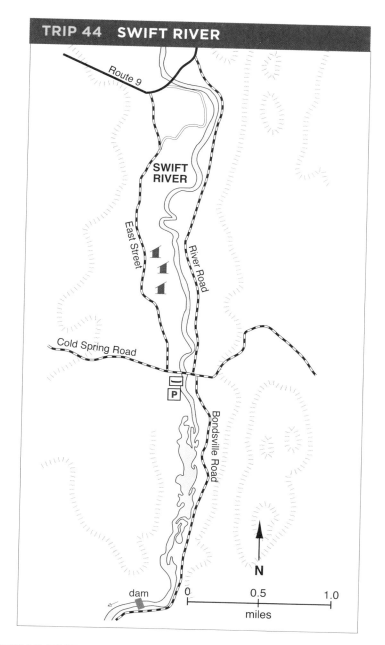

GETTING THERE

From the junction of Routes 9 and 202 in Belchertown, go 3.8 miles east on Route 9, and turn right on East Street. Drive 2.1 miles (5.9 miles), and turn left on Cold Spring Road. In 0.1 mile (6.0 miles), reach the access on the right, just before the bridge. **42° 14.564′ N, 72° 20.112′ W**

WHAT YOU'LL SEE

Although clusters of houses impinge somewhat on the Swift River, most of the section included here has a very wild feel. The Swift River's clear water, outlet for the mighty Quabbin Reservoir, meanders along slowly with a modest low-flow volume mandated by law. Shallow water, masses of aquatic vegetation, and occasional downed trees and logjams limit motors.

We watched muskrats harvest grasses and pickerelweed and saw evidence of beaver in the pruned-back streamside alders. What we reveled in most, though, was the huge number of birds of many species. We saw wild turkey, tufted titmouse, grackle, blue jay, flicker, kingfisher, veery, eastern kingbird, eastern wood-pewee, red-winged blackbird, robin, catbird, cardinal, song sparrow, yellow-rumped warbler, yellowthroat, northern waterthrush, goldfinch, crow, mourning dove, and great blue heron. We also saw broods of mallards and Canada geese and enjoyed treetop Baltimore orioles singing their melodious songs.

The river contains lots of aquatic vegetation, especially in late summer, which shows that high water rarely scours the channel. Pickerelweed, pondweed, and American white waterlily grow in profusion against the wooded shoreline. Downstream from the access—in the section backed up by a dam—lots of inlets, islands, and coves beg to be explored. Upstream from the access, Mass-Wildlife (the Massachusetts Division of Fisheries and Wildlife) maintains four lean-tos along the river within the Herman Covey Wildlife Management Area that visitors may use for free but must reserve in advance.

TRIP 45

CHICOPEE RIVER RESERVOIR

Chicopee River Reservoir offers scenic paddling along wooded shores on a relatively undeveloped section of river, just a stone's throw from Springfield, the state's third-largest city. At low water levels, you may be able to paddle all the way to Three Rivers, where the Ware, Quaboag, and Swift rivers converge to form the Chicopee. Here, you can also explore some early 1900s industrial mills. Expect to see wood ducks, great blue herons, and painted turtles.

LOCATION Wilbraham, Ludlow, and Palmer, MA

MAPS *Massachusetts Atlas & Gazetteer*, Map 48: A1; USGS Ludlow

AREA/LENGTH Reservoir, 106 acres; Chicopee River, 2.5 miles one way

TIME Half day or more

HABITAT TYPE Shallow reservoir; wooded shores

FISH Yellow and white perch; northern pike (see fish advisory, Appendix A)

CAMPING Wells State Park, Tully Lake

INFORMATION massriversalliance.org/chicopee-river

TAKE NOTE Keep clear of the dam; current can be swift after heavy rains

GETTING THERE

From I-90, Exit 54, turn right on Route 21/Center Street, go 0.5 mile, and turn right on Chapin Street. Continue 1.0 mile (1.5 miles), and turn left on East Street (becomes Red Bridge Road). At 2.6 miles (4.1 miles), reach the access on the left. Drop off your boat and go 0.2 mile back on Red Bridge Road. Park on the left (south) side of the road. **41° 56.783′ N, 71° 6.867′ W**

WHAT YOU'LL SEE

Chicopee River Reservoir, also known as Red Bridge Pool, impounds the Chicopee River, which is formed by the confluence of the Ware, Quaboag, and Swift rivers in the village of Three Rivers; the Chicopee River flows into the Connecticut River in—surprise!—Chicopee. The reservoir and several shallow extensions offer a pleasant half day of paddling—more if you bring a picnic lunch or do some hiking on the surrounding trails.

A diverse mix of deciduous trees—red and silver maples, gray and black birches, alder, red and white oaks, basswood, black locust—and hemlock, along with a few white pines, crowd the heavily wooded shoreline. Hemlock woods tend to have open understories, as is the case here, providing views into the needle-carpeted woodland. Unfortunately, invasive hemlock woolly adelgid insects heavily infest these hemlocks and are found throughout the Northeast's hemlock forests. The insects are too tiny to see, but if you inspect an overhanging branch, you will see the distinctive woolly white masses at needle bases. These aphid-like insects weaken—and eventually kill—the trees. Will the hemlock soon disappear from New England forests?

Huge granite boulders and cliffs reach down to the water's edge in places, many sporting carpets of moss, splotches of lichen, and clumps of polypody fern (*Polypodium vulgare*). You will also see interrupted, sensitive, and New York ferns. Understory shoreline shrubs include some that are quite colorful when in bloom: mountain laurel (*Kalmia latifolia*), swamp azalea (*Rhododendron viscosum*), and sweet pepperbush (*Clethra alnifolia*), along with highbush blueberry, witch hazel, and—in swampier areas—silky dogwood, buttonbush,

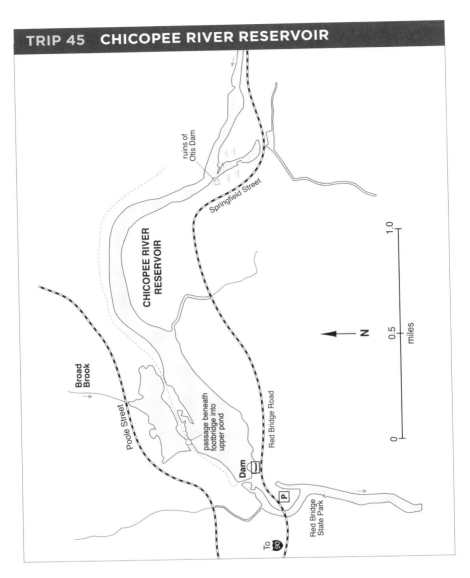

and swamp loosestrife. We spotted some Eurasian watermilfoil but were surprised at how few invasive plants we encountered.

Paddling east along the southern shoreline for about 2 miles, you'll reach an odd stone structure, a former hydroelectric plant, jutting out into the water. The Otis Company began construction of a dam and hydropower plant here in the early 1900s to power its cotton canvas manufacturing plant. At the same time, however, the Ludlow Mills company built the still-operating Red Bridge dam and hydropower facility. The Otis Company sued to stop the Red Bridge dam, which would flood the Otis turbine gates, but lost in court and abandoned its facility. Depending on water level, you might be able to paddle into the turbine rooms through the domed openings.

Beyond these ruins and off to the right (south), you can explore a beautiful, quiet backwater of the Chicopee River. Unlike most of the reservoir and river, this shallow impoundment is filled with emergent and floating vegetation, including pickerelweed, bur-reed, iris, bullrush, grasses, cattail, yellow pondlily, and watershield. In places, we paddled through bright green duckweed that totally covered the surface, parting it as we paddled along, then watching it fill in behind us. Watch for wood ducks and great blue herons here.

Back out on the main river, the current, swift from recent rains, had us working hard to paddle up another third of a mile to what remains of a second dam and hydropower facility, built by the same Otis Company after ceasing construction of the first. It was in use until the company went bankrupt in the late 1930s. We turned around here, but at lower water levels, with some effort, one could likely paddle up to Three Rivers.

Returning along the northern shore, pass a waterfall that offers a pleasant picnic spot. Then, not far from the dam and boat access, you can go under a small footbridge into a smaller pond to the north. We saw many more painted turtles here than on the main reservoir, along with one common musk, or stinkpot, turtle (*Sternotherus odoratus*), but otherwise the pond is more developed than the main reservoir and offers less to explore.

Paddlers on Chicopee River Reservoir can view the ruins of the ill-fated Otis hydroelectric facility; at lower water levels, one might be able to squeeze through the turbine gates shown in the photo.

SECTION 5

WESTERN MASSACHUSETTS

The nine entries in Western Massa-chusetts offer varied paddling opportunities. One out-of-the-way pond—Upper Highland Lake—though small, is a recreation destination for paddling, camping, and hiking and a great place to bring kids to learn about the outdoors. Bog and Burnett ponds, lying within Savoy Mountain State Forest, have much  to offer, including the best locations in the state to look for moose, high elevation for cooler summer temperatures, and northern fen habitats, characteristic of northern New England.

We include a 10-mile section of the Housatonic River for those who wish to paddle a lengthy slow-flowing stream filled with wildlife. Mostly small ponds compose the rest of the bodies of water. We're especially intrigued by Thousand Acre Swamp and remote East Indies Pond, with its spectacular late June mountain laurel bloom from plants reaching as high as 20 feet. Swampy Three Mile Pond warrants a visit; although paddling its circumference takes little time, we have seen plentiful wildlife there, including osprey, broad-winged hawk, barred owl, wild turkey, and more.

Other ponds also occur at higher, and therefore cooler, elevations on the Berkshire Plateau. You can study many plant species at Upper Spectacle Pond and admire the scenic hillsides surrounding Buckley Dunton Lake, with the Appalachian Trail traversing nearby hillsides. Plainfield Pond also offers a scenic backdrop, along with rafts of little floating heart, a relatively rare and delicate floating aquatic plant. At Littleville Lake, you may see beaver and deer in the evening, especially on the lake's north end.

TRIP 46

BOG POND AND BURNETT POND

These small mountain ponds are an excellent place to paddle when the surrounding valley floors suffer from summer heat. They lie within Savoy Mountain State Forest, the best location to look for moose in Massachusetts.

LOCATION Savoy, MA

MAPS *Massachusetts Atlas & Gazetteer*, Map 21: B5; USGS Cheshire (Burnett Pond) and North Adams (Bog Pond)

AREA Bog Pond, 40 acres; Burnett Pond, 30 acres

TIME 1 hour for each pond

HABITAT TYPE Swampy fen in state forest

FISH Largemouth bass, yellow perch, pickerel (see fish advisory, Appendix A)

INFORMATION Savoy Mountain State Forest, stateparks.com/savoy _mountain_state_forest_in_massachusetts.html

CAMPING Savoy Mountain State Forest, Clarksburg State Park, Mount Greylock State Reservation, Mohawk Trail State Forest

TAKE NOTE No motors; no development

GETTING THERE

Bog Pond From the junction of Routes 2 and 8 in North Adams, head 4.4 miles east on Route 2, and turn right on Central Shaft Road, at the sign for Savoy State Forest. Go 5.8 miles (10.2 miles) south on Central Shaft Road (becomes Florida Road, then Burnett Road), following state forest signs, veering left on Burnett Road at the T. As Burnett Road ends, go 1.2 miles (11.4 miles) straight (north) on New State Road to the access on the left. **42° 38.44′ N, 73° 1.991′ W**

From the east from Whitcomb Summit, go 1.9 miles west on Route 2, turn left on Central Shaft Road, and follow directions as above.

Burnett Pond From the junction of Burnett Road and New State Road, go 0.8 mile south on New State Road to the unmarked access on the right at a gate. Hike 100 yards down to the pond. **42° 37.003′ N, 73° 2.525′ W**

WHAT YOU'LL SEE

Savoy Mountain State Forest, one of the best places to see moose in Massachusetts, certainly warrants a visit, particularly during hot summer weather. Bog Pond, at an elevation of 1,858 feet, and nearby Burnett Pond are both nearly 1,300 feet higher than nearby valleys. Consequently, they can be several degrees cooler because of the so-called adiabatic lapse rate. The sun's heating of valley floors sends warm air masses skyward, which expand as they rise. Because the rising masses' heat content remains constant as they work

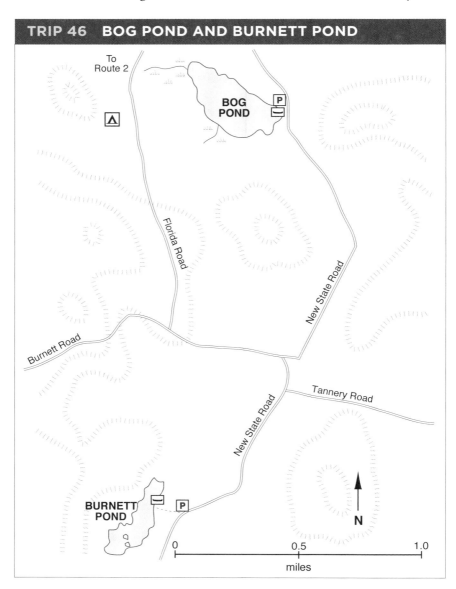

TRIP 46   BOG POND AND BURNETT POND

to expand against adjacent air masses, they cool. Dry air masses cool at the rate of 5.4 degrees Fahrenheit per 1,000 feet, while more humid air masses cool at 3.6 degrees. So, depending on humidity, on sunny days the shores of Bog Pond should be between 5 and 7 degrees cooler than the surrounding lowlands. In addition, cooling breezes often flow strongly across Bog Pond because no mountains lie to the west.

Bog Pond lies in a gorgeous setting, with lots of boggy islands to explore at your leisure. American white waterlily, watershield, and American eelgrass cover the water's surface, while hemlock, balsam fir, and red maple cover the shoreline. A large beaver lodge perches on a sphagnum-covered island, along with three species of carnivorous plant: purple pitcher plant, round-leaved sundew, and large patches of a beautiful terrestrial, yellow-flowered, horned bladderwort (*Utricularia cornuta*) that blooms in mid-July. The pond's shores—filled with ostrich fern, leatherleaf, sweetgale, sheep laurel, and several other shrubs—also provide habitat for a host of marsh birds, including yellowthroat, yellow warbler, cedar waxwing, song sparrow, black-capped chickadee, Canada goose, and great blue heron.

When we paddled here, beaver had dammed the spillway, raising the water level by more than a foot. Even with the added depth, this small, shallow pond demands that you paddle slowly, savoring the marsh's plants and animals.

Nearby Burnett Pond, with its higher proportion of conifers, has a more boreal feel, perhaps explaining the frequent moose sightings there.

A gorgeous, terrestrial, yellow-flowered bladderwort, *Utricularia cornuta*, bloomed in profusion when we paddled here in mid-July.

PLAINFIELD POND

This pond perches high on the Berkshire Plateau, surrounded by gorgeous forests, and is an excellent location to study trees, shrubs, and aquatic plants. Large granite slabs on the pond's north end add a scenic quality.

LOCATION Plainfield, MA

MAPS *Massachusetts Atlas & Gazetteer*, Map 21: C6; USGS Ashfield

AREA 65 acres

TIME 2 hours

HABITAT TYPE Shrubby wooded pond

FISH Largemouth bass, yellow perch, pickerel, northern pike (see fish advisory, Appendix A)

CAMPING Savoy Mountain State Forest, Clarksburg State Park, Mount Greylock State Reservation, Mohawk Trail State Forest

TAKE NOTE No motors; limited development

GETTING THERE

From Charlemont at the junction of Routes 2 and 8A, go 9.4 miles south on Route 8A, and turn right on Routes 8A/116. Continue 0.9 mile (10.3 miles) to the access on the right, just past the town beach. **42° 32.38′ N, 72° 57.522′ W**

From Adams, go east on Route 116 to the junction with Route 8A south. Stay straight on Routes 8A/116, and go 4.9 miles to the access on the left.

From Pittsfield, go east—and from Northampton, go west—on Route 9, turn north on Route 8A, and head 9.3 miles to the access on the left.

WHAT YOU'LL SEE

At the access, very tame mallards with broods greeted us, a sure sign that residents using the town beach feed these birds. Massive quantities of little floating heart (*Nymphoides cordata*), with tiny white flowers and heart-shaped leaves less than 2 inches across, also greeted us as we paddled out from the access. Rarely do we see these delicate aquatic plants growing in such profusion. Thick stands of shrubs layer the shoreline, with a profusion of highbush blueberry and mountain laurel, as well as lesser quantities of swamp azalea and arrowwood. When we paddled here in mid-July, arrowwood's umbel-like purple berries and blueberry's urn-like white flowers lent color to the shore, but we wished that we had visited earlier when the mountain laurel and swamp azalea bloomed.

Plainfield Pond perches high on the Berkshire Plateau, surrounded by forests of spruce, paper birch, white pine, red maple, and hemlock. These trees populate large, gorgeous, fractured granite slabs, some posing as islands, on the pond's north end. The pond's very clear water, harboring lots of freshwater mussels, gives way to yellow-brown water as you enter the marshes on the north end. Sweetgale, with lesser amounts of leatherleaf and swamp rose, lines the low banks, and beaver keep a channel open through the pickerelweed, watershield, yellow-flowered bladderwort, and yellow pondlily.

Beaver had gnawed away the bark of some hemlocks, killing them, a phenomenon that we have seen in several other locations. (Apparently, if you run out of the good stuff, you kill off the bad stuff in the hope that more palatable species will replace it.) The next time you see a dense stand of hemlock, look closely at the understory. Few hardwoods—preferred beaver food—take root under hemlocks. This phenomenon is called negative allelopathy, where plants produce chemicals that inhibit seedling growth.

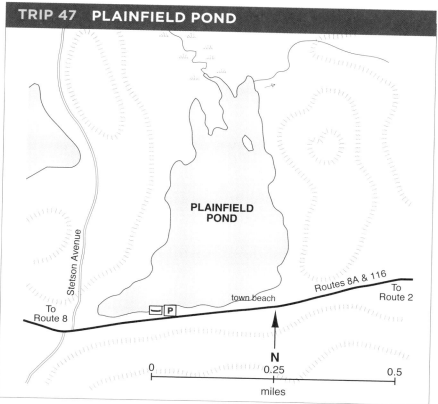

TRIP 47   PLAINFIELD POND

UPPER HIGHLAND LAKE

Nestled in Daughters of the American Revolution (DAR) State Forest, Upper Highland Lake is a recreation destination with camping, hiking, and paddling available. A beautiful stand of hemlock graces this site, but how long it can withstand the hemlock woolly adelgid onslaught is an open question.

LOCATION Goshen, MA

MAPS *Massachusetts Atlas & Gazetteer*, Map 34: A2; USGS Goshen

AREA 56 acres

TIME 2 hours

HABITAT TYPE Wooded pond

FISH Brook and rainbow trout, largemouth and smallmouth bass, yellow perch (see fish advisory, Appendix A)

CAMPING DAR State Forest

INFORMATION DAR State Forest, mass.gov/locations/daughters -of-the-american-revolution-dar-state-forest

TAKE NOTE No internal combustion motors; limited development

GETTING THERE

From the South From Northampton, go west on Route 9, turn right on Route 112, and go 0.7 mile north to the DAR State Forest entrance (Moore Hill Road) on the right. Continue 0.4 mile (1.1 miles) to the access on the left. **42° 27.441' N, 72° 47.511' W**

From the North Go west from Greenfield or east from North Adams on Route 2, turn south on Route 112 in Shelburne Falls, and go 13.7 miles to the DAR State Forest entrance on the left. In 0.4 mile (14.1 miles), the access is on the left.

WHAT YOU'LL SEE

Nestled within DAR State Forest in the Berkshires, Upper Highland Lake offers a great getaway spot for a relaxed weekend of camping, paddling, and hiking. Groves of gorgeous hemlocks, with streams of light filtering through the canopy, await hikers on the many trails that traverse the 1,020-acre DAR State Forest. The 52 campsites, including some that are universally accessible, fill up well before the weekend, so we recommend reservations. This small lake, with no development on it other than recreational facilities and Camp Holy Cross—a private youth camp—near the northwest corner offers quiet paddling in scenic surroundings.

The shoreline vegetation consists primarily of deciduous trees—birch, maple, beech, and some oak—with many white pine and hemlock mixed in. The hemlock woolly adelgid, an Asian import that has gradually marched northward, threatens the eastern hemlock here and in the rest of New England. The hemlock may not go the way of the chestnut, as some success in controlling the adelgid has been achieved through two imported beetles from the Northwest and one from Japan. However, while the chestnut continues to sprout from stumps, once a hemlock dies, that's it—no stump sprouting. Time is running out, so a lot is riding on biological control of the adelgid. Robert Frost, the eminent New England poet, penned the following poem, "Dust of Snow," about the hemlock.

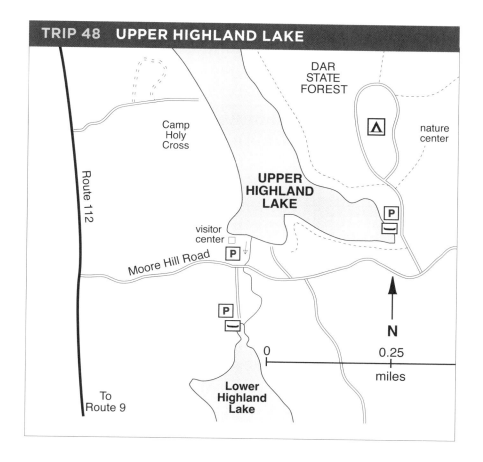

TRIP 48 UPPER HIGHLAND LAKE

DAR STATE FOREST

nature center

Camp Holy Cross

Route 112

UPPER HIGHLAND LAKE

P

visitor center

Moore Hill Road

P

P

N

0   0.25

miles

To Route 9

Lower Highland Lake

The way a crow
Shook down on me
The dust of snow
From a hemlock tree

Has given my heart
A change of mood
And saved some part
Of a day I had rued.

Highbush blueberry, mountain laurel, and other shrubs grow along the shore. An inlet and a cove extending to the northwest await exploration. A beaver lodge perches between the cove and inlet, which you might want to visit around dusk or dawn to look for beaver.

Just to the south and also largely within DAR State Forest lies the somewhat larger Lower Highland Lake. The state prohibits gasoline-powered motorboats here as well, but considerable development crowds the southern shores.

A ranger found a World War II photograph showing the boot-shaped Upper Highland Lake from the fire tower atop Moore Hill (on the east side of the lake and accessible by road or trails). Spotters used the tower, like others throughout southern New England in this uneasy time, to watch for warplanes. The photo shows a nearly bare summit with young growth of hemlock and pine, a reminder that much of this area had once been cleared for raising sheep. Enlargement of the dams by the Civilian Conservation Corps increased the size of both lakes, turning these small reservoirs—used for powering silk mills at Goshen—into today's lovely paddling lakes.

TRIP 49

LITTLEVILLE LAKE

This is a worthwhile trip for anglers and for paddlers who don't mind weaving their way through a stump-filled reservoir. The wooded hillsides and scattered islands lend a scenic beauty. Look for great blue heron prowling the west end marshes.

LOCATION Chester and Huntington, MA

MAPS *Massachusetts Atlas & Gazetteer*, Map 34: C1; USGS Chester

AREA 275 acres

TIME 3 hours

HABITAT TYPE Long, narrow, wooded reservoir

FISH Brook, brown, and rainbow trout; largemouth bass; yellow perch (see fish advisory, Appendix A)

CAMPING Chester-Blandford State Forest, DAR State Forest

INFORMATION Littleville Lake Recreation Area, nae.usace.army.mil/Missions/Recreation/Littleville-Lake/

TAKE NOTE No development; boats must be at least 12 feet long; motors allowed, 10 HP limit

GETTING THERE

Southern Access, from Northampton Go 13.6 miles west on Route 66 (initially West Street), and turn left on Route 112. Drive 2.2 miles (15.8 miles), and just after crossing the Westfield River, turn right on Littleville Road at the sign for Littleville Lake. At 0.7 mile (16.5 miles), veer right on Goss Hill Road. Go 0.7 mile (17.2 miles) to the access on the left. **42° 16.133′ N, 72° 52.798′ W**

Southern Access, from the South At the junction of Routes 20 and 112 in Huntington, go 1.4 miles north on Route 112, and turn left just before crossing the Westfield River, at the sign for Littleville Lake. Follow directions as above.

Northern Access From the junction of Routes 20 and 112, go 0.1 mile north on Route 112, and turn sharply left onto Basket Street (main road becomes Old Chester Road), just after crossing the bridge. Go 1.5 miles (1.6 miles), and turn right on Skyline Trail. Continue 2.5 miles (4.1 miles), and turn right on East River Road. In 2.0 miles (6.1 miles), turn right on Kinne Brook Road, and go 0.8 mile (6.9 miles) to the Dayville access. **42° 17.613′ N, 72° 53.975′ W**

WHAT YOU'LL SEE

Created in 1965 when the U.S. Army Corps of Engineers built a flood-control dam on the Middle Branch of the Westfield River to stem serious flooding that had occurred since the 1600s, Littleville Lake offers superb paddling, fishing, and picnicking in a scenic valley. To build the dam, a local fairground had to be relocated, but today's Littleville Fair continues to be a high point in late summer. The lake doubles as a backup water supply for Springfield, about 30 miles downstream, but has yet to be drawn upon.

The wooded hills amid 1,567 acres contain typical woodland tree species, including sugar and red maples, white ash, red oak, black and gray birches, quaking aspen, white pine, ironwood, and sycamore. The rocky shoreline leads to fairly steep wooded banks. A few marshy areas occur at the north end, along with the inlet. Signs of an abandoned farm appear about two-thirds of the way up the lake: old apple trees, stone walls, and pastures growing up into woodland. We found beaver and other wildlife to be more plentiful near the north end. You can paddle up the crystal-clear inlet river a short distance, but it becomes shallow fairly quickly with a lot of exposed rocks.

Anglers ply these waters for largemouth bass, yellow perch, and rainbow trout. Paddling around early one evening with the light just right, we saw about a dozen foot-long bass lurking beneath the surface along the west shore.

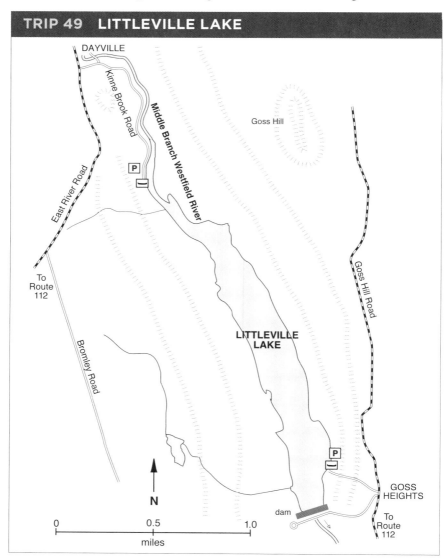

TRIP 49 LITTLEVILLE LAKE

Despite the general lack of inlets and coves to explore, Littleville Lake offers a pleasant morning or afternoon of paddling, with plenty of places to stop for a picnic. The Corps prohibits swimming, wading, and camping.

TRIP 50

HOUSATONIC RIVER

The Housatonic River is a deservedly popular place to paddle. It meanders through the namesake valley, loaded with wildlife, backed to the east by scenic October Mountain State Forest. Look for deer, otter, muskrat, beaver, herons, egrets, ducks, and geese. (We don't recommend bringing children here, for the reasons cited below.)

LOCATION Lee, Lenox, Pittsfield, and Washington, MA

MAPS *Massachusetts Atlas & Gazetteer*, Map 32: B3; USGS Pittsfield East

LENGTH 10 miles one way

TIME All day; shorter trips possible

HABITAT TYPE Dammed-up meandering river; shrubby marshlands; forested hillsides; some farmland

FISH The river holds 45 species of fish, but they cannot be eaten from this portion of the river because of polychlorinated biphenyl (PCB) contamination (see fish advisory, Appendix A).

CAMPING October Mountain State Forest, Beartown State Forest, Tolland State Forest, Pittsfield State Forest

INFORMATION PCBs, epa.gov/region1/ge/understandingpcbrisks.html; a clean boat certification is required, mass.gov/doc/clean-boat-certification -form-0/download

TAKE NOTE Little development; electric motors allowed; we recommend that no one, especially children, should come in contact with the water because of PCB contamination

GETTING THERE

New Lenox Road From the junction of Routes 7 and 20 west to Albany in Pittsfield, head 3.4 miles south on Route 7, and turn left on New Lenox Road.

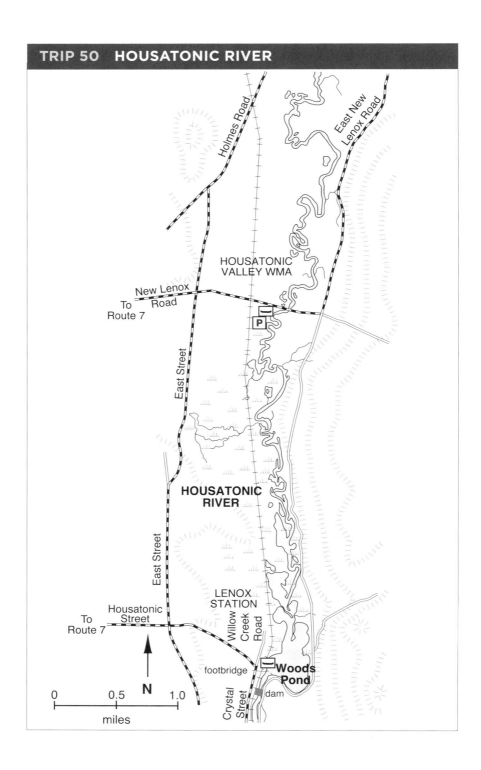

Holmes Road

East New Lenox Road

HOUSATONIC VALLEY WMA

New Lenox Road

To Route 7

P

East Street

HOUSATONIC RIVER

East Street

LENOX STATION

To Route 7

Housatonic Street

Willow Creek Road

footbridge

Woods Pond

Crystal Street

dam

N

0   0.5   1.0

miles

Go 1.4 miles (4.8 miles) to the John F. Decker canoe access on the right. **42° 23.62' N, 73° 14.539' W**

Lenox Station From the junction of East Street and New Lenox Road, go 2.9 miles south on East Street, and turn left on Housatonic Street. Drive 0.9 mile (3.8 miles) to the access by the footbridge at the junction of Housatonic Street, Willow Creek Road, and Crystal Street. **42° 20.985' N, 73° 14.628' W**

WHAT YOU'LL SEE

This very popular canoeing and kayaking stream teems with paddlers on busy summer weekends, making wildlife viewing more difficult. We recommend paddling here in spring or fall or during the week in summer months. You can escape the crowds somewhat by paddling off into the numerous, very large oxbows, leaving behind the troops of paddlers intent on just making it down the river.

Though the current barely flows by midsummer, paddling here during spring high water may necessitate a one-way trip. At times of high water, you can travel upstream from Lenox Station/Woods Pond; myriad bays and side channels sheltered by scenic hillsides invite exploration. If time is limited, paddle upstream from Lenox Station rather than downstream from New Lenox Road.

The relatively tame mallards that met us at the access did not seem to mind visitors, and we did manage to see abundant birdlife—the usual marshland species, including several broods of wood ducks. We did not paddle here in the evening, but judging from the size and number of lodges, beaver must be a routine evening sight. The Housatonic Valley Wildlife Management Area protects the river valley marshlands, and October Mountain State Forest protects the lovely forested hillsides to the east.

Except for farmland near New Lenox Road, trees cover the shoreline, arching out over the water and over the abundant, diverse shrubs and vines lining the shore. Silver maple dominates in some areas, its branches serving as launch pads for deerflies (a sight predator). We also saw willow, basswood, box elder, and many others. Thick patches of ostrich fern waved in the slight breeze, and wildflowers bloomed in profusion. As we listened to song sparrows calling from the underbrush and watched a phoebe bob its tail from a streamside perch, we understood why this is such a popular location. We did not understand, however, how so much trash could accumulate behind the numerous deadfalls; perhaps it had washed downstream from Pittsfield after heavy rains.

Paddling upstream from New Lenox Road, after about a mile you will reach several power lines and a complex of buildings on the right, a research station of the Electrical Power Research Institute (EPRI). Several years ago, we visited this facility to talk with researchers about their work with electromagnetic fields (EMF) for an article that Alex was writing for his publication *Environ-*

We saw many pairs of Canada geese raising their broods along the Housatonic River.

mental Building News on the effects of EMF on human health. EPRI had an entire house set up using different code-compliant wiring configurations to see how much EMF each produced.

Another electrical complex, however, was not so benign. For years, a General Electric (GE) plant making transformers dumped huge quantities of polychlorinated biphenyls (PCBs) into the Housatonic River. GE acknowledged dumping 20 tons into the river; the U.S. Environmental Protection Agency (EPA) says that it was between 50 and 300 tons. This is an astounding amount for a poison that acts lethally in animal species at parts per million concentrations. The highest concentrations are found in the sediment for the 10 miles of the river included here. Eating fish or waterfowl from this area is taboo, as is swimming. Here are the findings from a 1998 EPA report:

- Young children and teenagers playing in and near portions of the river face noncancer risks that are 200 times greater than the EPA considers safe. Noncancer effects from PCBs may include liver and nervous system damage and development abnormalities, including lower IQs.

- Teenagers growing up near portions of the river face a 1 in 1,000 cancer risk due to exposure to contaminated riverbank soils.

- Fish collected in the river had PCB concentrations of up to 206 parts per million, among the highest levels ever found in the United States and 100 times higher than the limits set by the U.S. Food and Drug Administration.

- Because it would take hundreds of years for the PCBs to degrade, the EPA is overseeing GE's clean-up of the river sediment.

BUCKLEY DUNTON LAKE

Buckley Dunton Lake, because of its higher elevation, is a pleasant place to paddle when the lowlands get hot. Surrounding Berkshire hillsides lend a scenic quality, with high tree-species diversity. Mountain laurel blooms in profusion in June, and patches of blueberry ripen in August.

LOCATION Becket, MA

MAPS *Massachusetts Atlas & Gazetteer*, Map 33: C4; USGS East Lee

AREA 195 acres

TIME 3 hours

HABITAT TYPE Wooded reservoir

FISH Largemouth bass, pickerel (see fish advisory, Appendix A)

CAMPING October Mountain State Forest, Beartown State Forest, Tolland State Forest, Pittsfield State Forest

TAKE NOTE Barely submerged stumps, rocks, and poor access limit motors; limited development

GETTING THERE

From I-90, Exit 10, go 4.0 miles east on Route 20, and turn left on Becket Road (becomes Tyne Road as it ascends Becket Mountain and crosses the Appalachian Trail). In 1.9 miles (5.9 miles), veer left on Yokum Road as Tyne Road goes right. Go 0.6 mile (6.5 miles), and turn left at the hidden access road, just before a garage (the turn is across from Leonhardt Road). Continue 0.4 mile (6.9 miles) to the put-in. **42° 18.335′ N, 73° 7.723′ W**

WHAT YOU'LL SEE

Buckley Dunton Lake nestles amid the Berkshires in the southeast corner of October Mountain State Forest, Massachusetts's largest tract of publicly owned land, which includes a 9-mile Appalachian Trail segment that passes over nearby scenic peaks. The damming of Yokum Brook in the 1800s to provide power for downstream mills created the lake.

Trees and shrubs typical of the moderately high Berkshire mountains dot the lake's heavily wooded shoreline, including hemlock, white pine, spruce, red and sugar maples, black cherry, ash, gray and yellow birches, and alder. Look for large patches of mountain laurel in bloom in late June; blueberries ripen in late

July or August. Large boulders that jut out into the water invite picnic stops, but thick vegetation makes most of the shoreline quite impenetrable.

Rotting logs and tree stumps in the shallow, marshy north end force paddlers to navigate carefully. Yellow pondlily, American white waterlily, pondweed, blue flag, and cattail grow here. Also, look closely for diminutive carnivorous sundews on mossy hillocks. Listen for bullfrogs in spring, and in the evening or early morning you may see the lake's resident beaver. We also observed ruffed grouse. On pleasant weekends you may see and hear heavy use of trails by off-road vehicles and see several people fishing on the lake.

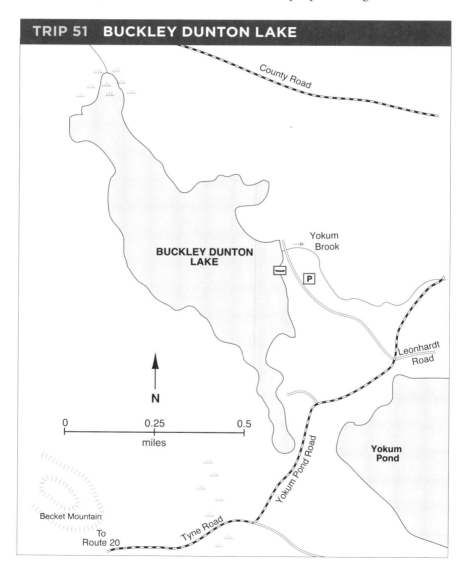

TRIP 51 BUCKLEY DUNTON LAKE

County Road

BUCKLEY DUNTON LAKE

Yokum Brook

P

Leonhardt Road

N

0   0.25   0.5
miles

Becket Mountain

To Route 20

Tyne Road

Yokum Pond Road

Yokum Pond

The heavily wooded hillsides of October Mountain State Forest surround Buckley Dunton Lake.

BEAVER: WETLANDS ENGINEER

The beaver, *Castor canadensis*, is one of the most remarkable animals found in New England's waters. Unlike most other animals, beaver actively modify their environment. The sole representative of the family Castoridae, this 30- to 100-pound rodent—the largest in North America—descends directly from a bear-sized ancestor that lived a million years ago.

Quietwater paddlers frequently see beaver dams and lodges, especially on more remote lakes and ponds. This industrious mammal uses branches pruned from streamside trees or downed timber to make the structures. Beaver now work mostly under cover of darkness, especially in areas heavily frequented by humans. In more remote, wild areas, however, many beaver labor in broad daylight. (We mention in our descriptions where we have seen beaver abroad during the day.)

Beaver build dams to raise water levels, providing the resident colony with access to trees growing farther away. The deeper water also allows beaver to cache branches underwater for later retrieval, even when thick layers of ice cover their winter stores. They also dig small canals through marsh and meadow to transport branches from distant trees. Just as we prefer paddling a boat to carrying it, beaver prefer swimming with a branch—taking advantage of water's buoyancy—to carrying it overland. They usually prune off leafy twigs to reduce drag.

Studies show that the sound of flowing water guides beaver in their dam building—they jam sticks into the dam where they hear the gurgle of water. In one experiment, researchers played a tape of gurgling water; beaver responded by jamming sticks into locations that emanated sound, even though no water actually flowed there. Beaver dams can be more than 10 feet high and hundreds of feet long. The largest dam ever recorded, near the present town of Berlin, New Hampshire, spanned 4,000 feet and created a lake with 40 lodges!

Beaver dams benefit many species, providing important habitat for waterfowl, fish, moose, muskrat, and other animals. Plus, the dams control flooding, minimize erosion along streambanks, increase aquifer recharge, and improve water quality, both by allowing silt to settle out and by providing biological filtration through aquatic plants. We credit beaver with creating much of America's best farmland by damming watercourses, thus allowing nutrient-rich silt to accumulate over many years. As the ponds fill in, meadows form.

The beaver lodge includes an underwater entrance and usually two platforms: a main floor about 4 inches above the water level and a sleeping shelf another 2 inches higher. Beaver may construct the lodge in a pond's center but more commonly site it on the edge. Before the onset of winter, beaver cover much of the lodge with mud, which they carry on their broad tails while swimming. The mud freezes to create an almost impenetrable fortress. The river otter—the only predator that can get in—can swim through the underwater entrance. Beaver leave the peak more permeable for ventilation.

Near the lodge, in deep water, beaver store up a winter's worth of branches in an underwater food cache. They jam branches butt-first into the mud to keep them under the ice and then swim out under the ice to bring back branches to eat.

The beaver has adapted remarkably well to its aquatic lifestyle. It has two layers of fur: long, silky guard hairs and a dense woolly underfur. By regularly grooming this fur with a special comblike split toenail and keeping it oiled, the beaver ensures that water seldom totally wets its skin. Special valves keep the beaver's nose and ears shut underwater, and skin folds in the mouth enable it to gnaw underwater and to carry branches in its teeth without getting water down its throat. Back feet have fully webbed toes to provide propulsion underwater, and the tail provides rudder control, helping the beaver swim in a straight line when dragging a large branch. Both the respiratory and circulatory systems have adapted to underwater swimming, enabling a beaver to stay underwater for up to 15 minutes. Finally, as with other rodents, its teeth grow constantly and remain sharp through use.

Beaver generally mate for life and maintain an extended family structure. Young stay with their parents for two years, so both yearlings and the current year's kits live with the parents in the lodge. Females usually bear two—sometimes three—kits between April and June. Born fully furred with eyes open, they can walk and swim almost immediately, although they rarely

leave the lodge until at least a month of age. Yearlings and both parents bring food to the kits, as well as help with dam and lodge construction.

The demand for beaver pelts, more than any other factor, prompted the early European exploration of North America. Trappers had nearly exterminated the beaver by the late 1800s, but last-minute legislative protection in the 1890s saved it from extinction. Trappers extirpated beaver in Connecticut in the mid-1800s, and the state began reintroducing them in 1914 as part of a restocking program. Then began what certainly must be the most successful endangered species reintroduction program ever. By 1955, beaver had repopulated the entire state. Reintroduction in Massachusetts began in 1932 with the release of three animals from New York. Beaver that immigrated from surrounding states started showing up in Rhode Island in 1976.

As you paddle the shoreline of lakes or quiet rivers, keep an eye out for telltale beaver signs, including gnaw marks on trees, distinctive conical stumps of cut trees, canals leading off into the marsh, alder branches trimmed back along narrow passages, and well-worn paths to the water's edge where beaver have dragged branches to the water.

We see beaver most often in late evening or early morning. Paddle quietly toward a beaver lodge around dusk. Wait patiently, and you will likely see the animals emerge for evening feeding and perhaps construction work on a dam or lodge.

TRIP 52

UPPER SPECTACLE POND

This out-of-the-way mountain pond offers a short, pleasurable paddle between wooded hillsides. A stand of majestic hemlock and white pine greets you at the access. Expect to see Canada geese; this is also a prime location to study aquatic vegetation. Mountain laurel puts on a spectacular display in June.

LOCATION Otis and Sandisfield, MA

MAPS *Massachusetts Atlas & Gazetteer*, Map 45: A4; USGS Otis

AREA 72 acres

TIME 2 hours

HABITAT TYPE Wooded mountain pond

FISH Pickerel (see fish advisory, Appendix A)

CAMPING Tolland State Forest, Beartown State Forest, Granville State Forest, Chester-Blandford State Forest

TAKE NOTE Hand-carry access limits motors; no development

GETTING THERE
From I-90, Exit 10, go 6.9 miles east on Route 20, and turn right on Route 8. Go 5.5 miles (12.4 miles), and turn right on Route 23. In 3.4 miles (15.8 miles), turn left on Cold Spring Road. Continue 0.8 mile (16.6 miles), and then veer left on unmarked dirt Webb Road. The access is 1.0 mile (17.6 miles) farther on the right fork. **42° 10.632′ N, 73° 7.082′ W**

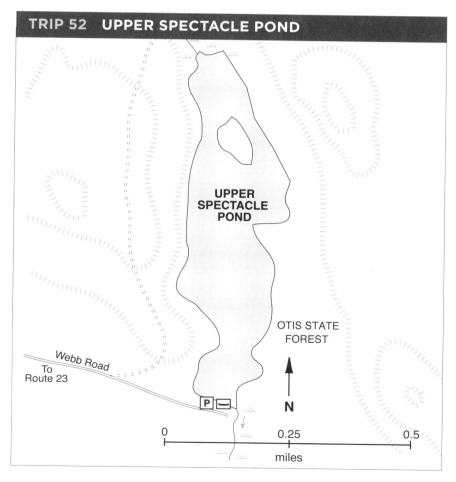

TRIP 52   UPPER SPECTACLE POND

UPPER
SPECTACLE
POND

OTIS STATE
FOREST

N

Webb Road
To
Route 23

P

0   0.25   0.5

miles

Water smartweed blooms abundantly on Upper Spectacle Pond.

From Great Barrington, go east on Route 23 to Monterey. From the church, general store, and post office, go 3.7 miles, turn right on Cold Spring Road, and follow the directions above.

WHAT YOU'LL SEE

Pass through a deep hemlock woods to arrive at the access amid a noble stand of large hemlock and white pine. If the hemlock does not withstand the hemlock woolly adelgid onslaught, the area surrounding the pond will be substantially diminished. (See Trip 45 for more information on the hemlock woolly adelgid.)

Although white pine occurs along the pond's shore, deciduous trees predominate here and on scenic hillsides, with mountain laurel the dominant shrub. The pond and its coves—including a beautiful island wooded with oaks—require only an hour or two to explore fully. (If geese haven't covered the granite slabs on the northeast with excrement, these slabs make an excellent picnic stop.)

Water smartweed (*Polyganum amphibium*) and pondweed (*Potamogeton spp.*)—both featuring elongated, floating leaves and small, vertical puffs of flowers—grow in profusion side by side. They bear a superficial resemblance, but look closely and note the leaf venation. Smartweed veins radiate out at roughly right angles to the midvein, whereas pondweed side veins start with the midvein at the stem and remain roughly parallel to the midvein all the way to the tip.

Lots of yellow-flowered and eastern purple bladderwort occur here, notable because invasive watermilfoil has not yet inundated this pond and crowded out native species. Gelatinous Bryozoa colonies, also susceptible to crowding, occur on many submerged logs and branches along the shore. As we paddled along, an immature bald eagle soared overhead, possibly from the nest at nearby Colebrook River Lake to the south.

TRIP 53

THREE MILE POND

This remote pond generally provides good opportunities to view wildlife. We saw an osprey, wild turkeys, a broad-winged hawk, Canada geese, and wood ducks and heard a barred owl on our trips here. Look for beaver in the evening.

LOCATION Sheffield, MA

MAPS *Massachusetts Atlas & Gazetteer*, Map 44: B2; USGS Sheffield

AREA 81 acres

TIME 2 hours

HABITAT TYPE Wooded pond with forested hillsides

FISH Largemouth bass, pickerel (see fish advisory, Appendix A)

INFORMATION Three Mile Pond Wildlife Management Area, mass.gov/info-details/three-mile-pond-wma

CAMPING Beartown State Forest, Tolland State Forest, Granville State Forest, October Mountain State Forest

TAKE NOTE Too weedy and shallow for motors; limited development; lies mostly within Three Mile Pond Wildlife Management Area

GETTING THERE

From Great Barrington From the junction of Routes 7, 23, and 41, go 0.9 mile south on Route 7, and turn left on Brookside Road (becomes Brush Hill Road, then Home Road). Drive 4.0 miles (4.9 miles), and turn left on a different Brush Hill Road. Go 1.1 miles (6.0 miles) to the sometimes muddy access on the right. **42° 8.785′ N, 73° 18.824′ W**

From Sheffield From Route 7, go 1.6 miles east on Maple Avenue (which becomes County Road), and turn left on Home Road. Drive 1.7 miles (3.3 miles), turn right on Brush Hill Road, and go 1.1 miles (4.4 miles) to the access on the right.

WHAT YOU'LL SEE

A broad-winged hawk soared overhead and dozens of tree swallows darted from their nest boxes as we carefully worked our way down the rutted road to the access one early May. Spring peepers beckoned to us while an osprey

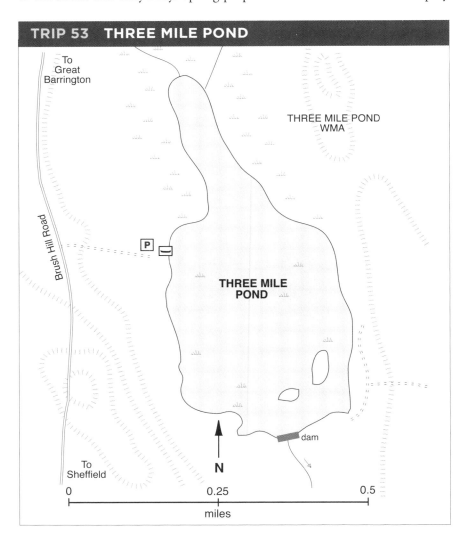

A white-tailed skimmer (*Plathemis lydia*) soaks up the sun on a dead tree on Three Mile Pond.

dove for fish. When we ventured onto the northern section of this shallow, weedy pond, wood ducks flew off into the marsh, and Canada geese swam out of sight. On another May trip several years later, a flock of wild turkeys greeted us at the access while a barred owl called from the surrounding woods.

On a late June return trip, the osprey had vanished, no doubt because dense rafts of invasive watermilfoil clogged the pond, leaving precious little open water. Though we had to slog through this sea of vegetation, we still enjoyed forging our way down to the large island off the southeast shore. The densely foliated island harbors quite a few tall, thin tamaracks—a tree that withstands saturated soil—along with sphagnum mats, pitcher plants, cranberries, and a large beaver lodge.

We gazed back up the pond, with clumps of blooming mountain laurel here and there, and drank in the scenic beauty of unspoiled, undulating, deciduous-tree-covered hillsides that include a section of the Appalachian Trail. A couple of cabins on the southeast shore and a low earthen dam on the south end provide the only evidence of civilization except, of course, for the invasive watermilfoil.

Returning to the access, we studied the several species of dragonflies that patrol the shallows and searched for frogs among the cattails. While you could paddle the entire perimeter of this pond in an hour, you could also linger, examining the myriad plants and wildlife in this picturesque spot.

THOUSAND ACRE SWAMP AND EAST INDIES POND

Thousand Acre Swamp offers a one- to two-hour leisurely paddle on a weed-filled pond surrounded by Cookson State Forest. We enjoy the swamp but much prefer the secluded East Indies Pond, especially in late June with its spectacular mountain laurel bloom. Look for beaver here in the evening, along with typical marsh species.

LOCATION New Marlborough, MA

MAPS *Massachusetts Atlas & Gazetteer*, Map 44: C3; USGS South Sandisfield

AREA Thousand Acre Swamp, 155 acres; East Indies Pond, 69 acres

TIME 4 hours to paddle both ponds

HABITAT TYPE Shallow, marshy, tree-lined ponds

FISH Largemouth bass, yellow perch, muskellunge (see fish advisory, Appendix A)

CAMPING Beartown State Forest, Tolland State Forest, Granville State Forest

INFORMATION Cookson State Forest, stateparks.com/cookson_state _forest_in_massachusetts.html

TAKE NOTE Few motors; no development

GETTING THERE

Thousand Acre Swamp From Great Barrington, go east on Routes 23 and 183; when they divide, continue 5.7 miles on Routes 57 and 183, and turn right on New Marlborough–Southfield Road. Go 1.3 miles (7.0 miles), and turn left on Norfolk Road. In 2.9 miles (9.9 miles), turn left on Hotchkiss Road. Go 0.6 mile (10.5 miles) to the access on the right. **42° 4.222′ N, 73° 12.661′ W**

East Indies Pond From the Thousand Acre Swamp access, paddle straight across the pond toward a grove of tall white pine to the trailhead for East Indies Pond. The half-mile trail begins here. Go about 600 paces to a T, turn right, go about 160 paces (cross the outflow stream at about 60 paces), and turn left on an obvious trail (look for a large rock) that leads to Mill Pond.

Go about 100 paces to Mill Pond. Alternatively, from the stream crossing, go about 1,000 paces, and take the left fork downhill for about 400 paces to a fire grate and East Indies Pond. **42° 4.039′ N, 73° 11.792′ W**

TRIP 54 THOUSAND ACRE SWAMP AND EAST INDIES POND

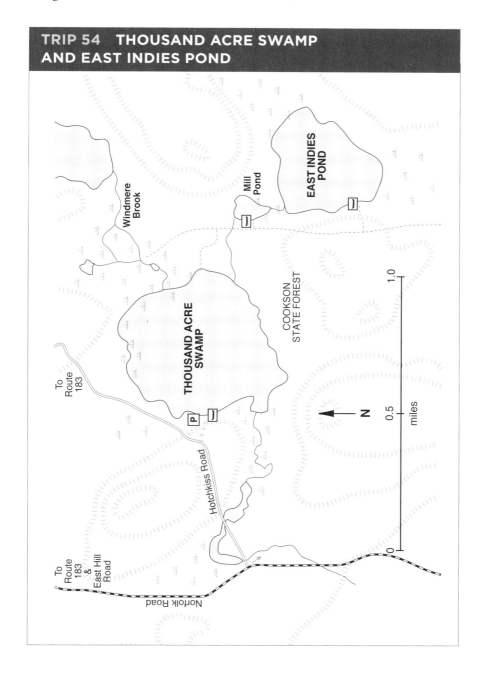

WHAT YOU'LL SEE
THOUSAND ACRE SWAMP

This out-of-the-way, scenic pond offers wonderful paddling within the borders of Campbell Falls State Park. Interestingly, Campbell Falls itself lies well outside the park, which has no development or conveniences. Though we enjoyed paddling through the abundant vegetation of this stump-filled pond, we noted luxuriant growths of invasive watermilfoil starting to crowd out the native watershield, American white waterlily, yellow pondlily, and pondweed. While some mountain laurel bloomed along the southern shore, it paled in comparison to the growth at East Indies Pond.

Mallard and Canada goose nest here, and if you visit in the evening, you may see some of the resident beavers as they work over the wooded shores. In the woodland during a mid-June visit, we watched a wild turkey hen herding her brood of six young. Although we did not paddle it, the outlet stream where it crosses Hotchkiss Road south of the pond looks like an interesting area to explore. We found loads of mussels on the sandy bottom, and we watched a great blue heron—up to its nether parts in yellow pondlily—hunting fish and frogs. In early summer, you may notice shallow depressions in the pond's sandy bottom, where calico bass keep their eggs aerated and protected from predators. You can paddle back into the Whiting River about 150 feet, past a large beaver lodge to a beaver dam 3 feet high.

The northwest entrance to East Indies Pond is secluded and marshy.

EAST INDIES POND

Launch your boat on East Indies Pond only if you crave adventure. Branches hang low over the trails, making portaging a challenge. A wheeled portaging cart would help. After reaching the access on Mill Pond, you have to portage over some swampy beaver dams to get to East Indies Pond.

We were not prepared for what greeted us upon reaching the pond in late June—probably the most spectacular mountain laurel display we had ever seen. Mountain laurel, with stems reaching 15 to 20 feet tall, all in electric bloom, formed dense stands along much of the shoreline. Cruising the shoreline in this gorgeous setting, we hardly noticed the little floating heart, American eelgrass, pondweed, waterlilies, or the complete lack of invasive watermilfoil. We expect that you would see beaver here in the evening, judging by the size of the lodges on the two ponds. A few clearings along the west shore looked enticing, as did some large granite boulders—perfect for an afternoon rest or picnic.

SECTION 6

RHODE ISLAND

Rhode Island, although our smallest state—30 Rhode Islands would fit within Maine's borders—offers truly spectacular paddling . . . and lots of it. The state is known for its rivers that, although short in length, flow with relatively large volumes, mostly through unspoiled habitat. The Wood River is the premier paddling destination. Expect to see large

numbers of birds and other wildlife as the river meanders through marshes. Another great paddle starts at Worden Pond and the beginning of the Pawcatuck River as it flows through Great Swamp.

Placid, relatively untrammeled Big River flows north through a broad marsh rich with wildlife; look for deer, great blue heron, osprey, muskrat, and beaver. We include two very different branches of the Pawtuxet River. The exceptionally clear water of the North Branch flows out of Scituate Reservoir, water supply to 60 percent of Rhode Island's population; check out the bloom on the extensive stand of mountain laurel in the upper reaches. The South Branch flows through an urban area, but the river corridor remains relatively untouched, other than some road noise. While here, consider using the 19-mile Washington Secondary Bike Path.

Just minutes from downtown Providence, you'll find lovely Olney Pond. While you can expect to find beauty here, don't expect solitude given its proximity to Rhode Island's capital. Shallow Brickyard Pond is a bird-watching paradise; despite the urban environment and the pond's small size, you can see osprey fishing here.

Highly productive Belleville Pond provides good fishing and excellent waterfowl habitat. We've watched anglers pull in sizable bass. Tucker Pond boasts an impressive stand of rosebay rhododendron, the largest member of the heath family. Because the small kettle-hole pond has no major inlet, water level varies with rainfall.

Bowdish Reservoir sits on the site of an ancient bog whose substrate now floats on parts of the lake, adding a northern fen character. Its large campground makes it a recreation destination. Watchaug Pond is also a recreation destination, with camping at Burlingame State Park, hiking on trails of Kimball Wildlife Refuge, and paddling on the pond and its outflow stream.

Ninigret Pond, Rhode Island's largest coastal pond, offers interesting opportunities for plant and wildlife viewing. Nineteen rare or endangered plant species inhabit the pond's shores and Ninigret National Wildlife Refuge, and more than 250 bird species have been recorded there.

TRIP 55

BOWDISH RESERVOIR

Bowdish Reservoir is a recreation destination, with camping, bicycling, hiking, and paddling available. The reservoir has some development and suffers from road noise, but an unusual plant assemblage graces some floating islands. Plants here include black spruce, Atlantic white cedar, leatherleaf, bog laurel, bog rosemary, and more.

LOCATION Glocester, RI

MAPS *Connecticut/Rhode Island Atlas & Gazetteer*, Map 24: C4; USGS Thompson

AREA 226 acres

TIME 4 hours

HABITAT TYPE Shallow reservoir

FISH Largemouth and calico bass, pickerel (see fish advisory, Appendix A)

CAMPING George Washington Camping Area

INFORMATION Bowdish Reservoir, exploreri.org/siteReport php?siteID=152&src=criteria

TAKE NOTE Motors limited to 10 HP; limited development; use caution in wind; when campground is open, boat launch available to registered campers only

GETTING THERE

From the junction of Routes 44, 100, and 102 in Chepachet, go 4.4 miles west on Route 44, and turn right at the George Washington Camping Area. Drive 0.3 mile (4.7 miles) to the third left, which leads to the access. **41° 55.409′ N, 71° 45.508′ W**

WHAT YOU'LL SEE

A large bog stood at this site before Bowdish Reservoir flooded it out. Today, a few floating sphagnum islands, the only remnants of the bog, appear near the reservoir's center. When the water level rose, these mats broke loose and floated to the surface. Tree roots anchor them in the reservoir's shallow waters. On these islands, look for rare bog plants usually seen much farther north, including black spruce (an extremely short-needled conifer), Atlantic white cedar, leatherleaf, bog laurel, bog rosemary, sundew, pitcher plant, and—rarest of all—dwarf mistletoe, which lacks roots and always grows in association with black spruce. (*Note*: These islands appear larger on older maps and may be disappearing.)

Bowdish Reservoir does not exude wilderness, but it offers a scenic location to get some exercise in your boat or on foot or bicycle. The southwestern edge, bounded by heavily traveled Route 44, supports some development. Even at the far eastern end, by the George Washington Camping Area, you can still hear cars and trucks. A mammoth private campground that caters to RVs occupies most of the northern shore, although quite a bit of space exists between heavily wooded sites.

Huge slabs of granite stretch down into the water in places, and the small private island in the reservoir's southern extension appears to be mostly solid rock. The forested land of George Washington Wildlife Management Area along the reservoir's eastern end remains readily accessible to hikers and picnickers. Several pleasant trails, reachable from the boat launch area, course through the surrounding oak-hemlock forests for several miles. Dominant species include hemlock; white, red, and scarlet oaks; black birch; white pine; and moun-

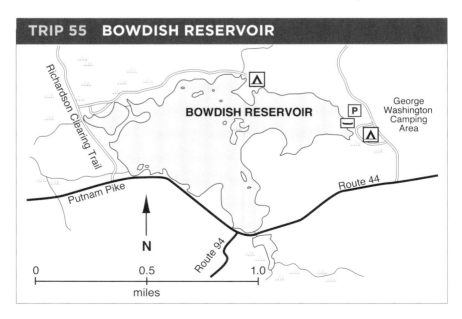

tain laurel. At the water's edge you will also find lots of highbush blueberry and sweet pepperbush, which has very fragrant, late-blooming white flower spikes.

The reservoir itself supports ample vegetation. Underwater plants include watermilfoil, Carolina fanwort, and bladderwort. Floating plants include watershield and yellow pondlily. Though the abundant aquatic vegetation damps waves somewhat, in a strong wind large waves build up across the open water, so use caution paddling here.

TRIP 56

OLNEY POND

Olney Pond is a lovely little wooded pond just minutes from downtown Providence. Because of that proximity, hikers, joggers, and bicyclists abound, especially on weekends. You can expect to find beauty here but not solitude.

LOCATION Lincoln, RI

MAPS *Connecticut/Rhode Island Atlas & Gazetteer*, Map 26, D3; USGS Pawtucket

AREA 120 acres

TIME 2 hours

HABITAT TYPE Wooded pond

FISH Rainbow and brown trout, largemouth bass, pickerel (see fish advisory, Appendix A)

INFORMATION Lincoln Woods State Park, riparks.ri.gov/parks/lincoln -woods-state-park

CAMPING George Washington Camping Area

TAKE NOTE No motors on weekends and holidays, otherwise 10 HP limit; recreational development only

GETTING THERE

From Route 146, about 4 miles north of I-95, take the Twin River Road exit for Lincoln Woods. Turn left at the end of the exit ramp, go 0.3 mile, and turn right at the stop sign, entering the 2.6-mile one-way loop road around the pond. In 1.4 miles (1.7 miles), reach the access on the left. **41° 53.364′ N, 71° 25.676′ W**

WHAT YOU'LL SEE

Just minutes from downtown Providence, Olney Pond offers surprisingly pleasant paddling. Gorgeous granite boulders—some striated with bands of quartz or blazoned with clusters of polypody fern—dot the heavily wooded shoreline. Only Lincoln Woods State Park recreational facilities occur along the pond—and herein lies the problem: Olney Pond abounds with recreational users on weekends and particularly pleasant days. Hikers, joggers, and bicyclists, many of whom come from nearby offices for a work break, fill the pond's perimeter road, removing any semblance of solitude.

Many sheltered coves beg to be explored, especially a particularly beautiful one at the pond's northern tip, where you must wend your way around huge boulders extending from the water. Red oak dominates the surrounding

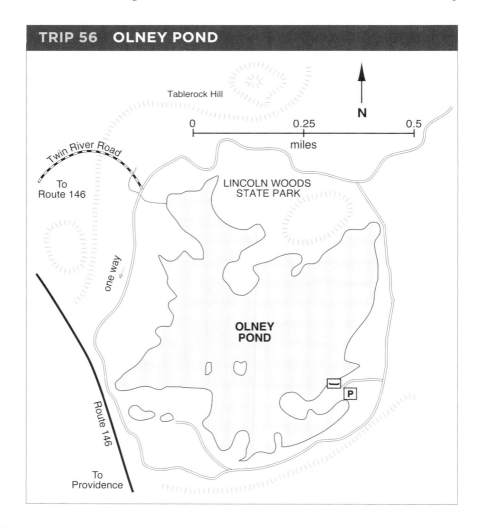

Huge granite boulders lend scenic character to Olney Pond's shores.

woods; other species include white oak, dogwood, white ash, hickory, and—close to shore—red maple.

At a trail junction near the pond's northernmost cove, a marker by an old spring commemorates the Zachariah Allen Woodlot, planted in 1820. About 0.3 mile from here, to the northwest on Quinsnicket Hill, Allen took ownership of a worn-out 40-acre pasture and planted acorns and chestnuts in an early silviculture experiment. Today, more than 170 years later, the marker describes this unusual businessman/botanist and his investment through planting acorns and chestnuts in plowed soil. Even before the area became a state park, city folk from nearby Providence visited the woodlot via steam cars to Lonsdale or "electrics" from Pawtucket. Wildflowers and ferns, including such uncommon species as maidenhair spleenwort and smooth yellow violet, fill the Quinsnicket Hill woods.

TRIP 57

BRICKYARD POND

This small, shallow urban pond is a bird-watching paradise. Expect to see osprey, mute swan, Canada goose, wood duck, great blue heron, spotted sandpiper, catbird, cardinal, goldfinch, and more.

LOCATION Barrington, RI

MAPS *Connecticut/Rhode Island Atlas & Gazetteer*, Map 39, C5; USGS Bristol

AREA 102 acres

TIME 2 hours

HABITAT TYPE Shallow wooded pond

FISH Rainbow and brown trout, largemouth bass, yellow perch, pickerel (see fish advisory, Appendix A)

TAKE NOTE No motors; limited development

GETTING THERE
From I-195, Exit 2B, in East Providence, head south on Route 114 to the first stoplight. Turn right on Federal Road, go 0.6 mile, and turn left on Middle Highway. Go 1.0 mile (1.6 miles), and turn left on Legion Way. Continue 0.2 mile (1.8 miles), and turn left to the access. **41° 44.121' N, 71° 19.153' W**

WHAT YOU'LL SEE
Brickyard Pond, in an urban location that abounds with housing developments and a golf course, offers a surprisingly wild place to paddle. An abandoned railroad bed converted into a beautiful hiking and biking trail borders the northern shore, and a few houses dot the southern shore. But a wooded shoreline and many shallow coves draped with grape arbors, Virginia creeper, and honeysuckle vines invite exploration. Several islands provide more shoreline to investigate, making the pond seem much larger than its 102 acres.

During our visit, dozens of catbirds skulked among the dense grapevines and Virginia creeper in the fingerlike western coves, while goldfinches and gnatcatchers gleaned seeds and insects from shoreside vegetation. A downy woodpecker pulled apart heads of narrow-leaved cattail, probing for insects, and a diving osprey came up with a fish. Families of Canada geese fed in the shallows, two brightly colored male wood ducks took off in front of us, and

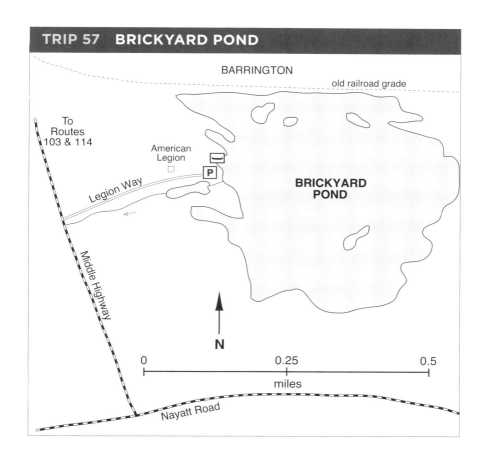

BARRINGTON

old railroad grade

To
Routes
103 & 114

American
Legion

Legion Way

P

BRICKYARD
POND

Middle Highway

N

| 0 | 0.25 | 0.5 |

miles

Nayatt Road

A downy woodpecker pecks apart a cattail, looking for insects.

we counted 23 mute swans. Although they are lovely, mute swans, introduced from Europe, aggressively compete with native species.

Four oak species—red, pin, white, and swamp white oaks—grace the shoreline, along with willow, sassafras, cottonwood, red and Norway maples, gray birch, and alder. We saw many other bird and plant species here and could have spent several hours exploring. As a spotted sandpiper fled before us, we reveled in the rich number of species harbored by this urban wildlife paradise.

TRIP 58

NORTH BRANCH PAWTUXET RIVER

The North Branch of the Pawtuxet River, with its exceptionally clear water, offers an outstanding paddling resource amid many interesting plant species. Extensive stands of mountain laurel, especially in the upper reaches, put on a glorious show, typically in mid-June.

LOCATION Scituate, RI

MAPS *Connecticut/Rhode Island Atlas & Gazetteer*, Map 37: C8; USGS Crompton, Kent

LENGTH 5 miles round trip

TIME 3 hours

HABITAT TYPE Narrow, meandering river with shallow coves, thick with emergent vegetation

FISH Trout, smallmouth bass, pickerel, northern pike (see fish advisory, Appendix A)

TAKE NOTE Motors allowed; limited development; avoid dam at access

GETTING THERE

From I-95, Exit 3, or I-295, Exit 5, go west on Route 12 (from I-295, west on Route 14 to Comstock Parkway south to Route 12). From the junction of Routes 12 and 116, go 2.3 miles south on Route 116, and turn right on Hope Furnace Road. Go 200 feet, and turn right onto the access road. **41° 43.865′ N, 71° 33.923′ W**

WHAT YOU'LL SEE

The North Branch Pawtuxet River is unlike any river we've paddled in Rhode Island in one major respect: it has extremely pure water. While most Rhode Island rivers suffer from heavy industrial pollution that began as far back as the 1700s, that's not the case here. The North Branch flows out of Scituate Reservoir, the rigorously protected water supply for 65 percent of the state's population. Upper sections flow with exceptionally clear water that lacks any chemical smell. Some development occurs along the shore, particularly in the river's lower portions, but it doesn't seem too intrusive.

You will see some relatively unusual vegetation along the river. Keep an eye out for sassafras (*Sassafras albidum*), with its varied leaf shapes—some oval,

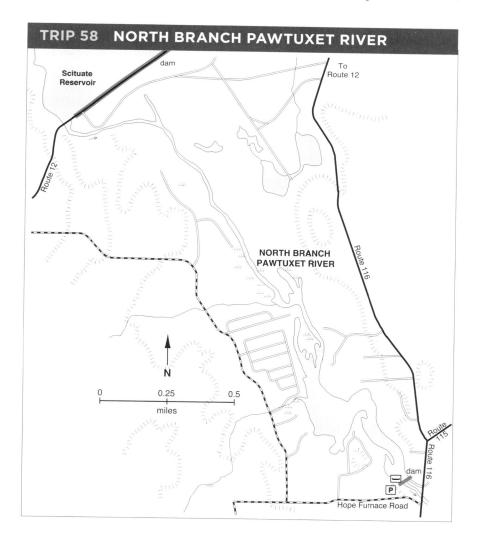

TRIP 58 NORTH BRANCH PAWTUXET RIVER

some with a rounded lobe on the left or right, and some with both lobes; crush a leaf to smell the characteristic sassafras odor. Look also for black gum (*Nyssa sylvatica*), with its horizontally layered branch structure; swamp white oak (*Quercus bicolor*); American hornbeam or ironwood (*Carpinus caroliniana*); red pine (*Pinus resinosa*); and more common species, such as white pine, red maple, gray birch, alder, and red oak.

Shrubs along the winding shoreline are a highlight of this trip. Mountain laurel (*Kalmia latifolia*) grows prolifically, particularly in the upper reaches, making this a spectacular place to paddle during the laurel bloom—typically mid-June. Laurel has developed an unusual pollination scheme. Tiny sacs tightly hold the ten pollen-containing anthers of unopened buds. As the buds open, the elastic filaments connected to the anthers bend backward, developing tension. Then, when a bumblebee—the plant's main pollinator—lands on a flower, the anthers release, and the filaments spring them forward to slap the pollen load against the bee's underside. When the bee visits the next flower, its pollen load rubs against the stigma, causing pollination. This method nearly eliminates self-pollination. It would be interesting to know whether natural selection has favored bees that fly off to the next plant after visiting just one flower, maximizing outcrossing and helping support genetic diversity.

When we paddled here later in the season, we saw lots of sweet pepperbush (*Clethra alnifolia*) in bloom, with its wonderfully sweet-smelling flower clusters. We also saw witch hazel (*Hamamelis virginiana*), a fall-blooming shrub whose seedpods mature in early August, getting ready to sling their seeds through a unique spring action as the seedpods open.

Extensive stands of yellow pondlily and American white waterlily populate the shallow coves, accompanied by lesser amounts of little floating heart (*Nymphoides cordata*), with small white flowers in early August; pondweed (*Potamogeton epihydrus*); yellow and purple bladderwort (*Utricularia spp.*); soft-stemmed bulrush (*Schoenoplectus tabernaemontani*, formerly *Scirpus validus*); and pickerelweed (*Pontederia cordata*). We spotted a single cardinal flower (*Lobelia cardinalis*) along the shore, with its brilliant red flower spike.

Farther north, the river narrows, the current becomes more rapid in places, and you have to dodge rocks. But the prodigious amount of mountain laurel here and the exceptionally clear water make paddling the upper reaches worth the effort. Eventually you reach the looming dam of Scituate Reservoir and the fencing and No Trespassing signs that help to keep the North Branch's water so pure.

SOUTH BRANCH PAWTUXET RIVER

The South Branch of the Pawtuxet River flows gently for a mile and a half between dams in Coventry. Surprisingly little development impinges on the river. Explore marshy areas, especially in spring. While here, you can also take advantage of the 19-mile Washington Secondary Bike Path.

LOCATION Coventry, RI

MAPS *Connecticut/Rhode Island Atlas & Gazetteer*, Map 37: D8, Map 38: D1; USGS Crompton, Kent

LENGTH 3 miles round trip

TIME 2 hours

HABITAT TYPE Narrow, meandering river with extensive marsh areas

FISH Trout, smallmouth bass, pickerel, northern pike (see fish advisory, Appendix A)

INFORMATION Washington Secondary Bike Path, dot.ri.gov/travel /bikeri/washington.php

TAKE NOTE Motors allowed; limited development; avoid dam at access

GETTING THERE

From I-95, Exit 10, go 4.0 miles west on Route 117 (jog right, then left at 2.6 miles; turn left at 3.3 miles), and turn left on Laurel Avenue. In 0.1 mile (4.1 miles), turn right on Pilgrim Avenue. Go 150 feet, and turn right into the access. **41° 41.678′ N, 71° 32.853′ W**

WHAT YOU'LL SEE

This section of the South Branch Pawtuxet River, which can be traveled in a few hours, flows gently between a dam at Laurel Avenue and another at South Main Street. Massive Anthony Mill, built in 1872 and converted into apartments in 2013, lies at the lower terminus of this trip. Although large amounts of development extend in every direction, little of it impinges on the waterway. You will hear a fair amount of road noise, however.

By midsummer, Carolina fanwort (*Cabomba caroliniana*)—an aquatic plant native to the Southeast that has become invasive in the Northeast—grows thickly, filling the water column with its lacy filaments. Like Eurasian water-milfoil, Carolina fanwort chokes waterways, as it is doing here.

From the Pilgrim Avenue access, paddle to the left, fairly quickly going under a trestle carrying the well-maintained rail-trail known as the Washington Secondary Bike Path. The 19-mile trail, following a Hartford, Providence & Fishkill Railroad spur, runs from Cranston to Central Coventry. The hope is that it will eventually encompass 25 miles, from the Connecticut state line nearly into Providence, connecting to the Blackstone River Bikeway and East Bay Bike Path. After the trestle, the river continues south and west, passing some development and a large marsh extending to Tiogue Avenue.

In early spring, you should be able to explore down to Tiogue Avenue, but by midsummer the thick floating and emergent vegetation makes paddling difficult. A fairly large stand of wild rice sways in the breeze here, along with pickerelweed, bulrush, arrowhead, bur-reed, yellow pondlily, American white waterlily, watershield, and various grasses and sedges.

Most of the South Branch shoreline is thickly wooded with such species as black gum, white oak, pin oak, red maple, gray birch, white pine, ironwood, and alder. Along the shore you will see sweet pepperbush, blueberry, and lots of other shrubs. As you continue upstream, the river flows under Sandy Bottom Road, narrows, and turns more to the north, passing behind strip malls. The current picks up and you need to watch out for rocks here.

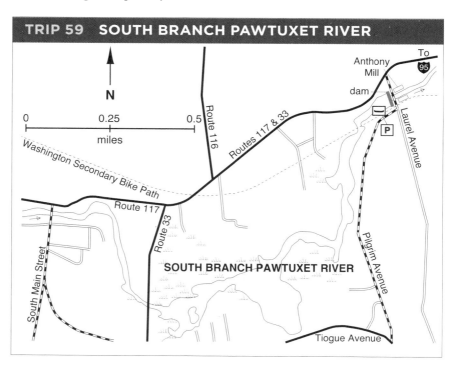

TRIP 59   SOUTH BRANCH PAWTUXET RIVER

This surprisingly wild, marshy section of the South Branch Pawtuxet River flows through Coventry.

After the river curves around to the west, with the concrete arch of the South Main Street bridge just visible through the trees, you will find a place where you can get out, climbing the steep bank to some commercial buildings on Main Street. (Avoid the not terribly inviting mounds of trash and broken glass here.) If you scramble up to Main Street, walk to the left and then turn left on South Main Street; from the bridge over the river, you can see the large dam just upstream.

TRIP 60

BIG RIVER

Big River flows north on an imperceptible current through a broad marsh rich with wildlife. Look for deer, great blue heron, osprey, muskrat, and beaver. Many species of aquatic plants fill the water column, making for slow paddling outside the main channel.

LOCATION Coventry and West Greenwich, RI

MAPS *Connecticut/Rhode Island Atlas & Gazetteer*, Map 37: D7, Map 49: A7; USGS Coventry Center, Crompton

LENGTH 2.3 miles one way

TIME 3 hours round trip

HABITAT TYPE Slow-flowing river through broad marsh

FISH Brook, rainbow, and brown trout; largemouth and smallmouth bass; yellow perch; pickerel; northern pike (see fish advisory, Appendix A)

CAMPING George Washington Camping Area; Arcadia Management Area (walk-in campground)

TAKE NOTE Most motors stay north of Harkney Hill Road; limited development

GETTING THERE

Northern Access From I-95, Exit 6 southbound, go 1.2 miles north on Route 3, and turn left on Harkney Hill Road. Go 1.0 mile (2.2 miles) to Zeke's Bridge Fishing Access on the right, just before the bridge. **41° 39.135′ N, 71° 37.133′ W**

Southern Access From I-95, Exit 6 southbound, go 0.6 mile south on Route 3, and park on the left past the bridge at the end of the guardrail. **41° 38.706′ N, 71° 36.741′ W**

WHAT YOU'LL SEE

Most boaters here venture out from the northern access into Flat River Reservoir; a low bridge and abundant aquatic vegetation keep most motors out of Big River's southern section. The river courses through a broad marsh, filled with aquatic vegetation and birdlife. Tons of Carolina fanwort and yellow-flowered and eastern purple bladderworts fill the water column, while pickerelweed, arrowhead, American eelgrass, American white waterlily, yellow pondlily, pondweed, little floating heart, and watershield crowd the surface, borne on an imperceptible current.

Along the shore, stands of Atlantic white cedar and white pine intermingle with the predominant deciduous trees. Stunted red maple, phragmites, cattail, buttonbush, royal fern, sweetgale, alder, and other shrubs hang out over the water. Paddling south, you can explore a couple of large coves before the river channel narrows just ahead of the culverts that slice through the I-95 embankment. Noise from the roadway far overhead does not intrude too much on the solitude. After passing under the Route 3 bridge, the riverbed continues to narrow through tight, twisting turns. About 0.25 mile south of Route 3, narrow passageways block further progress.

We saw a couple of anglers in motorboats in the northern reaches, but as you progress upstream to the south, you should pretty much have the water to yourself. We spent most of our time identifying and photographing the various bladderwort species, but we also enjoyed seeing many of the marsh birds that congregate here.

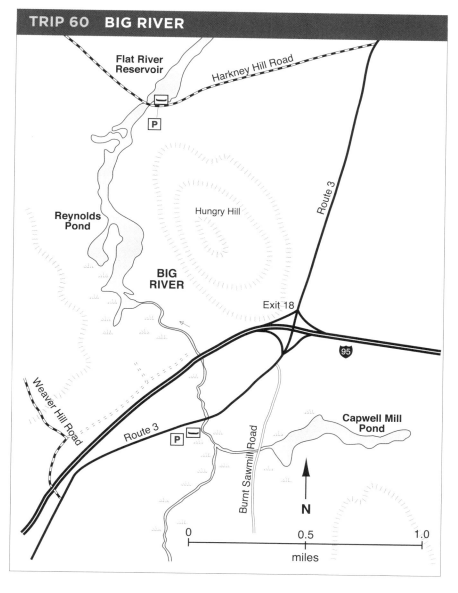

TRIP 60   BIG RIVER

BELLEVILLE POND

Highly productive Belleville Pond boasts ample fishing and great waterfowl habitat. We've watched anglers pull sizable bass out of the pond, and during fall migration, we've seen many species of waterfowl. Marshy islands on the north end provide plenty of opportunities for exploration.

LOCATION North Kingstown, RI

MAPS *Connecticut/Rhode Island Atlas & Gazetteer*, Map 50, B2; USGS Wickford

AREA 159 acres

TIME 3 hours

HABITAT TYPE Shallow, marshy pond

FISH Largemouth and calico bass, yellow perch, pickerel (see fish advisory, Appendix A)

CAMPING Burlingame State Park; walk-in camping, Arcadia Management Area

INFORMATION Belleville Pond, exploreri.org/siteReport.php?siteID =152&src=criteria

TAKE NOTE No gasoline motors; no development

GETTING THERE
From Route 4, Exit 3, go 2.6 miles east on Route 102, and turn right on Route 1. Drive 0.7 mile (3.3 miles), and turn right on Oak Hill Road. In 0.6 mile (3.9 miles), turn right at Ryan Park. Stay left on the loop road to the access. **41° 33.626' N, 71° 28.541' W**

WHAT YOU'LL SEE
Belleville Pond boasts some of the best inland marsh habitat that we've seen. Waterfowl abound, and the shoreline provides hours of quiet exploration. The shallow water, highly productive biologically, supports waterfowl populations that draw hunters in fall.

During an October visit—with both summer residents and migrants present—we saw many species, including pied-billed grebe, mallard, black duck, bufflehead, wood duck, American coot, green-winged teal, Canada goose, mute swan, cormorant, great blue heron, and marsh wren. During the warmer months, many painted turtles sun on logs. Marsh plants include cattail, phragmites, swamp loosestrife, bulrush, pickerelweed, yellow pondlily, American white waterlily, watershield, duckweed, Carolina fanwort, and bladderwort. The pond's water column used to host large quantities of bladderwort, but that is being crowded out by invasives, including Carolina fanwort, twoleaf watermilfoil, and water chestnut (in 2008, Belleville Pond became the first body of water in Rhode Island where water chestnut was found). The abundant underwater vegetation provides welcoming habitat for chain pickerel, largemouth bass, and yellow perch. A fish ladder at the outlet (Annaquatucket River, which flows 3 miles into Narragansett Bay) enables alewife to swim upstream into Belleville Pond to spawn.

At the pond's poorly defined north end, marshy islands abound. You should see lots of birds as you quietly navigate these islands and the increasingly narrow channels of open water between them.

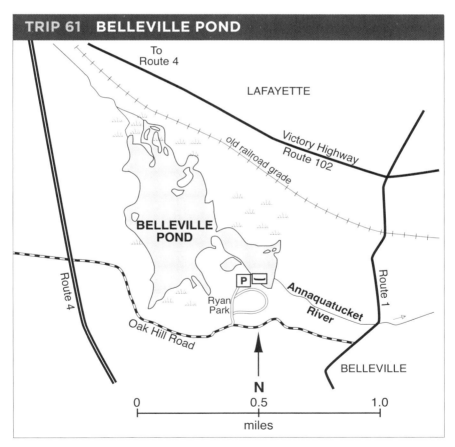

TRIP 61 BELLEVILLE POND

To Route 4

LAFAYETTE

Victory Highway
Route 102

old railroad grade

BELLEVILLE POND

Route 4

Route 1

P

Annaquatucket River

Ryan Park

Oak Hill Road

BELLEVILLE

N

0   0.5   1.0

miles

Around the less marshy sections of the pond, deciduous trees dominate: red, white, and scarlet oaks; red maple; aspen; gray birch; and black gum. On the more solid sections of shoreline, highbush blueberry, sweet pepperbush, and alder provide shelter and food for a wide variety of songbirds. You can hear traffic noise from Route 4 through the trees, but it doesn't detract too much from the solitude.

TRIP 62

WORDEN POND, GREAT SWAMP, CHIPUXET RIVER, AND PAWCATUCK RIVER

This area and the Wood River (Trips 66 and 67) are the two premier paddling destinations in Rhode Island. Stick to the rivers on windy days. Expect to see large numbers of birds and other wildlife, along with diverse trees and shrubs. The narrow rivers meander through Great Swamp on their way to join the Wood River as the major tributaries of the Pawcatuck.

LOCATION South Kingstown, RI

MAPS *Connecticut/Rhode Island Atlas & Gazetteer*, Map 49: D7, D8, Map 50: C1, D1, Map 61: A7, A8; USGS Kingston

AREA/LENGTH Worden Pond, 1,075 acres; Chipuxet and Pawcatuck rivers, 9 miles one way

TIME All day; shorter trips possible

HABITAT TYPE Marshy, meandering rivers through a swamp with overhanging shrubs and trees

FISH Largemouth and calico bass, pickerel, northern pike (see fish advisory, Appendix A)

CAMPING Burlingame State Park; walk-in camping, Arcadia Management Area

TAKE NOTE No development; no motors on rivers; little development on Worden Pond, but watch out for motors and treacherous wind; beware of poison ivy and tight curves on the Pawcatuck River

GETTING THERE

Chipuxet River From the junction of Routes 1 and 138, go 5.2 miles west on Route 138, through the Route 110 intersection. Cross the Chipuxet River, and turn immediately left on Liberty Lane to the parking area for Taylor's Landing. **41° 28.955′ N, 71° 33.075′ W**

Pawcatuck River From the junction of Routes 2 and 138, go 4.1 miles south on Route 2/South County Trail, and turn left on the access road. Go 0.1 mile (4.2 miles) to the access. To reach the Pawcatuck River, paddle downstream under the railroad bridge. At the Pawcatuck, a left turn (upstream) leads to Worden Pond. **41° 27.05′ N, 71° 36.951′ W**

Worden Pond From the junction of Routes 110 and 138, go 3.8 miles south on Route 110, and turn right on Wordens Pond Road. The access is in 0.5 mile (4.3 miles) on the right. **41° 25.77′ N, 71° 34.07′ W**

WHAT YOU'LL SEE

Worden Pond and its inlet and outlet rivers—which weave through 3,350-acre Great Swamp—vie with the Wood River as the best paddling in Rhode Island. From the public boat access point at Worden Pond's south end, you can reach all the areas covered in this section. When the wind blows across Worden Pond, we would put in on either of the rivers. You can also paddle one way from the Taylor's Landing access down the Chipuxet River, across Worden Pond, and down the Pawcatuck River to the Route 2 access, a distance of about 6 miles.

CHIPUXET RIVER AND THIRTY ACRE AND HUNDRED ACRE PONDS

We recommend paddling here only during times of high water. From Taylor's Landing, paddle upstream on the Chipuxet River into Thirty Acre and Hundred Acre ponds. You may encounter beaver dams that require portaging. Brush and low water may also block access up the narrow channel. Above the beaver dam, the river widens into Thirty Acre Pond—a gorgeous body of water rich in wildlife. Woodland and University of Rhode Island agricultural research fields surround the pond—you may notice irrigation pumps along the shore. Only one residence sits near the pond, although you may see (and hear) a small brick pump house near the south end that draws drinking water from an underground aquifer (beneath the shallow pond) for the town of South Kingstown.

We saw many pied-billed grebes amid the pond's thick vegetation (waterlilies, Carolina fanwort, pickerelweed, bur-reed, swamp loosestrife), as well as great blue herons, kingfishers, and painted turtles. An occasional train speeds past the pond's north end. At the north end, paddle under the cavernous, arched, stone-and-concrete railroad bridge and a second much lower bridge to get into Hundred Acre Pond. Though marked by some development, Hundred Acre Pond still offers wonderful paddling on a quiet morning in spring or fall. Along the perimeter, look for black gum, whose leaves turn crimson in early fall. Mountain laurel, highbush blueberry, and sweet pepperbush grow thickly along the less developed eastern shore. The state record northern pike, at 35 pounds, was caught here in 1987.

Paddle through the pond's marshy northern end, following the winding Chipuxet River up through the dense swamp of red maple, cedar, alder, and swamp loosestrife, full of songbirds. The channel narrows, and the vegetation converges from the sides until it finally blocks further progress near Wolf Rocks Road. Paddling from Taylor's Landing up to here takes a couple of hours if you allow time for watching birds and investigating both ponds' plant life.

TRIP 62 CHIPUXET RIVER, HUNDRED ACRE POND, AND THIRTY ACRE POND

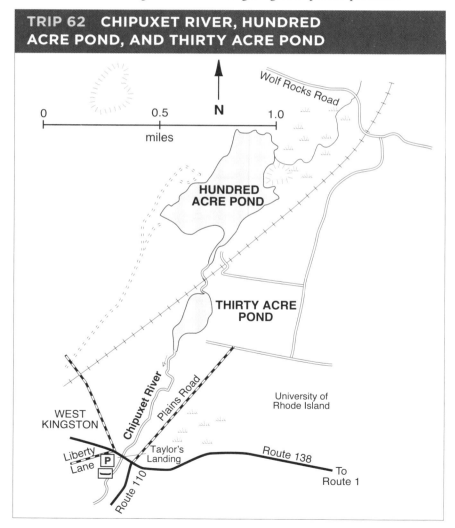

CHIPUXET RIVER DOWNSTREAM TO WORDEN POND THROUGH GREAT SWAMP

More commonly, people paddle from Taylor's Landing downstream into Worden Pond—a distance of about 3 miles. The narrow river tightly twists through Great Swamp. The current, though noticeable, allows paddling in both directions. Along the way, you pass through a red maple swamp, with patches of cattail, bulrush, and phragmites on the oxbow curves and thick stands of sweetgale, dogwood, winterberry, and sweet pepperbush. Wild rice also grows sparingly here—look for the tall, delicate grass in early fall, when the tasty grain can be shaken from the fruiting heads. It's likely you will have to portage over beaver dams to get to Worden Pond.

When you reach 1,000-plus-acre Worden Pond, take note of the wind conditions. Strong winds, typically from the south in summer, send up sizable waves across more than a mile of open water. If possible, try to reach Worden Pond before 10 A.M. to improve your chances of avoiding windy conditions.

Because development impinges on the eastern and southern shores and Wordens Pond Road traverses the southern shore, you will likely find more enjoyment in the northern shore. Pass a privately owned island on your left (used as a hunting and fishing camp) and then aptly named Stony Point—which makes a great picnic stop—on the right. Large, seemingly out-of-place granite boulders extend out into the pond. On higher ground, beech, white oak, red oak, and sassafras grow, along with more water-tolerant red maple and black gum found throughout Great Swamp. At one point, state-record largemouth bass and northern pike came from Worden Pond, and anglers continue to entice lunkers to their landing nets.

This natural basin's maximum depth is 7 feet, with an average depth of only 4 feet. Extensive areas of bulrush grow in the shallows. In the cove west of Stony Point, a large seaplane hangar seems oddly alone at the pond's edge. From a sandy spot just east of the hangar, you can reach a network of trails that crisscross Great Neck and travel along a dike built to maintain wildlife habitat in the swamp. Great Neck rises to a surprisingly high 182 feet.

The Great Swamp Fight occurred on Great Neck in 1675 as part of King Philip's ill-fated rebellion against the onslaught of European settlers. When the Pilgrims arrived in New England in 1620, American Indians befriended them and kept them alive, teaching them how to plant corn and how to live off the New England environment. For several decades, peace reigned. But pressure built as more and more shiploads of settlers arrived in the New World, cleared land, built settlements, and through deeds and treaties pushed the American Indians onto smaller and smaller corners of remaining wilderness. Chief Massasoit of the Wampanoags had been a friend to settlers, but when he died in 1662, his son Metacom became chief and saw what was happening in a different light. Dubbed King Philip of Pokanoket by the colonists, Metacom convinced the Narragansetts and other tribes in the region to join in resisting the settlers.

In 1675, Metacom led his alliance in a series of offensives—known as King Philip's War—attacking and destroying settlements. As the first heavy snow of December fell on Great Neck, Colonial soldiers from Connecticut joined those from the Massachusetts and Plymouth colonies and set out on a march inland from the burned-out garrison at Pettaquamscutt. They intended to attack a fortress somewhere in a vast swamp near Kingston. Their "enemy"—a band of about 1,000 Narragansetts, including women and children, plus King Philip's raiders—had gathered with winter stores inside the freshly built fort. The battle seriously depleted the numbers of native warriors. It did not end King Philip's War, but it turned the tide.

PAWCATUCK RIVER

Either put in at the Route 2 access or continue from the Chipuxet River down around the northern shore of Worden Pond from the seaplane hangar, rounding Case Point to reach the Pawcatuck River outlet. The Pawcatuck—along with the Wood River, the major source of the Pawcatuck (Trips 66 and 67)—flows through a seemingly denser and more magical part of Great Swamp and twists even more tightly than the Chipuxet. Tall scarlet oak and red maple shade the river, while buttonbush, cinnamon fern, dogwood, swamp rose, swamp loosestrife, and arrowhead claim the shore. Dense canopies of grape, greenbrier, and other vines sweep down to the water's surface. You can almost imagine yourself in a tropical jungle and expect to see howler monkeys and colorful macaws in the trees. In places, poison ivy drapes over fallen trees so thickly that you have a hard time avoiding brushing against it as you paddle underneath. (If you are allergic to poison ivy, be wary and plan your attire appropriately; if you wash exposed skin with soap when you get home, you may not develop a rash.) You may also have to carry your boat over or around an obstruction or two. Because of tight curves along the Pawcatuck, you will do much better in a shorter boat.

About a mile from Worden Pond, look for a built-up bank on the right and an obvious spot to pull up your boat by some concrete abutments. This dike creates the Great Swamp Waterfowl Impoundment, a 138-acre wetlands providing nesting habitat for numerous waterfowl species. Climb the bank to the trail that extends along the dike and over to Great Neck. Bird-watching here is fantastic. On an early July trip, in a couple of hours we saw and heard perhaps 50 species of waterfowl, warblers, woodpeckers, flycatchers, thrushes, sparrows, and other species. On a mid-October trip, we were treated to the rare sight of a peregrine falcon and its nearly successful efforts to catch a teal.

You will likely see osprey here, diving for fish. Osprey nest atop the power line poles that cross the swamp. You can actually walk out into the swamp for quite a way on a plank boardwalk. Sections of boardwalk may have deteriorated, so be careful. You might be tempted to carry your boat over the dike to explore the water on the east side, but please leave that area to the wildlife.

From the landing by the dike, the tightly twisting river continues west, passing under the power line and then joining the Usquepaug River, which enters from the northeast. You can explore a little of this river—it parallels the railroad tracks for about a mile and then turns north, crossing under the railroad bridge. Continuing downstream at the rivers' confluence, you will reach the railroad tracks and the Route 2 access in about 0.75 mile. Paddle along the tracks for a short distance and watch for a fork to the right (look for a Boat Landing sign nailed to a tree). Take this fork and paddle under the railroad tracks to the landing just ahead. If you miss the fork, you will soon reach the Biscuit City Road bridge, followed by the Route 2 bridge. Aromatic swamp azalea and swamp rose bloom in profusion in late June and early July along the section down to the Route 2 bridge.

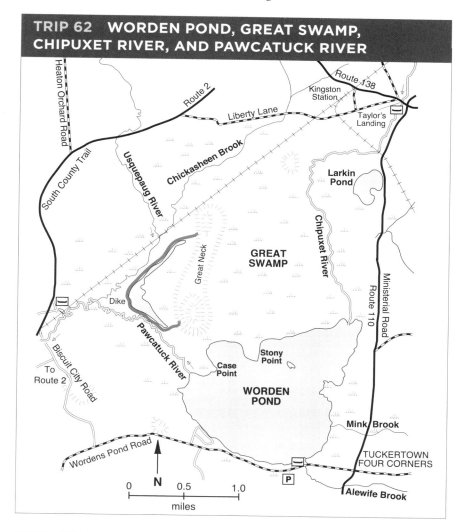

TRIP 62   WORDEN POND, GREAT SWAMP, CHIPUXET RIVER, AND PAWCATUCK RIVER

TRIP 63

TUCKER POND

This small kettle-hole pond features a noteworthy stand of rosebay rhododendron, the largest member of the heath family. The pond has no major inlet, so the water level varies with rainfall. This is a good location to paddle when the wind blows up big waves on nearby Worden Pond.

LOCATION South Kingstown, RI

MAPS *Connecticut/Rhode Island Atlas & Gazetteer*, Map 61: A8, Map 62: A1; USGS Kingston

AREA 101 acres

TIME 2 hours

HABITAT TYPE Wooded, natural kettle-hole pond

FISH Largemouth bass, white and yellow perch, pickerel (see fish advisory, Appendix A)

CAMPING Burlingame State Park; walk-in camping, Arcadia Management Area

INFORMATION Tucker Pond, exploreri.org/siteReport.php?siteID =258&src=criteria

TAKE NOTE Motors limited to 10 HP; limited development

GETTING THERE

From the junction of Routes 110 and 138 in West Kingston, go 3.8 miles south on Route 110, and turn left on Tuckertown Road. In 0.5 mile (4.3 miles) reach the access on the right. **41° 24.564′ N, 73° 32.945′ W**

From the junction of Routes 1 and 110, go north on Route 110, and turn right on Tuckertown Road. Go 0.5 mile to the access on the right.

WHAT YOU'LL SEE

Tucker Pond, just southeast of Worden Pond in southern Rhode Island, has perhaps the most dramatic display of rosebay rhododendron (*Rhododendron maximum*) that we have seen north of the southern Appalachians. This largest member of the heath family—which includes mountain laurel, azalea, blueberry, cranberry, and leatherleaf—covers most of the shoreline. Although we haven't been here when these 15- to 20-foot rhododendrons bloom (typically late

June or early July), they ought to be spectacular. On the pond's steeper south and east sides, they extend up quite high on the banks, with taller white oak, black gum, and pitch pine rising above—as if emerging from a sea of green.

About a dozen houses appear around the pond but do not seem terribly imposing, and the 10 HP limit keeps boating activity to quiet fishing. A state-record white perch, a 2-pounder, was caught here in 1974; that record wasn't broken until 2018. Because this natural kettle-hole pond has no major inlet, the water level fluctuates with rainfall. In a dry year, the level can drop considerably. The last glacier, which receded about 12,000 years ago, created the hilly area that extends south from Tucker Pond for a few miles, known as the Charlestown recessional moraine or the Matunuck Hills. Tucker Pond and the collection of smaller kettle-hole ponds to the south, formed from chunks of glacial ice, have shoreline ecosystems (some protected by The Nature Conservancy) that support a number of plant species quite rare in Rhode Island. Enjoy this vegetation from your boat.

A band of floating plants surrounds much of the perimeter, but most of the pond consists of open water. Where rhododendrons don't dominate the

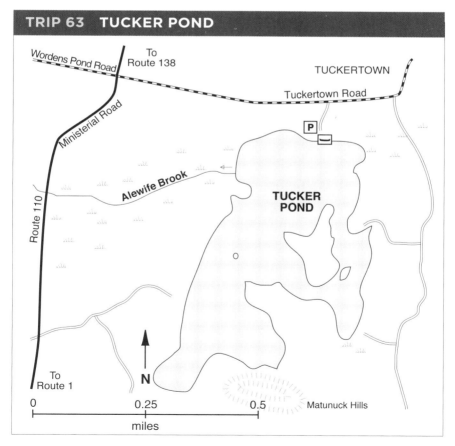

shoreline, highbush blueberry, sweetgale, sweet pepperbush, and red maple occur. Swamp loosestrife, pickerelweed, and bulrush populate the few marshy coves. Several islands rise from the pond, including a large one (with a house fairly well hidden near the peak).

TRIP 64

NINIGRET POND

Ninigret Pond, Rhode Island's largest coastal pond, offers ample opportunities for observing plants and wildlife. Nineteen rare or endangered plant species inhabit the pond's shores and Ninigret National Wildlife Refuge; bird-watchers have recorded more than 250 bird species here. We don't recommend this pond for novice paddlers because of tides, wind-driven waves, and boat traffic.

LOCATION Charlestown, RI

MAPS *Connecticut/Rhode Island Atlas & Gazetteer*, Map 61: B6, B7; USGS Carolina, Quonochotaug

AREA 1,700 acres

TIME All day; shorter trips possible

HABITAT TYPE Coastal tidal pond; shrubby marshlands; many islands and protected bays

FISH Bluefish, flounder (see fish advisory, Appendix A)

INFORMATION Tide charts, usharbors.com; Ninigret National Wildlife Refuge, fws.gov/refuge/ninigret

CAMPING Burlingame State Park

TAKE NOTE Development; motors allowed; use caution due to boat traffic, wind, and tides; not recommended for novice paddlers; always wear your PFD

GETTING THERE

Park Lane From the junction of Routes 1 and 116, go 2.7 miles north on Route 1 and veer right on Route 1A. Drive 0.4 mile (3.1 miles), and turn right on Park Lane. In 1.1 miles (4.2 miles) reach the access at Grassy Point. **41° 21.619′ N, 71° 39.267′ W**

Charlestown From Route 1 northbound, take the Cross Mills/Charlestown Beach exit. From Route 1 southbound, make a U-turn onto Route 1 north, just after the Route 2 exit, and turn right on Cross Mills. Go straight across Route 1A onto Town Dock Road. The access is at road's end, adjacent to Ocean House Marina. Jam your vehicle into the Japanese knotweed that lines the road's west side. **41° 22.881′ N, 71° 38.698′ W**

Charlestown Beach From the Cross Mills/Charlestown Beach exit, turn left on Route 1A, following signs for the Breachway. Go 0.6 mile, and turn right at the Breachway sign. In 0.4 mile (1.0 mile), turn right on Charlestown Beach Road. Go 1.3 miles (2.3 miles) to the access on the right, just after the causeway bridge. **41° 21.825′ N, 71° 37.598′ W**

WHAT YOU'LL SEE

Although quite developed in places, Ninigret Pond, Rhode Island's largest coastal pond, offers enjoyable paddling and superb wildlife viewing opportunities. However, strong winds, tidal currents, and moderate motorboat traffic during summer weekends can present hazards. Use caution, wear your PFD, and paddle the nearby Pawcatuck or Wood rivers instead when the wind howls. Novice paddlers should avoid Ninigret Pond. We recommend that you

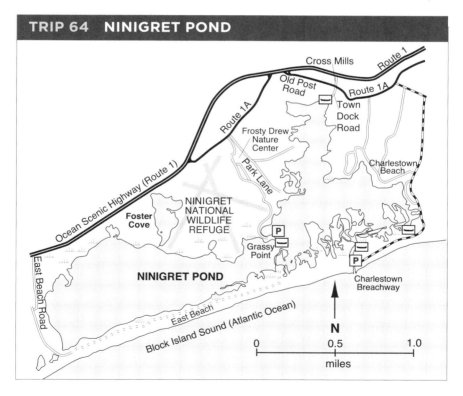

TRIP 64   NINIGRET POND

launch from Grassy Point, which provides better access to the pond's wilder west end and avoids some of the heavier boat traffic.

Away from Charlestown's congestion, the western two-thirds of Ninigret Pond remain relatively wild, with much of it included in Ninigret National Wildlife Refuge. Most of this 868-acre refuge was once a U.S. Navy landing field, which explains the extensive paved areas. More than 70 acres of pavement have been ripped up and carted away. Hike around the old airfield to see how nature gradually reclaims miles of runway. More than 250 bird species have been recorded at the refuge, with prime birding during spring and fall migrations. But plants provide the real attraction for naturalists. More than half the total number of known plants of yellow fringed orchid (*Platanthera ciliaris*) in New England occur here, along with at least eighteen other rare or endangered plant species.

The northern and southern shores of Ninigret Pond vary considerably. Northern shore vegetation consists primarily of shrubby grassland, along with bayberry, blueberry, beach plum, shadbush, wild cherry, dogwood, cedar, and seaside goldenrod—an ecosystem that provides excellent bird habitat, especially as a stopover for migrating warblers. The marshier tidal coves and inlets sport tall stands of phragmites, with patches of cordgrass (*Spartina*) occupying the lower, regularly flooded sections.

Along the pond's southern shore, next to the Ninigret Conservation Area barrier beach, salt marsh grasses—*Spartina patens* and *S. alterniflora*—dominate. Carolina sea lavender (*Limonium carolinianum*), a delicate plant with tiny lavender flowers resembling baby's breath, mixes with the *Spartina*. So much Carolina sea lavender has been collected for dried-flower arrangements that in some areas of the Northeast it no longer adds its subtle lavender blush to the salt marsh. Enjoy the plant where it grows, and avoid the temptation to pick it.

The sand here appears almost white, and the water is quite clean. You will see scallop shells washed up, patches of eelgrass flowing with tidal currents, and clumps of seaweed and sponge on rocks as you paddle the shallows. Anglers here catch lots of winter flounder, as well as bluefish in summer when they enter to feed on young flounder.

With the cleaning up of coastal waters after decades of dumping raw sewage and industrial wastes, commercial harvesting of soft-shell clams, quahogs, bay scallops, and oysters has ramped up once again. The huge shellfish industry of centuries past, decimated by hurricanes and by diseases that affected both the shellfish and the humans who ate the tainted products, has risen to help fill our burgeoning population's insatiable demand for seafood. However, around the world, we are already beginning to see the effects of global warming on shellfish production. With increasing amounts of carbon dioxide dissolved in the oceans, the water's acidity increases, which runs directly counter to the needs of shellfish larvae to develop their hard calcium carbonate shells in a low-acidity environment. And with warming waters, diseases that cause shell-fish mortality and sickness in humans and that normally die back in winter may be present year-round, further stressing shellfish production.

To enjoy the crashing waves of the Atlantic, beach your boat and walk across the dunes to East Beach, accessible only by boat, foot, or four-wheel-drive vehicle. The wildlife refuge section of Ninigret's south shore remains closed to the public to protect nesting least terns and piping plovers—both threatened species in Rhode Island.

CLIMATE CHANGE AND ITS IMPACT ON OUR WATERWAYS

Climate change's catastrophic impacts—from longer and more intense heat waves to more severe storms, flooding, drought, and wildfire—have taken hold worldwide. So, how will a changing climate affect our paddling in New England?

A few changes might improve our outdoor experience, such as a possible reduction in flying insect populations, which could mean less swatting as we explore marshy wetlands. But the vast majority of changes will be negative.

Hotter summer days may limit midday paddling. While breezes generally help keep us cool, that only goes so far. When temperatures rise into the 90s and beyond, accompanied by high humidity, more and more of us will not venture from our air-conditioned enclaves.

Increasingly variable precipitation patterns will result in lon-ger and more severe drought in some areas, shrinking river flows and lowering pond and lake levels. Such droughts may damage wetlands vegetation and the forested landscapes bor-dering waterways. At the other end of the spectrum, increased rainfall will cause flooding that can make normally calm sec-tions of river swollen and frenzied—far from the quiet water we expect. The most extreme conditions may limit our access to coastal paddling destinations—even washing away bridges and flooding access sites. Sea level rise in the coming decades will exacerbate coastal flooding. Tidal flooding—flooding that results even in pleasant weather at high tide—will become more common and may block more access locations.

Beyond these disruptions to our paddling adventures, climate change is already having an impact on wildlife and biodiversity.

Half of the world's 10,000 bird species are in decline, while one in eight faces extinction. Habitat loss due to agricultural and residential development is the primary culprit, but climate change will also cause habitat loss and further species reductions.

Many other animal species also face adverse conditions. Warmer water temperatures will dramatically change wetlands ecosystems. Coldwater fish species such as trout will disappear from some waterways. Populations of freshwater mussels, frogs, salamanders, insects, and Bryozoa will decline, while blooms of toxic cyanobacteria (blue-green algae) in warmer waters will increase health risks to both wildlife and humans recreating in those waters.

One concrete example of climate change's effect on wildlife is the moose. While moose populations have always been low in southern New England, moose are likely to completely disappear with a warmer climate. Warmer winters have already had a dramatic effect on Maine's moose population. In 2022, winter ticks wiped out 90 percent of moose calves tracked by biologists. Cow moose, weakened by ticks, are having fewer offspring. Typically, about 30 percent of births were twins; recently, that has dwindled to zero. Although the long-term effect of lower reproduction is not clear, we likely will see other adverse effects crop up over time.

The impact on plants will be complicated. Increased CO_2 concentrations may increase growth rates, but warmer temperatures will give insect pests more time to multiply. Incursion of invasive plants into wetlands will further interfere with the ecological balance, in part because native insects that did not co-evolve with these plants often cannot feed on them. Droughts and flooding will undoubtedly have adverse effects, as will wildfires. Paddlers will have a ringside seat for wetlands changes.

TAKING ACTION

Those of us who enjoy paddling the less developed bodies of water in this guide—and others in the AMC Quiet Water series—often share an environmental ethic that calls for protecting these places from development. When we see litter, we pick it up and pack it out to keep these waterways more pristine. Some of us lobby for restrictions on high-impact motorboat use. We may donate to land-protection organizations, such as AMC and The Nature Conservancy.

We should also act at the microscale, recognizing that all of us have an impact on the environment and contribute—in various ways—to climate change. Our consumption of fossil fuels results in carbon emissions, as does our fuel use in heating homes or apartments, our choices about travel, our buying habits, and our decisions about what we eat. While driving to a quietwater lake probably consumes gasoline, a paddling trip might actually be reducing our carbon emissions if it is in place of flying across the country or across the ocean.

The bottom line is that we should think about our lifestyles and how we are influencing climate change. A bit of alteration in behavior or travel—if enough of us do it—can have a huge beneficial impact.

Finally, we should consider how we can support organizations that work to make a difference with climate, such as AMC, the Environmental Defense Fund, the Natural Resources Defense Council, The Nature Conservancy, and the many state and local groups that do such beneficial work throughout our region.

TRIP 65

WATCHAUG POND AND POQUIANT BROOK

Watchaug Pond is a recreation destination, with camping at Burlingame State Park, hiking on trails of Kimball Wildlife Refuge, and paddling on the pond and its outflow stream as possibilities.

LOCATION Charlestown, RI

MAPS *Connecticut/Rhode Island Atlas & Gazetteer*, Map 61: B5, B6; USGS Carolina

AREA/LENGTH Watchaug Pond, 573 acres; Poquiant Brook, 0.75 mile one way

TIME 4 hours

HABITAT TYPE Large, open pond

FISH Rainbow and brown trout, largemouth and calico bass, yellow perch, pickerel, northern pike (see fish advisory, Appendix A)

INFORMATION Kimball Wildlife Refuge, visitrhodeisland.com/listing/kimball-wildlife-refuge/8635/

CAMPING Burlingame State Park

TAKE NOTE Motors and water-skiers; personal watercraft prohibited; limited development

GETTING THERE

From the junction of Routes 1 and 216, go 3.0 miles north on Route 1, and turn left. Cross the median, make a U-turn, and then turn immediately right on Prosser Trail, following signs to Burlingame State Park. Go 0.8 mile (3.8 miles), passing the Kimball Wildlife Refuge entrance on the left, and turn left to the picnic area. In 0.1 mile (3.9 miles), turn left. The Barton C. Hurley Landing access is 0.2 mile (4.1 miles) on the right. **41° 22.714′ N, 71° 40.787′ W**

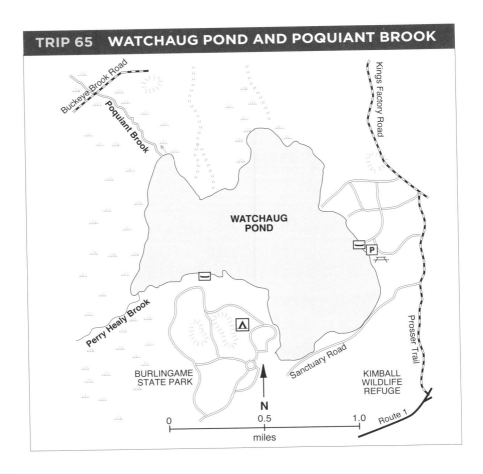

TRIP 65 WATCHAUG POND AND POQUIANT BROOK

WHAT YOU'LL SEE

Watchaug Pond, a large body of water near Rhode Island's southern tip, sees heavy recreational use but can offer enjoyable paddling, particularly for a family camping at Burlingame State Park. Visit either early or late in the season to avoid the crowds.

All the activity at the southeastern end near the public boat launch area, along with shoreline development on the pond's east side, may provide strong incentive to concentrate on the northern and western sections. While traveling on the pond for this book's first edition, we encountered several noisy personal watercraft, but the town of Charlestown banned them in January 2002. The marshy western end feels much more remote and wild; we paddled through acres of little floating heart here. As dusk approached, we watched an otter near the outlet at the northwestern tip. Even though otter sightings are rare in southern New England, if you spend much time paddling around less developed lakes, ponds, and rivers around dawn or dusk, you should see this delightful mammal sooner or later.

You can get away from most Watchaug Pond action by paddling down the outlet, Poquiant Brook, at the pond's northwestern tip. We followed this peaceful, meandering waterway for at least 0.5 mile through thick marsh. When the wind blows up whitecaps on Watchaug Pond, the brook offers a welcome escape into a quiet, secluded area. Look for blueberry bushes, along with cedar, black gum, and a wide assortment of marsh plants. Keep an eye out for the elusive wood duck. The state-record calico bass, a 3-pounder, was caught in Watchaug Pond in 1976.

Kimball Wildlife Refuge, protected by the Audubon Society of Rhode Island and then

The best time to visit popular Watchaug Pond is in May or after Labor Day.

sold to the state's Department of Environmental Management, abuts lands near the pond's southern end, with wonderful trails through oak and laurel woodland. With 755 campsites, Burlingame State Park provides one of the largest camping areas in New England. Nonetheless, the campground often fills to capacity during summer months.

TRIP 66

PAWCATUCK RIVER

The wide Pawcatuck River offers a great paddling opportunity along generally secluded wooded shores, with understory shrubs that bloom in profusion in spring. You will see osprey that nest here, along with myriad other bird species. Access is difficult, except for the Bradford put-in.

LOCATION Charlestown, Hopkinton, and Westerly, RI

MAPS *Connecticut/Rhode Island Atlas & Gazetteer*, Map 60: A4, B4, Map 61: A5; USGS Ashaway

LENGTH 8 miles one way

TIME All day, round trip

HABITAT TYPE Wide, undeveloped river; wooded shores

FISH Brook, rainbow, and brown trout (see fish advisory, Appendix A)

CAMPING Burlingame State Park

INFORMATION Pawcatuck River, wpwildrivers.org/the-rivers /pawcatuck-river/

TAKE NOTE Motors allowed; some small dams downstream from the Bradford access must be portaged on the right, but experienced paddlers might be able to paddle over them; wear your PFD

GETTING THERE

Potter Hill From I-95, Exit 1, drive 2.2 miles south on Route 3, and turn right on Hillside Avenue. Go 0.2 mile (2.4 miles), and turn left on Laurel Street. In 0.5 mile (2.9 miles), turn right on Potter Hill Road. Launch at the Flora Whiteley Preserve, just across the bridge on the left. Finding a place to park can be quite difficult. **41° 24.829′ N, 71° 47.85′ W**

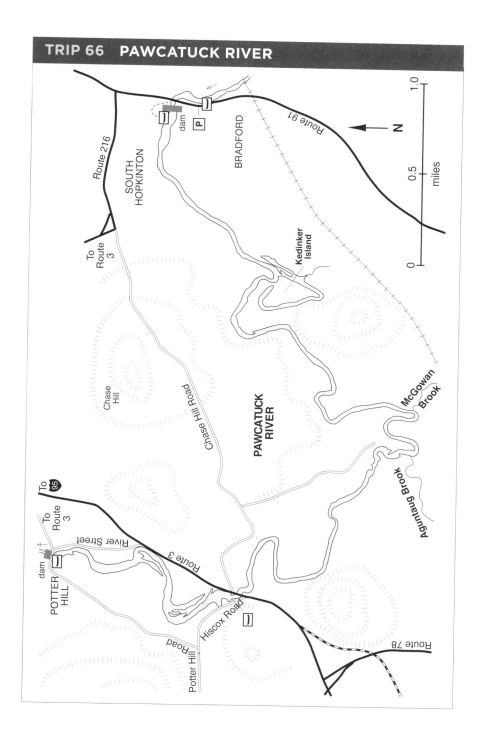

Hiscox Road It might be easier to park on Hiscox Road at the junction with Route 3, with parking for three vehicles. From I-95, Exit 1, go 3.7 miles south on Route 3, and turn right on Hiscox Road. **41° 23.966' N, 71° 48.03' W**

Bradford From Ashaway, go south on Route 216 until it joins Route 91. Continue south 0.4 mile to the access on the left, just after the bridge. This is the easiest access. **41° 24.382' N, 71° 44.888' W**

WHAT YOU'LL SEE

After the Wood River joins the Pawcatuck River (also called the Charles River above the Wood) just south of Alton Dam, the combined waters form a broad, slow-flowing river between wooded shores. We paddled upstream from Potter Hill Dam, although with two cars you could paddle this one way from Bradford (8 miles; the upstream put-in is here)—or from Alton Dam (13 miles) or Hope Valley (19.5 miles), both on the Wood River (Trip 67).

When we visited here in July, we saw no other boats upstream of the Route 3 bridge. We loved the sculptural lateral branches of the black gum trees (*Nyssa sylvatica*) that clustered along the shores in spots and looked like splayed fingers. In early fall, their leaves turn crimson, and occasional white pines offer a dark, contrasting green to the fall foliage. Surprisingly, beaver have girdled a lot of the black gums. We often see hemlocks girdled because, presumably, they have resinous bark unpalatable to beaver, but why would beaver want to kill off deciduous trees? Black gum bark may also be resinous, given that the trees can withstand submersion for decades.

Lacy branches of black gum (*Nyssa sylvatica*) extend out over the Pawcatuck River's banks.

Several active osprey nests, some on utility poles and some on artificial platforms, sit along this stretch of the Pawcatuck. We saw several ospreys perched or fishing as we paddled along. We also saw and heard many other bird species, including great blue heron, green heron, wood duck, Canada goose, mute swan, cardinal, eastern wood pewee, cedar waxwing, eastern towhee, chickadee, veery, tufted titmouse, catbird, and yellow warbler.

Lots of swamp rose, swamp loosestrife, swamp azalea, and dogwood form an understory beneath the mature canopy of red maple, ash, willow, gray birch, scarlet oak, beech, black gum, and white pine. Occasional marshy areas occur along the normally wooded river course.

TRIP 67

WOOD RIVER AND ALTON POND

This and the rivers of Great Swamp (Trip 62) are the two premier paddling destinations in Rhode Island. Expect to see large numbers of birds and other wildlife, along with diverse trees and shrubs. The river meanders through marshes on its way to join the Pawcatuck River as it exits Great Swamp.

LOCATION Hopkinton and Richmond, RI

MAPS *Connecticut/Rhode Island Atlas & Gazetteer*, Map 49: D5, Map 61: A5; USGS Carolina

LENGTH 6.5 miles one way

TIME All day; shorter trips possible

HABITAT TYPE Dammed-up meandering river; shrubby marshlands; many oxbows

FISH Brook, rainbow, and brown trout; largemouth bass (see fish advisory, Appendix A)

CAMPING Burlingame State Park; walk-in camping, Arcadia Management Area

TAKE NOTE Little development; no motors

GETTING THERE

Alton Dam From I-95, Exit 2 southbound, go 3.5 miles south on Woodville-Alton Road to the access on the left. **41° 26.284' N, 71° 43.344' W**

Hope Valley From the junction of Route 3 and Mechanic Street in Hope Valley, go 0.9 mile south on Mechanic Street to the access on the left, at the end of the guardrail just after the I-95 bridge. **41° 29.61' N, 71° 42.96' W**

WHAT YOU'LL SEE

The Wood River offers an outstanding paddling resource, certainly one of the most pristine in Rhode Island. The section included here, from Hope Valley to Alton Dam, can occupy you for anywhere from a few hours to a full day or two. We prefer putting in at Alton Dam and paddling upstream, although spring high water could preclude making it all the way to Woodville. With two cars, you could paddle downstream from the Hope Valley access to Alton Dam.

As you paddle north from Alton Dam, after passing a few houses, the 39-acre pond narrows to a winding, deep channel, and you leave most fishing activity behind. Along the wild Wood River, numerous oxbows, side channels, eddies, and hidden ponds harbor lots of wildlife. We saw several pairs of wood ducks, plus cormorants, green herons, mallards, kingfishers, and songbirds galore. Osprey wheeled overhead, occasionally diving for fish. Scattered shoreline piles of mussel shells bore evidence of successful raccoon or otter feasting. Paddling along quietly, you should see literally hundreds of painted turtles on a sunny day, basking on floating logs or on tussocks of grass that extend out into the water along the marshy shoreline.

Ancient blueberry bushes, black gum, red maple, and white pine grow along the shore. Where the ground rises steeply from the water, dense, lush stands of mountain laurel bloom spectacularly in June. With the river flowing so slowly, we lost the main channel several times, finding ourselves on one of the oxbow ponds.

A couple of miles upstream, the channel forks. Paddling up the smaller left fork, you quickly come to an old farm, a long-abandoned mill building, and a dead end. The main channel curves right, where you soon reach the Woodville Road bridge over the river and a beautiful dam just beyond. Water was diverted here for the mill. Ruins of a much older stone mill building occur here. Take out on the right bank before the bridge, carry up and over the bridge, and put in on the left side.

Upstream from Woodville Dam, the stream meanders through more marshland, similar to that below the dam, except with less mountain laurel. Large patches of swamp rose make up for the lack of laurel, and arrowhead and pickerelweed line the shores. After about a mile, the marshland and streambed

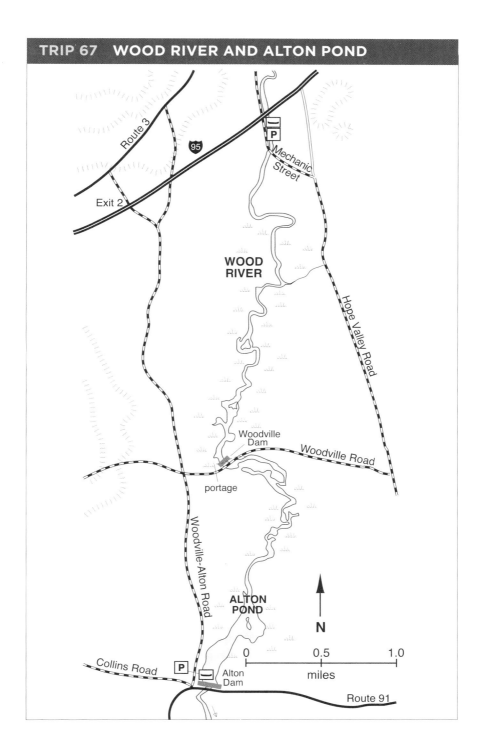

Eastern kingbirds appear often along the shores of New England's rivers and ponds. Note the dark head and back, white underbelly, and white-tipped tail.

narrow to a shore lined with red maple, gray birch, oaks, ash, and black gum. Painted turtles sun on the numerous snags and overhanging branches. We also enjoyed several iridescent green damselflies with black wings that landed on our boats. Two great horned owls eyed us warily from perches above.

Alton and Woodville, part of a string of old textile towns almost hidden along the Wood and Pawcatuck rivers in southern Rhode Island, made up the economic pillar of this area. Alton Pond formed behind the power-producing dam built by David L. Aldrich in 1860. His mill changed hands over the years but still produces textiles—elastic webbing rather than the cotton and wool of old. And, just like a hundred years ago, fishing remains the favorite activity on the quiet pond.

SECTION 7

EASTERN CONNECTICUT

The ten entries for Eastern Connecticut include mostly ponds and
lakes, with a few interesting rivers
thrown in. Five small ponds offer
paddling among abundant aquatic
vegetation. Stump Pond is a great
place to observe waterfowl: wood
duck, great blue heron, and many
more species. Ross Marsh—a quiet,

out-of-the way pond—also contains a lot of waterfowl; watch for muskrat and
beaver in the evening.

Look for Bryozoa colonies in Mono Pond if they have not been crowded
out by invasive aquatic weeds. Also look for great blue heron, wood duck, and
other marsh birds. We saw an otter family on Bishop Swamp, and you could
also see muskrat and beaver. Canada goose and wood duck both nest there,
and we watched crows mob a great horned owl. Bigelow Pond is the last of
the shallow, weed-choked bodies of water in this section. It's part of Bigelow
Hollow State Park; we saw an osprey fish on this tiny pond.

Standing in marked contrast to the five ponds mentioned above, Mashapaug
Lake also lies within Bigelow Hollow State Park; you can see down at least 20
feet in the clear, oligotrophic (low-nutrient) waters. Few trips in this book can
boast that kind of clarity. Popular Mansfield Hollow Lake offers many hours
of varied paddling opportunities, including open lake, deep coves, islands, and
several streams. Although motors are allowed, you will see more canoes and
kayaks. In the evening, watch for beaver and muskrat in the inlet rivers.

Other entries in this section include small ponds with rivers that provide
miles of paddling. West Thompson Lake is fun to paddle, and it's great to
camp there and to hike the nearby trails. Then paddle up the Quinebaug
River, enjoying the vine-draped shoreline, listening to birds calling from the
canopy. After paddling 41-acre Somersville Mill Pond, head up the narrow,
meandering Scantic River, leading through a bird-filled swampland. A very
diverse set of aquatic and semi-aquatic plants lines the shores, and in the upper
reaches, branches and vines provide an ever-encroaching canopy.

Oneco Pond and the Moosup River start in Connecticut, with portions of the upstream river winding into Rhode Island. Marshy Eagleville Pond, at 80 acres, has more nooks and crannies to paddle, and the Willimantic River offers hours of exploration. Great blue and green herons patrol the shoreline, while song sparrows, cardinals, catbirds, and common yellowthroats fill dense shrubs along the water's edge. Canada goose and wood duck also appear here. Watch for beaver and muskrat in the evening.

TRIP 68

QUADDICK RESERVOIR AND STUMP POND

Stump Pond is an excellent place to observe waterfowl amid a sea of aquatic plants. You will see wood duck, great blue heron, and many more species. Avoid this area when the speedway is running races.

LOCATION Thompson, CT

MAPS *Connecticut/Rhode Island Atlas & Gazetteer*, Map 24: B3, C3; USGS Thompson

AREA Quaddick Reservoir and Stump Pond, 467 acres

TIME 2 hours for Stump Pond

HABITAT TYPE Marshy reservoir

FISH Largemouth and calico bass, yellow perch, pickerel, northern pike (see fish advisory, Appendix A)

INFORMATION Thompson Speedway Motorsports Park race dates, thompsonspeedway.com

CAMPING Mashamoquet Brook State Park, West Thompson Lake

TAKE NOTE Motors allowed; no development on northern section

GETTING THERE

From I-395, Exit 50 northbound, drive 0.6 mile east on Route 200, and turn left on Route 193. Go 1.5 miles (2.1 miles), and turn right on Brandy Hill Road. In 0.4 mile (2.5 miles), bear left on Baker Road. Go 1.4 miles (3.9 miles) to the access by the bridge. **41° 58.141' N, 71° 19.015' W**

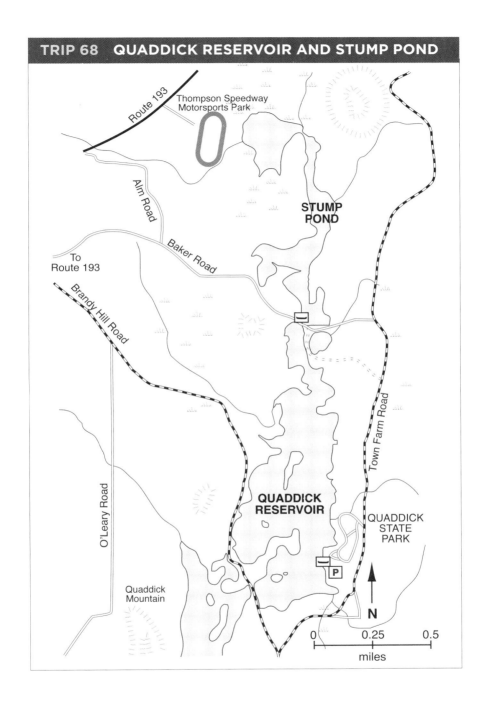

Route 193

Thompson Speedway
Motorsports Park

Alm Road

Baker Road

To
Route 193

Brandy Hill Road

O'Leary Road

STUMP
POND

QUADDICK
RESERVOIR

QUADDICK
STATE
PARK

Town Farm Road

P

N

Quaddick
Mountain

| 0 | 0.25 | 0.5 |

miles

When Thompson Speedway Motorsports Park is not in use, a paddle on relatively wild and marshy Stump Pond should be quiet and relaxing.

SECTION 7: EASTERN CONNECTICUT

WHAT YOU'LL SEE

Long, narrow Quaddick Reservoir nestles into the extreme northeastern corner of Connecticut, next to the Rhode Island and Massachusetts borders. Those seeking solitude should avoid the two southern sections, especially on sunny summer weekends, because they feature heavy development and teem with motorboats. The reservoir's northern section, described here—one of our favorite paddling spots in northeastern Connecticut—receives much less boat traffic because of abundant aquatic vegetation.

Floating waterlilies and submerged bladderworts, Carolina fanwort, and coontail clog the northern section's clear, shallow water. Water birds abound, especially mallard, black duck, wood duck, and great blue heron. The shallow coves and the far northern end—known as Stump Pond—provide the richest bird habitat. Thick woods of white pine and mixed deciduous trees surround the northern reservoir, along with sweet pepperbush, highbush blueberry, and sweetgale. Cattail, bulrush, and bur-reed embellish the shallow coves and inlets.

The only drawback to the northern section—besides the few motorboats that muscle their way in—is the noise that wafts in on a blue haze from Thompson Speedway Motorsports Park. The track backs right up to the Stump Pond marsh, filling it with race noises. To avoid the cacophony, check race dates on the speedway's website. Listening to your paddle dip methodically into water while you watch wood ducks circle low over the marsh presents a stark contrast to the roar of several thousand auto racing buffs who congregate a few hundred yards away. Although a sad commentary that so many more people watch car races than go out to enjoy nature, we would rather have the marsh teem with birds than with paddlers or, worse, motorboats. We wonder what those wood ducks think about our species . . . .

TRIP 69

WEST THOMPSON LAKE AND QUINEBAUG RIVER

This is a recreation destination, with camping, paddling, and hiking opportunities. The lake offers great paddling, free from development, but we prefer paddling up the river, enjoying the vine-draped shoreline, listening to birds calling from the canopy.

LOCATION Thompson, CT

MAPS *Connecticut/Rhode Island Atlas & Gazetteer*, Map 24: B1, B2, C1, C2; USGS Putnam

AREA/LENGTH West Thompson Lake, 239 acres; Quinebaug River, 3 miles one way

TIME: 5 hours

HABITAT TYPE Reservoir; wide, shallow river

FISH Largemouth, smallmouth, and calico bass; yellow perch; pickerel; walleye; also trout in the river (see fish advisory, Appendix A)

INFORMATION U.S. Army Corps of Engineers, West Thompson Lake, corpslakes.erdc.dren.mil/visitors/projects.cfm?Id=E619760

CAMPING West Thompson Lake, Mashamoquet Brook State Park

TAKE NOTE Motors limited to 5 MPH; no development

GETTING THERE

From I-395, Exit 47 northbound, go 0.8 mile west on Route 44, and turn right on Route 12. Head 1.9 miles (2.7 miles) north, and turn left, following signs to West Thompson Lake. Go 0.3 mile (3.0 miles), and turn right on Reardon Road. In 0.5 mile (3.5 miles), turn left into West Thompson Lake Recreation Area. **41° 57.209′ N, 71° 53.983′ W**

WHAT YOU'LL SEE

This 200-plus-acre lake, managed by the U.S. Army Corps of Engineers, provides enjoyable paddling and camping opportunities. Indeed, only a few lakes in southern New England—most of them Corps of Engineers facilities—can boast no development along their shorelines. With a 5 MPH speed limit, you will encounter mostly canoes and kayaks.

The sandy, pebbly shore provides easy access around nearly the entire perimeter, where you can get out for a picnic or foray into the oak-hickory woods in the 2,200-acre recreational area surrounding the lake. The Corps maintains two picnic areas and a campground, which was less than half full on a mid-August Sunday. This lake used to suffer from expanses of muddy banks because of fluctuating water levels related to flood control, but since the early 1990s the Corps has raised the pool level, eliminating the band of exposed shoreline.

From the boat ramp on the east shore, paddle north and explore the inlets on the east shore and the small islands and rock outcroppings on the west shore. In one inlet that expands into a pickerelweed-choked pool about 125 feet across, we came across a very large snapping turtle hanging lazily near the surface, head pointed downward, searching for its next meal. Paddling north

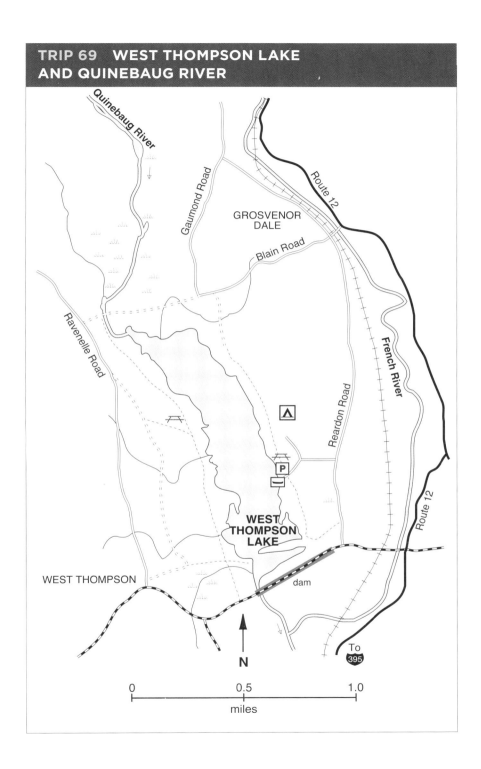

Quinebaug River

Gaumond Road

Route 12

GROSVENOR DALE

Blain Road

Ravenelle Road

French River

Reardon Road

WEST THOMPSON LAKE

Route 12

WEST THOMPSON

dam

To 395

N

0   0.5   1.0

miles

into the Quinebaug River, you soon pass under an old bridge on a 3.6-mile hiking trail that extends around the lake.

Wild grapevines drape the wooded shoreline along the river, and a broad marsh opens up just above the footbridge, where we observed great blue and green herons, along with a pair of kingbirds chasing a sharp-shinned hawk. We saw a cuckoo feeding on tent caterpillars, and we spied another large snapping turtle, along with dozens of painted turtles out sunning on logs. Look carefully in the clear water, and you might also see the elusive underwater rubber donut (*Goodyearis submergicus*); though many of them populate these waters, their bottom-dwelling habits frequently hide them from view. The farther upriver you paddle, the shallower it becomes, and the swifter the current; we paddled nearly 3 miles upstream before a riffle and very shallow water blocked our way.

TRIP 70

MASHAPAUG LAKE AND BIGELOW POND

Mashapaug Lake stands in contrast to most entries in this book because it is oligotrophic (has low-nutrient water). You can see down at least 20 feet in the clear water. Tiny Bigelow Pond, where we watched an osprey fish, is a shallow, marshy, nutrient-laden pond, more typical of entries in this book.

LOCATION Union, CT

MAPS *Connecticut/Rhode Island Atlas & Gazetteer*, Map 23: A5, B5; USGS Wales, Westford

AREA Mashapaug Lake, 287 acres; Bigelow Pond, 26 acres

TIME 4 hours

HABITAT TYPE Oligotrophic natural lake; little aquatic vegetation; small, marshy pond

FISH Trout, largemouth and smallmouth bass, yellow perch, pickerel, walleye (see fish advisory, Appendix A)

INFORMATION Bigelow Hollow State Park, Nipmuck State Forest, portal.ct.gov/DEEP/State-Parks/Parks/Bigelow-Hollow-State-Park-Nipmuck-State-Forest

CAMPING Mashamoquet Brook State Park, West Thompson Lake

TAKE NOTE Some development and motors (10 MPH limit) on Mashapaug; no internal combustion motors or development on Bigelow

GETTING THERE

Bigelow Pond From I-84, Exit 74, go 3.6 miles east on Route 171, and turn left into Bigelow Hollow State Park. In 0.3 mile (3.9 miles) the access is on the left. **41° 59.835' N, 72° 7.521' W**

Mashapaug Lake Go another 0.8 mile (4.7 miles) to the road's end. Just before the Mashapaug access, you pass the 1.2-mile trail to Breakneck Pond on the right. **42° 0.303' N, 72° 7.732' W**

WHAT YOU'LL SEE
MASHAPAUG LAKE

This large, natural lake in northeastern Connecticut boasts deep coves, rocky shores, and beautiful surrounding hemlock and white pine woods. Bigelow Hollow State Park, with picnic tables on needle-carpeted ground overlooking the lake's blue water, hugs the southern shore. Trails here wind among ancient stands of laurel, and the light filtering through the hemlock, pine, and oak canopy seems just right to support a wide array of wildflowers. Whether the hemlocks will withstand the hemlock woolly adelgid onslaught is an open question (see Trip 45). Most of the lake's eastern shore, with the land rising steeply from the water's edge, lies within 8,000-acre Nipmuck State Forest. In some areas, huge stone slabs extend down into the water.

While the south end of Mashapaug remains undeveloped except for the picnic area, some limited development fans out along the western and northern shores. Besides the development, road noise from I-84—just 0.5 mile away at the closest point—provides the only other reminder of civilization while you paddle this gorgeous place.

Few aquatic plants grow in these oligotrophic (low-nutrient) waters that boast 20-foot visibility. The state-record largemouth bass (12 pounds, 14 ounces) emerged from Mashapaug in 1961, and the state-record channel catfish (29 pounds, 6 ounces) was caught in Mashapaug in 2004.

BIGELOW POND

On a clear September day, we watched an osprey fish the clear water of Bigelow Pond. With only 26 acres, the pond takes little time to explore. It may be better just to picnic here and soak in the scenic beauty.

In contrast with Mashapaug, this quite shallow pond abounds with floating vegetation and sphagnum-covered hillocks where tree stumps have long since rotted away. Look for sundews amid the sphagnum moss. In early October, we noticed quite a few nodding ladies' tresses (*Spiranthes cernua*)—a small white orchid occasionally found in boggy areas. Along the shoreline, look for blueberry, sweet pepperbush, and laurel, along with hemlock and white pine farther from the water's edge. American white waterlily, yellow pondlily, and watershield grow in the shallows. Beaver occur here at times, and you may see the occasional wood duck.

TRIP 70 MASHAPAUG LAKE AND BIGELOW POND

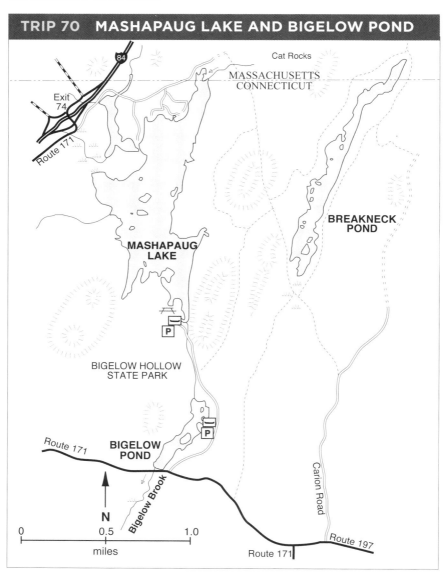

BREAKNECK POND

In Nipmuck State Forest, a mile or so east of Mashapaug Lake, Breakneck Pond offers a wonderful paddling experience in a thick marshland. Intrepid explorers can reach this long, narrow pond only by hiking in—a very long carry with a boat.

TRIP 71

SOMERSVILLE MILL POND AND SCANTIC RIVER

It is a joy to paddle the Scantic River through a bird-filled swampland. A very diverse set of aquatic and semi-aquatic plants lines the shores, and in the upper reaches, branches and vines provide an ever-encroaching canopy. Somersville Mill Pond, which you quickly leave behind, has an interesting history.

LOCATION Somers, CT

MAPS *Connecticut/Rhode Island Atlas & Gazetteer*, Map 21: B6; USGS Ellington

AREA/LENGTH Somersville Mill Pond, 41 acres; Scantic River, 3 miles one way

TIME 3 hours

HABITAT TYPE Shallow, marshy pond; narrow, winding river through swamp

FISH Trout, largemouth and calico bass, yellow perch, pickerel (see fish advisory, Appendix A)

CAMPING Mashamoquet Brook State Park

TAKE NOTE Few motors, 6 MPH speed limit; development near dam

GETTING THERE

From I-91, Exit 47E, go east on Route 190 for 5.0 miles, and turn right on Maple Street. The access is on the left in 0.2 mile (5.2 miles) at the junction with School Street. **41° 58.974′ N, 72° 29.224′ W**

WHAT YOU'LL SEE

Several small central Massachusetts brooks join to form the meandering Scantic River as it drains extensive wooded marshlands. The section included here backs up behind a Somersville dam that, at the time of the second edition, was flanked by gorgeous old redbrick mills. Those mills burned in 2012, leaving behind an unsightly heap of twisted steel and charred bricks. In 2023, the town of Somers chose a developer to replace the ruins with a mixed-income apartment complex.

Paddling out from the access, you quickly leave civilization behind. In the river's upper reaches, a golf driving range's net backs up to the riverbank, and twin high-voltage power lines appear overhead. Neither intrudes too much on the solitude.

Mist drifted off the water as we paddled out early one morning along the wooded shoreline. A kingfisher fled before us as cardinals, catbirds, song sparrows, and eastern towhees called from the dense undergrowth, and mourning doves sounded their plaintive coos overhead. We noted some big red oaks and huge swamp white oaks hanging out over the water. Shoreside shrubs, vines,

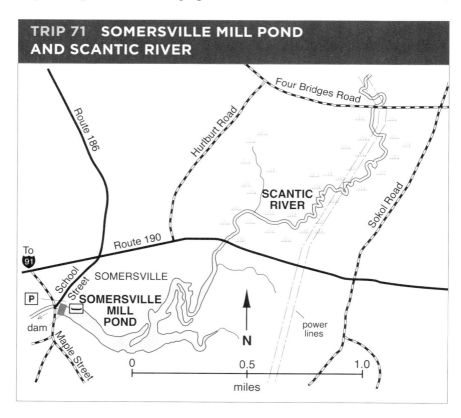

TRIP 71 SOMERSVILLE MILL POND AND SCANTIC RIVER

The Scantic River meanders slowly through scenic marshlands.

and flowers stand out most, though, as you paddle up the picturesque Scantic River. Red osier dogwood, alder, pickerelweed, arrowhead, willow, buttonbush, purple loosestrife, cattail, pondweed, grapes, bur-reed, jewelweed, and American eelgrass line the shallow waterway's banks. We found lots of cardinal flowers in bloom and many grapevines draped out over the water.

A beaver lodge just upstream from the Route 190 bridge had so many winter-forage branches surrounding the lodge that we almost couldn't get by. If you paddle far enough upstream, expect to find beaver dams. Check out the oxbows and side channels for birds; we saw or heard several species, including eastern phoebe, robin, chickadee, tufted titmouse, grackle, great blue heron, spotted sandpiper, crow, goldfinch, flicker, and red-bellied woodpecker.

Upstream, the channel narrows through tight-twisting turns with no perceptible current. Though plenty of water filled the main channel, we could not make it to Four Bridges Road because of overhanging grapevines and red osier dogwoods. (Maybe someone would be willing to prune back some of the more offending branches.)

TRIP 72
ROSS MARSH

Ross Marsh is a quiet, out-of-the way pond, where you should find a lot of waterfowl, along with seas of aquatic vegetation. Look for muskrat and beaver in the evening.

LOCATION Killingly and Sterling, CT

MAPS *Connecticut/Rhode Island Atlas & Gazetteer*, Map 36: B4; USGS East Killingly

AREA 55 acres

TIME 2 hours

HABITAT TYPE Shallow, marshy pond

FISH Largemouth bass, pickerel (see fish advisory, Appendix A)

CAMPING Mashamoquet Brook State Park

TAKE NOTE No motors; no development; watch out for stumps

GETTING THERE
From the North From I-395, Exit 37 southbound, drive 3.5 miles east on Route 6, and turn right on Sawmill Hill Road. Go 1.7 miles (5.2 miles) to the access on the left, just over the bridge. **41° 46.329′ N, 71° 47.757′ W**

From the South From the Lodge Turnpike, go 1.6 miles south on Cucumber Hill Road, and turn right on South Killingly Road. Continue 0.4 mile (2.0 miles), and turn right on Sawmill Hill Road. Go 0.2 mile (2.2 miles) to the access on the right, just before the bridge.

WHAT YOU'LL SEE
Ross Marsh, within Ross Marsh Wildlife Management Area, provides an outstanding paddling opportunity. Weaving our way north up the winding, open-water channel, we reveled in the solitude as mallards fed on abundant vegetation and hundreds of painted turtles slid off myriad stumps and logs into the water as we glided by. When we paddled here, beaver had dammed up the outlet, maintaining a slightly elevated water level. We startled a couple of fishing great blue herons and several flocks of wood ducks.

The diversity of aquatic vegetation and streamside shrubs and trees impressed us, especially the huge amount of eastern purple bladderwort in electric bloom.

In most years, a few blossoms appear here and there, but once or twice a decade, the blossoms erupt as though a brilliant lavender carpet has unfolded over the waterway. From late August through early September, we found dozens of ponds awash with color from *Utricularia purpurea*. When we visited here years later, it was too early in the season to determine whether invasives, such as Eurasian or twoleaf watermilfoil, were crowding out the bladderwort.

On the pond's north end, among the buttonbush and bur-reed, phragmites and cattails fight for dominance. You can paddle a couple of hundred yards up the narrow, winding inlet stream through a broad marsh, perhaps having to portage over a beaver dam. Dwarf red maple, streamside alder, and occasional swamp rose line the way. Watch out for stumps here and anywhere else in the pond outside the main channel.

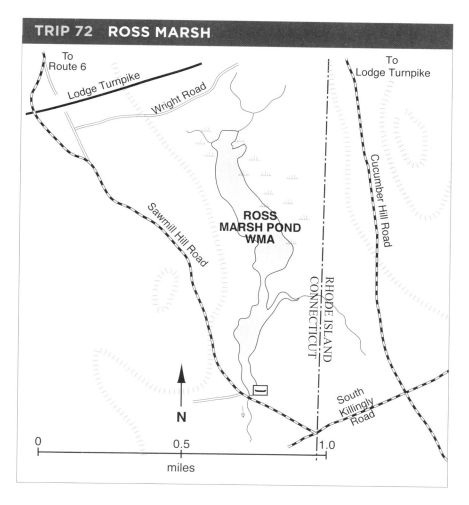

TRIP 72   ROSS MARSH

TRIP 73

MOOSUP RIVER AND ONECO POND

The Moosup River and Oneco Pond provide wonderful paddling just a few minutes from I-395 and close enough to Providence to escape for a morning or afternoon trip. Expect to see lots of painted turtles as well as the less common stinkpot turtle.

LOCATION Sterling, CT, and Coventry, RI

MAPS *Connecticut/Rhode Island Atlas & Gazetteer*, Map 36: D3, D4; USGS Oneco

LENGTH 2 to 4 miles one way, depending on water level

TIME 2 to 4 hours round trip

HABITAT TYPE Shallow, meandering stream with wooded shores beginning at Oneco Pond

FISH Trout (see fish advisory, Appendix A)

CAMPING Hopeville Pond State Park, Pachaug State Forest (Green Falls and Mount Misery campgrounds)

TAKE NOTE Family camping at private River Bend Campground on Oneco Pond, riverbendcamp.com

GETTING THERE

From I-395, Exit 29, go 5.5 miles east on Route 14A to the access on the right, just over the bridge, at the Sterling Municipal Building. **41° 41.566′ N, 71° 48.467′ W**

WHAT YOU'LL SEE

When we launched our boat on shallow, marshy Oneco Pond on an early October afternoon, thick mats of Eurasian watermilfoil floated on the surface, and exposed mud flats greeted us. But as we paddled generally east into the Moosup River channel, our initial negative impression turned around completely.

The fairly wide river has a generally sandy bottom, although more rocks appear as you paddle upstream into Rhode Island. Many downed trees had fallen into the water some years earlier—judging from the decay—likely from a storm event, providing superb sunning locations for turtles, which you will see in profusion.

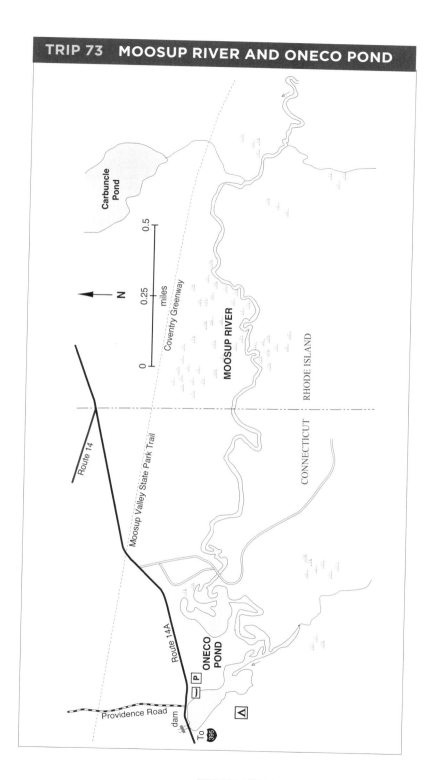

We saw probably more than a hundred painted turtles, but most skittered into the water long before we got too close. Another species found here, the stinkpot, or common musk, turtle (*Sternotherus odoratus*), tolerates a much closer approach. We often paddled right up to this small turtle, which has a more steeply humped carapace than that of the painted turtle and is often coated with algae. Its more sharply pointed snout often tilts upward as the turtle basks on its chosen log. We have also found this somewhat more dexterous turtle fairly far up steeply pitched tree trunks, whereas the painted turtle almost always hovers close to the water.

We've never seen more stinkpot turtles than we saw here, counting seven in a three-hour afternoon paddle. Although we didn't see any snapping turtles, which is not unusual, there should be lots of them as well.

Fortunately, we didn't find watermilfoil in the Moosup River. Shrubs along the banks include mountain laurel, winterberry, highbush blueberry, and sweet pepperbush. While white pine and red maple dominate the high ground, we also saw some black gum, red and white oaks, American hornbeam or ironwood (*Carpinus caroliniana*), sassafras, alder, gray birch, and sugar maple.

In early October, the water level seemed to be down 8 to 12 inches—as evidenced by the undercut banks and high-and-dry eddies in the marshy ponds just east of Oneco Pond. We suspect that beaver may have dug some deeper channels in these ponds, but we couldn't find clear evidence of that.

The low water hampered our paddling upstream. We didn't quite make it into Rhode Island but believe we could in spring or during higher water levels. The current also flowed more quickly upstream, and in spring,

Deciduous trees line the Moosup River's banks, lending spectacular colors in the fall.

stronger current could be an issue in some places. After getting out a few times to ease our boat over downed logs or shallow gravel, we turned around and made our way back to the access.

From Oneco Pond, if you paddle under the Route 14A bridge (north), you'll get to a dam and waterworks that we think originally served a mill. Learning more about this installation would be an interesting research project.

TRIP 74

MANSFIELD HOLLOW LAKE

Popular Mansfield Hollow Lake offers many hours of varied paddling opportunities, including open lake, deep coves, islands, and several streams. Although motors are allowed, expect to see more canoes and kayaks. In the evening, watch for beaver and muskrat in the inlet rivers.

LOCATION Mansfield and Windham, CT

MAPS *Connecticut/Rhode Island Atlas & Gazetteer*, Map 34: B4; USGS Spring Hill, Willimantic

AREA 500 acres

TIME All day

HABITAT TYPE Wooded reservoir; deep coves, islands, and inlet rivers

FISH Trout, largemouth and calico bass, yellow perch, pickerel, northern pike (see fish advisory, Appendix A)

INFORMATION Mansfield Hollow State Park, portal.ct.gov/DEEP /State-Parks/Parks/Mansfield-Hollow-State-Park

CAMPING Mashamoquet Brook State Park, Devil's Hopyard State Park

TAKE NOTE Recreational development only; boats limited to 8 MPH

GETTING THERE

From I-84, Exit 68, go south on Route 195, through Storrs, to Mansfield Center. Continue 0.5 mile past the Route 89 junction, and turn left on Bassett Bridge Road. Go 1.4 miles (1.9 miles) to the access on the left. **41° 46.099′ N, 72° 10.53′ W**

From the junction of Routes 6 and 195 just north of Willimantic, go 2.1 miles north on Route 195, and turn right on Bassett Bridge Road. Drive 1.4 miles (3.5 miles) to the access on the left.

WHAT YOU'LL SEE

Its large size, by southern New England standards, makes Mansfield Hollow Lake (or Naubesatuck Lake) a prime recreation destination, particularly

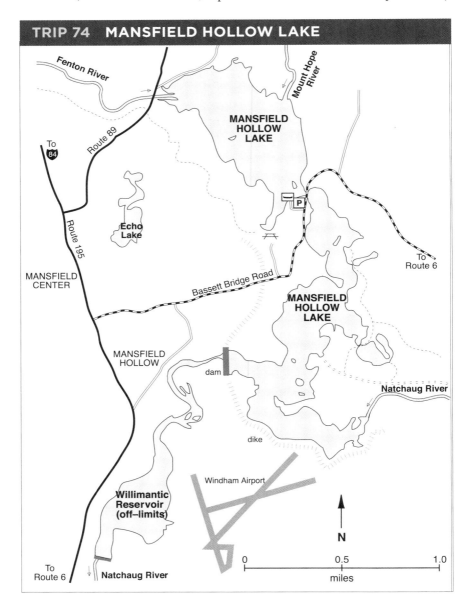

TRIP 74   MANSFIELD HOLLOW LAKE

Fenton River

Mount Hope River

MANSFIELD HOLLOW LAKE

Route 89

To 84

Echo Lake

Route 195

P

To Route 6

MANSFIELD CENTER

Bassett Bridge Road

MANSFIELD HOLLOW LAKE

MANSFIELD HOLLOW

dam

Natchaug River

dike

Windham Airport

Willimantic Reservoir (off–limits)

N

To Route 6   Natchaug River

0   0.5   1.0

miles

for those who crave lots of exercise. Because of an 8-MPH speed limit, more hand-powered than motor-powered craft ply these waters. It would take at least a day to explore the entire shoreline, every island, and the reservoir's deep coves. You can also paddle up the three inlet rivers, adding greatly to your exploration time.

Bassett Bridge Road causeway divides the waterway roughly in half. The U.S. Army Corps of Engineers, in response to devastating flooding of the town of Willimantic in 1936, created the lake in 1952 with a dam and dikes along the Natchaug River. Like many flood-control reservoirs, Mansfield Hollow Lake's water level fluctuates, although the Corps tries to keep it bank-full in summer. Paddling here after early October, you may have to contend with an exposed gravelly shoreline.

The narrower southern section of Mansfield Hollow Lake, below Bassett Bridge Road, offers more coves and islands to explore. From the access, paddle through one of two large steel culverts into the northeast end of this lower section, where a hidden pond off to the east connects with the main lake by a small channel. This small pond feels very remote and quiet—especially on a windy day. You can carry in to another, slightly larger pond farther to the southeast. As you travel into the southern end, a massive dike looms over the lake, like the Great Wall of China. The primary inlet into the lake, the Natchaug River, which can be paddled for a short distance upriver, flows in at the southeastern tip.

The northern, wider section of the lake, with fewer twisting coves to explore, has a somewhat more natural feel, particularly at the north end. Two inlets enter here: Mount Hope River, coming from the north, and the Fenton River, coming from the northwest. A few hundred yards up Mount Hope River, a beaver lodge stands sentinel over the rapids and rocks that block your way. You can travel under Route 89 and up the Fenton River much farther. We've gone about 0.5 mile here and found the paddling very easy on the slow-moving, meandering channel. Beaver lodges occur along here as well, and numerous muskrats call the banks home; in the late afternoon, you should see both beaver and muskrat.

White pine and red oak dominate the lake's shoreline, along with white oak, shagbark hickory, pitch pine, red maple, gray birch, alder, aspen, elm, willow, and various shrubs, including sweetgale, buttonbush, blueberry, red osier dogwood, wild grape, swamp azalea, swamp rose, swamp loosestrife, and winterberry. You will also see royal fern and the invasive purple loosestrife. Look for mussels on the sandy bottom and for the round, gelatinous balls of Bryozoa colonies clinging to underwater logs. Common reed (*Phragmites*) and other grasses populate the few small pockets of marsh. In early October, we saw osprey, red-tailed hawk, mallard, black duck, red-breasted merganser, and kingfisher species and quite a few eastern bluebirds in migration. The Connecticut state-record rainbow trout (14 pounds, 10 ounces) was caught here in 1998.

EAGLEVILLE POND AND WILLIMANTIC RIVER

Marshy Eagleville Pond and the Willimantic River offer hours of exploration. Great blue and green herons patrol the shoreline, while song sparrows, cardinals, catbirds, and common yellowthroats fill dense shrubs along the water's edge. Canada geese and wood ducks appear here. Watch for beaver and muskrat in the evening.

LOCATION Coventry and Mansfield, CT

MAPS *Connecticut/Rhode Island Atlas & Gazetteer*, Map 34: B1, B2; USGS Coventry

AREA/LENGTH Eagleville Pond, 80 acres; Willimantic River, 1.5 miles one way

TIME 3 hours round trip

HABITAT TYPE Shallow, marshy pond; vines and trees overhanging river

FISH Largemouth and smallmouth bass, yellow perch, pickerel (see fish advisory, Appendix A)

CAMPING Mashamoquet Brook State Park, Devil's Hopyard State Park

TAKE NOTE Limited development; cartop access and shallow water limit motors; 8 MPH speed limit

GETTING THERE
From I-84, Exit 59, go east on I-384. When I-384 ends, go 7.7 miles east on Route 44, and turn right on Route 32. Drive 1.8 miles (9.5 miles), and turn right on Route 275 (South Eagleville Road). In 0.3 mile (9.8 miles), reach the access on the right, just across the bridge. **41° 47.062′ N, 72° 16.905′ W**

WHAT YOU'LL SEE
Eagleville Pond and the Willimantic River offer hours of wonderful paddling through labyrinthine channels around dozens of low, marshy islands and coves. Swamp loosestrife lines many of these channels, particularly at the pond's north end where the river enters. Carolina fanwort is the dominant underwater species. A railroad track parallels the pond's east shore, with a

gravel pit beyond, and a few houses occur along the pond's southwest shore. Very little development impinges on most of the rest of this gorgeous habitat.

As we paddled up the pond, wood ducks rose from weed-choked coves, while red-winged blackbirds called from the streambanks. Skulking birds— song sparrows, cardinals, catbirds, and common yellowthroats—called from the dense undergrowth. Muskrats harvested pickerelweed along the shore, among the yellow pondlily and watershield. Swamp azalea, jewelweed, joe-pye weed, and lots of alders lined the banks, along with lush arbors of grapes overhanging the bankside shrubs. We spied a completely overgrown beaver

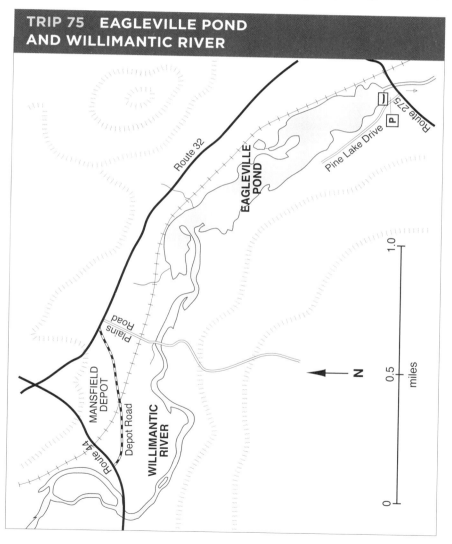

TRIP 75   EAGLEVILLE POND AND WILLIMANTIC RIVER

lodge, noticeable only because of the large array of alders and other branches stuck butt-first into the mud for winter fodder.

Along the river, shagbark hickory, red maple, and basswood formed arching canopies in places. Red maple and red oak dominate the shoreline, along with the occasional gray birch, ash, willow, American hornbeam, black cherry, and black birch (twigs have a wintergreen odor when scratched). The first part of the river upstream from the pond has no discernible current, but shallow riffles that make paddling difficult start to occur well before the Route 44 bridge.

As we paddled back downstream, a red-tailed hawk gave out its piercing cry from the treetops, while a green heron stalked the shoreline. Canada geese tried to look inconspicuous, and a great blue heron stood knee-deep among the lily pads. We hated to leave all the wildlife and beautiful scenery in this special place.

TRIP 76
MONO POND

If the Bryozoa have not been crowded out by invasive aquatic weeds, they offer a real treat when paddling Mono Pond's shores. Look for great blue heron, wood duck, and other marsh birds. Paddling can become difficult in summer because of copious amounts of aquatic vegetation.

LOCATION Columbia, CT

MAPS *Connecticut/Rhode Island Atlas & Gazetteer*, Map 34: D1; USGS Columbia

AREA 113 acres

TIME 2 hours

HABITAT TYPE Shallow, marshy pond

FISH Largemouth bass, yellow perch, pickerel (see fish advisory, Appendix A)

INFORMATION Aquatic plant survey, portal.ct.gov/CAES/OAIS/M /Mono-Pond/Mono-Pond-2012

CAMPING Devil's Hopyard State Park

TAKE NOTE Limited development; small size and aquatic vegetation limit motors; 8 MPH speed limit; no water-skiing

GETTING THERE

From the junction of Routes 6 and 66 just west of Willimantic, drive 2.7 miles west on Route 66, and turn left on Pine Street. Go 1.0 mile (3.7 miles), and turn right on Hunt Road. Continue 0.2 mile (3.9 miles) to the access on the left. **41° 40.735′ N, 72° 18.639′ W**

WHAT YOU'LL SEE

When we paddled Mono Pond in 2002, it sported a new concrete boat ramp, a huge disappointment for this scenic location. Though we could detect no Carolina fanwort or watermilfoil, boat trailers inevitably bring the plants in, infecting yet another pond with these invasive, nearly impossible-to-remove species. We fear that the underwater, gelatinous Bryozoa colonies will disappear, as they seem to have done in nearby Holbrook Pond, smothered out by dense rafts of Carolina fanwort and watermilfoil. When we visited in 2013, it was too early in the season to see whether invasives had arrived; however, a 2012 plant survey revealed the presence of three invasives: twoleaf watermilfoil (*Myriophyllum heterophyllum*), Carolina fanwort, and Brazilian waterweed. Quoting from

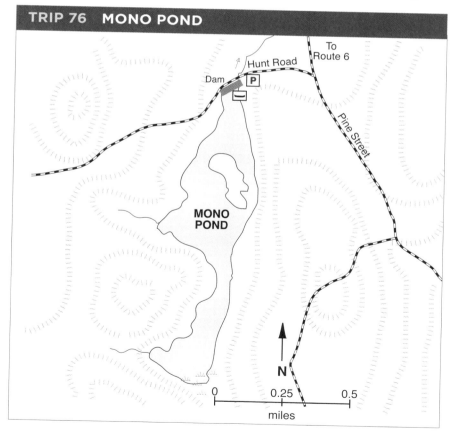

A great blue heron takes a break from fishing.

the survey, "*M. heterophyllum* was the most dominant plant in the lake." Since the third edition of this book, the state has eradicated the watermilfoil.

Bryozoa had colonized many submerged logs in the pond's north end, and huge rafts of both yellow-flowered and eastern purple bladderwort filled the water column at the south end. The bladderworts—whose underwater pods devour mosquito larvae—will become much reduced, if not eliminated, if invasives take over again.

But the Bryozoa would be the real loss, because we see these colonies only rarely. They require pure water, and we believe that choking vegetation causes either stagnation, which compromises water quality, or reduced ability for the cilia to sweep the water for the microscopic algae, protozoa, and diatoms that compose their diet.

Thick stands of mostly deciduous trees cover the hillsides, hiding some limited development. Sweet pepperbush, highbush blueberry, swamp azalea, buttonbush, and swamp loosestrife line the banks, while seas of watershield and American white waterlily cover the water's surface on the south end. By August, paddling through this blanket of vegetation becomes difficult, but our foray into it gave us clear looks at many wood ducks and an immature great blue heron as it stalked and ate sunfish along the shore.

TRIP 77

BISHOP SWAMP

Paddling is slow going on this weed-choked pond. We observed an otter family; you might find muskrat and beaver. Canada goose and wood duck both nest here, and we saw crows mob a great horned owl.

LOCATION Andover, CT

MAPS *Connecticut/Rhode Island Atlas & Gazetteer*, Map 33: C8; USGS Marlborough

AREA 53 acres

TIME 2 hours

HABITAT TYPE Shallow, marshy pond

FISH Largemouth and calico bass, pickerel (see fish advisory, Appendix A)

CAMPING Devil's Hopyard State Park

TAKE NOTE No development; no internal combustion motors

GETTING THERE

From I-84, Exit 59, go east on I-384. When I-384 ends, continue 5.7 miles east on Route 6, and turn right on Route 316. Go 0.5 mile (6.2 miles), and turn right on Boston Hill Road. Go 1.4 miles (7.6 miles), and turn left on Jurovaty Road. In 0.8 mile (8.4 miles), the access is on the right. **41° 42.964′ N, 72° 23.358′ W**

WHAT YOU'LL SEE

Although beaver maintain channels through the abundant surface vegetation—mostly American white waterlily and watershield—you can't escape the even more abundant invasive Eurasian watermilfoil and Carolina fanwort that fill the water column here. The copious vegetation, of course, suited the Canada geese and wood ducks just fine, and amazingly it did not seem to affect the family of otters that cavorted on the pond's south end. Every time

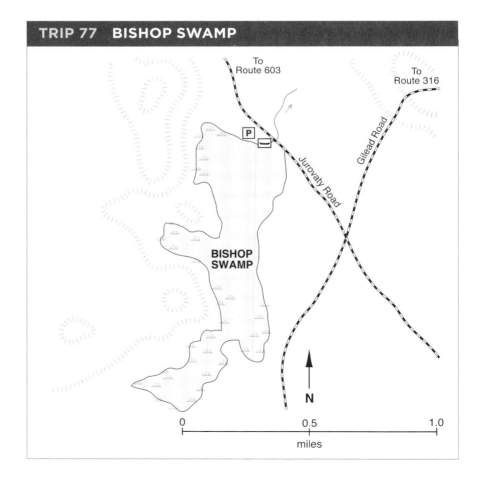

A male green frog (*Rana clamitans*) eyes us warily from the lily pads.

they surfaced, either to crunch loudly on fish or to cast a wary eye in our direction as we watched them through binoculars, aquatic vegetation clung to their heads and necks—a quite comical scene.

Though we did not see any beaver in the early morning, we did find several large, jewelweed-encrusted beaver lodges, a couple of them quite close together. We wondered whether otters had evicted the beaver from one of the lodges, causing them to construct another nearby.

We observed a lot more in this wildlife paradise, a stone's throw away from Hartford. We watched crows mob a great horned owl on an island on the pond's south end. A couple of great blue herons stalked the shoreline, and dozens of tree swallows perched on limbs of dead trees standing in the water of the larger coves. Other birds foraged for food above the water or in the shoreside foliage. We saw robins, goldfinches, mourning doves, red-bellied woodpeckers, kingbirds, red-winged blackbirds, and phoebes. Frogs hopped off the lily pads as we paddled along, trying to avoid the stumps and barely submerged logs.

This idyllic setting suffers, though, from alien invaders. The aforementioned watermilfoil and Carolina fanwort (not a foreign invader but often introduced from elsewhere) crowd out the yellow-flowered and eastern purple bladderworts, and purple loosestrife crowds out the native swamp loosestrife, cattail, button-bush, and joe-pye weed.

SECTION 8

SOUTHERN CONNECTICUT

The sixteen entries here include the Housatonic River estuary, embedded in Charles E. Wheeler Wildlife Management Area, and the Connecticut River's Great Island Estuary, along with four tributary streams. The coastal East River also has a small estuary. Mystic River, a tidal river, offers a different paddling experience. The other entries all consist of ponds and reservoirs.

The Housatonic River salt marsh is a birder's paradise, especially during shorebird migration in August, with more than 300 bird species observed here. The area is off-limits to motors until September 1, making for delightful paddling in the extensive channels that crisscross the marsh. Great Island Estuary also offers an extraordinary paddling opportunity. Birdlife abounds, which is why Roger Tory Peterson, the famed naturalist, chose to live in Old Lyme. The estuary center and wildlife area there both bear his name. East River provides a wonderful chance to explore an extensive *Spartina* salt marsh, or you can paddle upriver away from Long Island Sound. Look for fiddler crabs, herons, egrets, ospreys, and northern harriers.

Lord Cove, just upriver from Great Island, is one of the best places to watch osprey dive for fish. Look for herons and egrets, along with many shorebirds, on the mud flats during spring and fall migrations. Labyrinthine waterways lace the marsh. Farther upstream, tiny Whalebone Creek penetrates an extensive, pristine freshwater marsh, filled with birds and wild rice. Adjacent Selden Creek offers excellent paddling and also camping on a gorgeous Connecticut River island. Across from the island, more marshlands beg to be explored.

Even farther upstream on the Connecticut River, you can paddle several miles up the Salmon River, a choice location for bird-watchers. See osprey dive for fish in the clear water, and look for songbirds in the tall trees on the shore and hillsides. Marshy coves harboring wild rice await exploration.

Several bodies of water populate the Pachaug State Forest area, including Hopeville Pond and the Pachaug River. Hopeville Pond is a recreation destination, with camping, paddling, swimming, and hiking available. Another section of the Pachaug River, along with Beachdale Pond, makes a convenient spot to paddle up the river through a pristine swamp. Hiking and mountain biking trails course through the surrounding 23,000-acre Pachaug State Forest. Green Falls Pond, a recreation destination with camping, backpacking, hiking, biking, and paddling available, lies deep within Pachaug State Forest. A mix of tall trees surrounds the pond and the shrub-lined shore. The woods have an open understory with loads of wildflowers in spring.

Powers Lake boasts ample tree diversity along its shores, including four oak species. We were fortunate to see a rare spotted turtle, along with a stinkpot turtle, painted turtles, and several northern water snakes. Nehantic State Forest borders one side of nearby Uncas Pond and offers an extensive network of hiking trails. Uncas Pond's clear water is surrounded by a very diverse forest.

Babcock Pond lies within the 1,500-acre Babcock Pond Wildlife Management Area. The best paddling is in spring. Look for wood duck and other waterfowl and muskrat. Nearby Moodus Reservoir is a popular lake with a fair amount of development and high-speed boating; the best paddling is in early spring and in fall. For more solitude in summer, head to the deep southeast cove with its dense patches of watershield.

Undeveloped Pattaconk Reservoir sits amid Connecticut's second-largest state forest and does not allow motors. Although a great place to paddle amid gorgeous hillsides, it also draws large crowds for hiking, biking, and swimming—as well as paddling—particularly on weekends. In contrast, nearby Messerschmidt Pond, surrounded by a wildlife management area, is a much quieter place to paddle. On our visits, we've seen painted and snapping turtles and listened to many birds calling from the woods.

TRIP 78

HOPEVILLE POND AND PACHAUG RIVER

Hopeville Pond is a recreation destination, with camping, paddling, swimming, and hiking available. Besides exploring here, you can paddle upstream through Pachaug Pond into Glasgo Pond. Look for beaver in the evening. Expect to see great blue herons, ducks, geese, and turtles.

LOCATION Griswold, CT

MAPS *Connecticut/Rhode Island Atlas & Gazetteer*, Map 48: A1, B1; USGS Jewett City

AREA/LENGTH Hopeville Pond, 150 acres; Pachaug River, 3.6 miles one way

TIME 4 hours; all day to paddle into Glasgo Pond

HABITAT TYPE Dammed-up meandering river

FISH Largemouth bass, yellow perch, walleye, pickerel, northern pike (see fish advisory, Appendix A)

CAMPING Hopeville Pond State Park, Pachaug State Forest (Green Falls and Mount Misery campgrounds)

INFORMATION Hopeville Pond State Park, portal.ct.gov/DEEP /State-Parks/Parks/Hopeville-Pond-State-Park

TAKE NOTE Some development; state campground; motors limited to 8 MPH

GETTING THERE
From I-395, Exit 24, go 1.4 miles east on Route 201 to Hopeville Pond State Park on the right. **41° 36.465′ N, 71° 55.583′ W**

WHAT YOU'LL SEE
Hopeville Pond, a widened 3-mile section of the Pachaug River, offers very pleasant, relaxing paddling. Its shores include Hopeville Pond State Park, the site of a former waterpower-driven woolen mill. The federal government purchased the property in 1930, and the Civilian Conservation Corps managed it until transferring it to the state in 1959. Today, the pond offers fine waterside family camping, hiking, swimming, and boating. The park adjoins Pachaug State Forest, whose 14-mile Nehantic Trail wan-

We often see blue flag (*Iris versicolor*) growing along the banks of marshy ponds in New England.

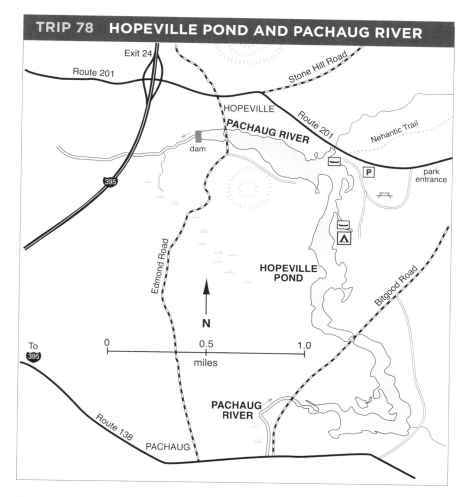

Exit 24

Route 201

Stone Hill Road

HOPEVILLE

PACHAUG RIVER

Route 201

Nehantic Trail

dam

395

park entrance

P

HOPEVILLE POND

Edmond Road

Bitgood Road

N

0   0.5   1.0
miles

To 395

PACHAUG RIVER

Route 138

PACHAUG

ders over low, hilly terrain, connecting the northeast side of Hopeville Pond with Green Falls Pond in Voluntown.

The pond winds through woodland, farmland, and areas with light cottage development between a dam at the north end close to I-395 and a section of river at the south end, connecting to other ponds farther upstream. To reach larger, more developed Pachaug Pond (831 acres) and much nicer Glasgo Pond (184 acres), continue upstream on the Pachaug River, carrying around the dam (Trip 79).

Like other bodies of water in this part of the state, Hopeville Pond's shallow water has a deep reddish brown color caused by natural tannins. You will see lots of painted turtles along here, as well as great blue herons, kingfishers, black ducks, mallards, and possibly wood ducks. Several male wood ducks in full breeding plumage landed right in front of our boats near the south end of the pond where we had paused under cover of a tree. Upon seeing us, they immediately took to the air, emitting their high-pitched distress call. We also saw signs of beaver here and a lodge at the south end where the pond narrows to a river channel.

EASTERN PAINTED TURTLE: QUIETWATER COMPANION

You won't have to spend much time paddling before spotting your first painted turtle, but getting a really close look may prove a little more difficult. The eastern painted turtle (*Chrysemys picta*) is the most visible of our turtle species but may not be the most common. That distinction may belong to the much larger snapping turtle, whose bottom-dwelling habit keeps it out of sight most of the time. On marshy ponds you might see literally hundreds of painted turtles basking in the sun on stumps, partially submerged logs, rocks, and vegetation—but always within easy reach of underwater safety. The painted turtle remains alert to danger; if you paddle along noisily, it disappears from view long before you draw near.

The painted turtle's carapace—the smooth, gently arched top shell—reaches a length of 7 inches. The colorful, patterned carapace lends the species its name. Narrow lines of yellow separate the dark olive-green scutes (interlocking plates evolutionarily adapted from vertebrae to form the shell), and a wider orange band defines the outer edge of the shell (a brownish deposit on the shell may obscure these colors). The head and neck sport distinctive yellow stripes, and dark blotches sometimes mark the yellow plastron (bottom shell).

The painted turtle, found throughout much of the United States, ranges farther north than any other turtle species. Of the four subspecies, two occur in southern New England. The much more common eastern painted turtle (*Chrysemys picta picta*) has carapace scutes that line up in rows across the back, while the midland painted turtle (*C.p. marginata*), found mostly in western parts of the region, has scutes that alternate instead of running straight across. You need to get a really close look to distinguish these subspecies.

Diet consists of both plant and animal material, and you may see painted turtles underwater, feeding on submerged vegetation and various crustaceans, tadpoles, snails, and insect larvae. Mostly you will see them basking, a habit attributed to having a body temperature that fluctuates with environmental temperature—emerging from cold water, they absorb solar radiation to raise their body temperature and, therefore, their metabolic rate, helping them grow faster. However, some evidence suggests that they also bask to dislodge attached leeches.

The painted turtle mates during spring or summer, usually from late April through mid-June. During courtship, one or more males swim around a stationary female. If she accepts a male's advances, she dives to the bottom, where mating takes place. One to two months later, the female leaves the water to deposit a clutch of five to eleven eggs in a nest excavated on open, sloping sand or gravel banks, or even lawns not too far from water. She digs the shallow nest with her hind feet and deposits the soft-shell eggs. She may also build several false nests, probably to mislead skunk, raccoon, and other predators that dig up and consume about 90 percent of turtle nests. Incubation temperature determines hatchling gender: males emerge from cool nests (around 75 degrees Fahrenheit) and females from warmer ones (around 85 degrees Fahrenheit).

Amazingly, hatchling painted turtles can withstand freezing. In northern parts of their range, the young overwinter in their nests after hatching in fall. With the nest just a few inches deep, temperatures drop well below freezing. The hatchlings' muscle activity, breathing, heartbeat, and blood flow totally stop—yet they usually recover fully when the temperature rises. While most biological functions cease, some minimal brain activity continues, and only about half of their body fluids actually freeze solid. Ice forms in the turtle's extremities and grows inward, but high concentrations of sugars in the blood work like antifreeze to keep the critical core fluids from solidifying, down to 25 degrees Fahrenheit. In years with sparse insulating snow cover, nest temperature drops below this point, and most hatchlings do not survive. A few other reptiles and amphibians exhibit similar freezing adaptations, but none is as well adapted as the painted turtle hatchling. After the first year, however, the painted turtle loses the ability to survive freezing.

The painted turtle hibernates at above-freezing temperatures in the pond's bottom mud—an area almost devoid of oxygen. Other turtle species also have the ability to hibernate underwater for periods of up to four months without coming up for air. During times of very low activity, many turtles and frogs absorb oxygen and release carbon dioxide through specialized membranes. But painted turtles, and closely related sliders, survive in totally deoxygenated water for a period of several months. Indeed, these turtles have the greatest known tolerance for oxygen deprivation of any vertebrate in the animal kingdom, with an ability to survive in water totally devoid of oxygen for up to 150 days. Specialized biochemical adaptations make survival possible. The turtles store large reserves of the carbohydrate fuel glycogen, which breaks down to produce energy without using oxygen in a process called glycolysis. Because glycolysis produces lactic acid, another adaptation is required: the release of calcium and magnesium from the turtle's shell to buffer the acid.

And you thought you were looking at just an ordinary pond dweller! Instead, the painted turtle's veritable treasure trove of fascinating and unique biological adaptations enables it to survive the harsh conditions of New England and southern Canada. For more information on turtles, see David Carroll's *The Year of the Turtle: A Natural History*, a naturalist's wonderful account of 40 years of turtle observation in New Hampshire (see Appendix B).

PACHAUG RIVER AND BEACHDALE POND

*Look for osprey, mute swan, wood duck, and possibly otter.
Paddle up the Pachaug River through a pristine swamp. Take
advantage of the hiking and mountain biking trails available
in the surrounding 23,000-acre Pachaug State Forest.*

LOCATION Voluntown, CT

MAPS *Connecticut/Rhode Island Atlas & Gazetteer*, Map 48: B2, B3;
USGS Voluntown

AREA/LENGTH Beachdale Pond, 46 acres; Pachaug River, 2.5 miles one
way, could be shorter if vines or downed trees block the river

TIME 4 hours round trip

HABITAT TYPE Dammed-up pond; narrow, meandering river with dense
overhanging shrubs; marshlands

FISH Trout, largemouth bass, yellow perch (see fish advisory, Appendix A)

CAMPING Hopeville Pond State Park, Pachaug State Forest (Green Falls
and Mount Misery campgrounds)

INFORMATION Pachaug State Forest, portal.ct.gov/DEEP/State-Parks
/Forests/Pachaug-State-Forest

TAKE NOTE Campground but otherwise little development; aquatic
vegetation limits motors; 8 MPH speed limit

GETTING THERE

From I-395, Exit 22, go 6.4 miles east on Route 138, and turn left on Route
49. Continue 0.6 mile (7.0 miles) to the access on the right, just after crossing
the bridge. **41° 35.079' N, 71° 51.309' W**

WHAT YOU'LL SEE

Paddle downstream from the Pachaug River access to reach small, shallow
Beachdale Pond with its extensive cover of marshy vegetation. Watch for
painted turtles and frogs hiding amid the abundant arrowhead, pickerelweed,
waterlilies, and grasses. Carolina fanwort, with white flowers and yellow stamens, bloomed when we visited here in August. We watched an osprey fish,
and a pair of mute swans swam about with four cygnets. To the northwest,

you can paddle up Mount Misery Brook, which winds through the marsh. We traveled upstream for about 0.5 mile or so before an approaching thunderstorm convinced us to turn around.

Though the pond is a pleasant diversion, the Pachaug River upstream from the access offers the real attraction. Once you clear Nature's Campsites, a private campground, you enter Pachaug–Great Meadow Swamp, winding your way upstream, dipping your paddle in the yellow-brown water of a pristine swamp on a gradually narrowing waterway. Red maple, grapevine, Virginia creeper, and ubiquitous poison ivy branches overhang the water. Eventually these branches and possibly downed trees block the way, unless some enterprising soul has hacked a path through them. Besides surprising an occasional

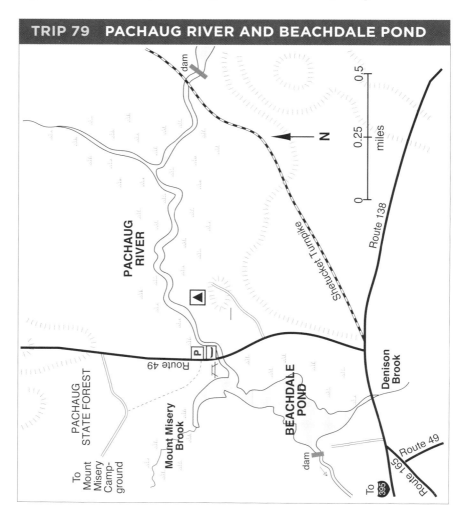

TRIP 79   PACHAUG RIVER AND BEACHDALE POND

wood duck brood, we saw many turtles out sunning themselves and reveled in the large patches of bright crimson cardinal flower growing along the banks.

Appropriately, Pachaug derives from a Narragansett word meaning "bend or turn in the river." Pequot, Narragansett, and Mohegan tribes inhabited this area before the arrival of Europeans. During the latter half of the seventeenth century, a combined force of colonists and Mohegans defeated the Narragansetts and Pequots, and in 1700, a 6-by-6-mile tract of land was granted to the Mohegan war veterans. Eventually the central portion of this tract became "Volunteer Town," incorporated as Voluntown in 1721.

Numerous hiking and mountain biking trails wend their way through various sections of the 23,000-acre Pachaug State Forest, the largest state forest in Connecticut. Nearby, a short loop trail traverses the wonderful Rhododendron Sanctuary—a quite unusual isolated stand of ancient rhododendron and white cedar. The Mount Misery camping area and Rhododendron Sanctuary are on the other side of Route 49 from the boat access.

Although graceful and elegant, mute swans (imports from Eurasia) drive away native species. Here, adults paddle with nearly fully grown cygnets.

TRIP 80

GREEN FALLS POND

Remote Green Falls Pond is a recreation destination offering camping, backpacking, hiking, biking, and paddling. A mix of tall trees surrounds the pond and the shrub-lined shore. The woods have an open understory with loads of wildflowers in spring. Look for eastern purple bladderwort on the pond.

LOCATION Voluntown, CT

MAPS *Connecticut/Rhode Island Atlas & Gazetteer*, Map 48: C3; USGS Voluntown

AREA 48 acres

TIME: 2 hours

HABITAT TYPE Wooded pond

FISH Trout, largemouth bass (see fish advisory, Appendix A)

INFORMATION Pachaug State Forest, portal.ct.gov/DEEP/State-Parks /Forests/Pachaug-State-Forest

CAMPING Hopeville Pond State Park, Pachaug State Forest (Green Falls and Mount Misery campgrounds)

TAKE NOTE No development; no internal combustion motors

GETTING THERE

From I-395, Exit 22, drive 8.5 miles east on Route 138, and turn right at the sign for Green Falls Reservoir. Go 2.5 miles (11.0 miles) to the access, passing the picnic area on the right. **41° 32.069′ N, 71° 48.645′ W**

WHAT YOU'LL SEE

Green Falls Pond, one of the most remote bodies of water in this guide, is a real treasure, ideal for a morning or afternoon of quiet paddling and a superb spot for family camping. Like Beachdale and Glasgo ponds, Green Falls Pond lies within southeastern Connecticut's sprawling Pachaug State Forest—the largest tract of public land in southern New England. Well off the beaten path, the state forest generally attracts only hiking, paddling, or camping enthusiasts.

The beautiful woods surrounding Green Falls Pond—with a tall canopy of red, chestnut, and white oaks; sugar maple; yellow birch; hemlock; sassafras; and shagbark hickory—shade a fairly open, leaf-carpeted understory of mountain laurel, flowering dogwood, and a wide variety of spring wildflowers. Blueberry, mountain laurel, and other shrubs line the rocky shoreline, with plenty of places to pull out for a rest, walk in the woods, or picnic. Look for eastern purple bladderwort along the shore. A few islands dot the pond, and several trails weave through Pachaug State Forest, including Nehantic and Narragansett trails. From the pond's south end by the dam, you can walk downstream through a deep gorge, with majestic hemlock trees towering more than 100 feet overhead. Let's hope they can withstand the hemlock woolly adelgid onslaught (see Trip 45).

Pachaug State Forest permits backpacking, one of the few areas in Connecticut to do so, with special shelters and campsites available along trails for backpackers only (advance registration required).

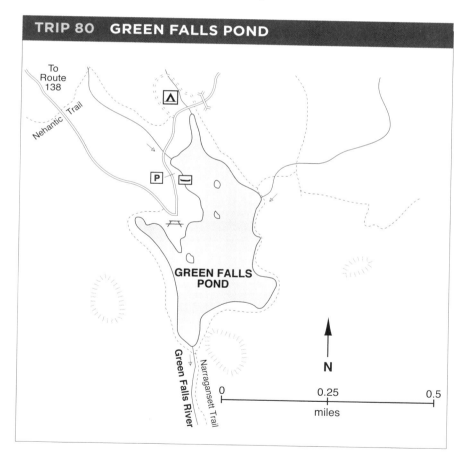

TRIP 80   GREEN FALLS POND

MYSTIC RIVER

Mystic River, though quite different from most trips in this book because of boat traffic and road noise, is still a worthwhile paddle, especially to view the historical ships at the Mystic Seaport Museum and to watch two interesting bridges in operation. Expect to see osprey; greater black-backed, ring-billed, and herring gulls; double-crested cormorant; kingfisher; and marsh wren.

LOCATION Stonington and Groton, CT

MAPS *Connecticut/Rhode Island Atlas & Gazetteer*, Map 59: B8; USGS Old Mystic, Mystic

LENGTH 6.5 miles round trip, upstream and downstream

TIME Half day or more

HABITAT TYPE Tidal river and salt marsh

FISH Striped bass, bluefish (see fish advisory, Appendix A)

CAMPING Rocky Neck State Park

INFORMATION Mystic Seaport Museum, mysticseaport.org; tide charts, usharbors.com

TAKE NOTE Many docks and marinas; substantial boat traffic, especially on weekends; best to paddle near high tide

GETTING THERE

From I-95, Exit 89, drive south on Route 614/Allyn Street, and turn left on Sandy Hollow Road. Go 0.4 mile, and turn left on Cow Hill Road. After 0.1 mile (0.5 mile), turn right on Bindloss Road. Continue 0.2 mile (0.7 mile), and bear left at the stop sign on River Road. In 0.4 mile (1.1 miles) the access is on the right, just after passing under I-95. **41° 22.433′ N, 71° 57.967′ W**

WHAT YOU'LL SEE

Mystic River, a 3.5-mile-long tidal river, offers a pleasant half day of paddling, particularly if you enjoy checking out boats of all shapes and sizes, including one of the largest collections of historical vessels in the country. The waterway gets its name from the Pequot term *missi-tuk*, or "tidal river." In the nineteenth century, the river harbored three large shipbuilding companies; it now hosts the Mystic Seaport Museum, which celebrates maritime heritage.

From the access, you can paddle left, upstream, for about 1.5 miles to a small, private bridge and, just past the bridge, Haley's Brook coming in from the left. If you make it this far given tidal conditions, turn around because you'll soon enter quickwater with a rocky bottom.

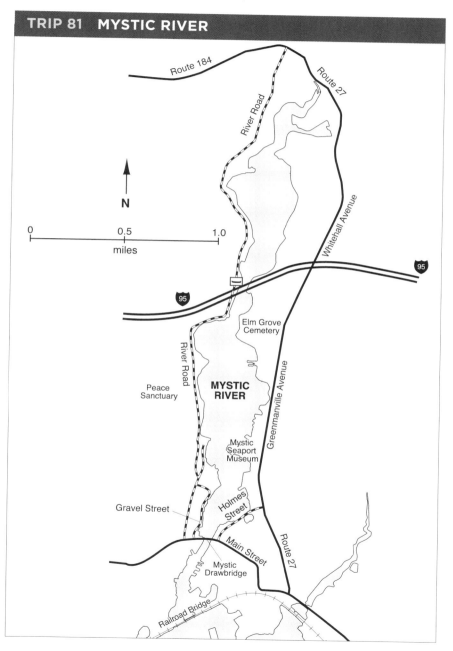

TRIP 81 MYSTIC RIVER

Route 184

Route 27

River Road

N

0   0.5   1.0
miles

Whitehall Avenue

95

95

Elm Grove
Cemetery

River Road

Greenmanville Avenue

Peace
Sanctuary

MYSTIC
RIVER

Mystic
Seaport
Museum

Gravel Street

Holmes
Street

Main Street

Route 27

Mystic
Drawbridge

Railroad Bridge

It makes sense to visit close to high tide, paddling upstream with the incoming tide and then heading downstream around high tide to explore the river's lower section. When you return to the access, a south wind often counteracts the outgoing tide, easing the paddling effort. Check tides and wind conditions and plan accordingly.

Some houses occur along the river north of I-95, interspersed with expanses of wilder salt marsh. Along with salt marsh cordgrass (*Spartina*), you'll see common reed (*Phragmites*), narrow-leaved cattail (*Typha angustifolia*), and various other sedges and grasses. Trees include white oak, red oak, Atlantic white cedar, white pine, cherry, and gray birch. A huge sycamore stands near the small bridge where you turned around.

Although this is not a premier birding location, listen for marsh wrens as you paddle along. You will see osprey here, either fishing the waters or raising young on nesting platforms. We saw a few great blue herons; a green heron; cormorants; kingfishers; solitary sandpipers along exposed shorelines; and herring, ring-billed, and greater black-backed gulls.

Paddling south from the access, just after the massive I-95 bridges, look along the eastern shore for Elm Grove Cemetery, established in the 1850s and serving as the resting place of numerous ancestors of one of this book's co-authors (Alex). In the 1890s, the removal of two huge elm trees at the cemetery entrance to make way for a granite arch sparked protests by town residents.

On the western shore, after paddling past houses along River Road, you pass the undeveloped Peace Sanctuary, with little evidence of the natural area from the water. Across from that sanctuary, as the river narrows, sits the Mystic Seaport Museum, the nation's largest maritime museum. While a quarter-million visitors enjoy the museum each year, exploring it from the water affords a less crowded view of the historical ships docked here.

Established in 1929, the Mystic Seaport Museum was one of the first living history museums in the United States, where visitors get a sense of what life was like in an earlier period of U.S. history. The museum includes more than 60 historical buildings—most relocated here from elsewhere and meticulously restored—arranged into an 1800s village.

The site features four National Historic Landmark vessels, including the world's last remaining wooden whaling ship: the *Charles W. Morgan*. The ship offers daily demonstrations of activities such as sail rigging and whale oil loading/offloading. More than 20 million visitors have walked the ship's deck since it arrived in 1941. The museum also houses the Henry B. du Pont Preservation Shipyard, which restores historical vessels. The shipyard built and launched a replica of the slave ship *La Amistad* here in 2000.

Mystic River Boathouse Park, at the museum's north edge, was under construction in 2023. It will include hand-launch facilities and should provide a

Paddlers on the Mystic River can get an up-close view of the *Charles W. Morgan*, the world's last remaining wooden whaling ship, which is on display with other historical ships at the Mystic River Seaport Museum.

convenient location for pulling your boat out of the water to explore the museum. Future parking and launching options remain unknown at this time.

Paddling south from the museum, you pass under Mystic River Bascule Bridge, where Main Street crosses the river. This drawbridge uses huge counterweights to lift the roadway to allow boats to pass. Builders often hide the counterweights, but here they made the two 200-ton concrete counterweights fully visible. During summer, the bridge typically rises at 40 minutes past the hour with boats queued upstream and downstream awaiting its opening. Paddlers can pass beneath the bridge at any time.

Farther south, a very different type of bridge—a center-pivoting, truss-style, swing bridge—carries Amtrak trains over the river. This bridge normally remains open, only closing for passing trains, and provides a convenient turnaround spot for most paddling adventures.

POWERS LAKE

Powers Lake boasts impressive tree diversity along its shores, including four oak species. Shrubs grow thickly along the water's edge, but you can get out on some protruding granite slabs. Expect to see lots of wildlife; we were fortunate to see a rare spotted turtle, along with a stinkpot turtle, painted turtles, and several northern water snakes.

LOCATION East Lyme, CT

MAPS *Connecticut/Rhode Island Atlas & Gazetteer*, Map 58: B2, B3; USGS Hamburg, Montville

AREA 144 acres

TIME 3 hours

HABITAT TYPE Wooded pond

FISH Largemouth and calico bass, yellow perch, pickerel (see fish advisory, Appendix A)

CAMPING Rocky Neck State Park, Hammonasset Beach State Park, Devil's Hopyard State Park, Hopeville Pond State Park

TAKE NOTE Limited development; motors limited to 8 MPH; no water-skiing

GETTING THERE

From I-95, Exit 74 northbound, go 0.4 mile north on Route 161, and turn left on Route 1 (Post Road). Drive 0.6 mile (1.0 mile), and turn right on Upper Pattagansett Road. In 2.7 miles (3.7 miles), turn right on Whistletown Road, and follow it for 0.6 mile (4.3 miles) before turning right on the access road. **41° 23.601' N, 72° 15.409' W**

WHAT YOU'LL SEE

Except for the state-owned boat access, Yale University owns the entire property surrounding Powers Lake (some 2,000 acres). Yale students, faculty, and associated groups use the recreation area at the lake's southwest end for retreats, picnics, and outdoor activities. The paddling is pleasant, the woodland flora varied, and the wildlife abundant. A surprising diversity of deciduous trees grows along the shoreline: four different species of oaks (red, white, scarlet, and chestnut), American chestnut, sassafras, yellow birch, red maple, tulip tree, hickory, black gum, beech, and Atlantic white cedar. Mountain laurel, blueberry, alder, and other shrubs form thick stands along the shore, making landing difficult, but some protruding granite slabs provide access to land for a picnic lunch or a break from paddling.

Two long fingers of this horseshoe-shaped lake make it seem larger than 144 acres. The longer finger frames a beautiful marshy area, though various waterlilies pretty well block access to the northernmost section by midsummer. In this part of the lake, look for tiny, delicate sundews on hummocks of grass and sphagnum moss. You should find two different species of this unusual plant—round-leaved sundew (*Drosera rotundifolia*) and spatulate-leaved sundew (*D. intermedia*)—that gains sustenance from insects caught by sticky hairs on its leaves. Also look for the four species of carnivorous bladderwort that inhabit the pond.

Most exciting to us, however, was the reptile life around the lake. We saw numerous northern water snakes, lots of painted turtles, a stinkpot turtle, and a quite rare spotted turtle (*Clemmys guttata*).

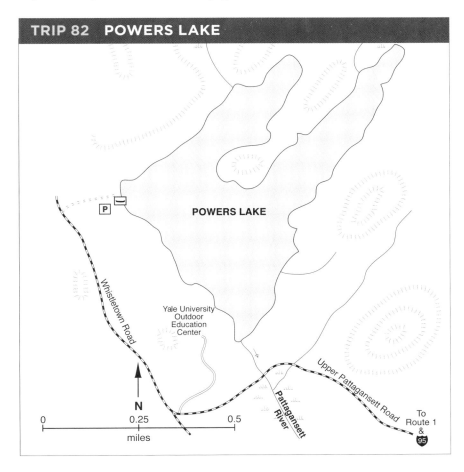

TRIP 82　POWERS LAKE

POWERS LAKE

Yale University
Outdoor
Education
Center

Whistletown Road

Upper Pattagansett Road

Pattagansett River

To
Route 1
&
95

N

0　　　　0.25　　　　0.5

miles

While close to major population centers, Powers Lake remains undeveloped. Vegetation covers the surface of the northeastern end.

TRIP 83

UNCAS POND

Nehantic State Forest borders one side of Uncas Pond and offers an extensive network of hiking trails. A very diverse forest surrounds the clear water of the pond. With no motors allowed, the location is usually pretty quiet.

LOCATION Lyme, CT

MAPS *Connecticut/Rhode Island Atlas & Gazetteer*, Map 58: B1; USGS Hamburg, Old Lyme

AREA 69 acres

TIME 2 hours

HABITAT TYPE Small, elongated wooded pond

FISH Trout, largemouth bass, yellow perch, pickerel (see fish advisory, Appendix A)

CAMPING Rocky Neck State Park, Hammonasset Beach State Park, Devil's Hopyard State Park, Hopeville Pond State Park

INFORMATION Nehantic State Forest, portal.ct.gov/DEEP/State-Parks /Forests/Nehantic-State-Forest; aquatic plant survey, portal.ct.gov/CAES /OAIS/U/Uncas-Lake/Uncas-Lake-2019

TAKE NOTE Limited development; no motors

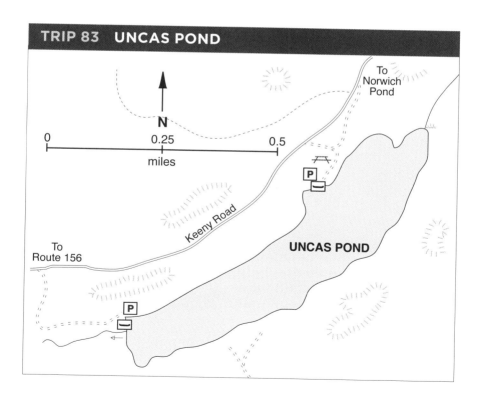

TRIP 83   UNCAS POND

GETTING THERE

From I-95, Exit 70, go 3.7 miles north on Route 156, and turn right on Keeny Road at the access sign for Nehantic State Forest. In 1.2 miles (4.9 miles), stay right at the fork (left goes to the picnic area), and continue 0.3 mile (5.2 miles) to the access. An alternate access is at the picnic area. **41° 22.371' N, 72° 19.334' W**

WHAT YOU'LL SEE

Uncas Pond in Nehantic State Forest offers a wonderful paddling experience. Though the pond is small, with some development on the southwest shore, the forested hillsides, clear water, and absence of motors beckon paddlers. The pond bears the name of Chief Uncas of the Pequot Nation. Uncas, which means "fox," evokes different images, depending upon your viewpoint. James Fenimore Cooper's *The Last of the Mohicans* transplanted this chief into the forests of upper New York. To his rivals—the Niantic and Narragansett—and even to his adopted Pequot, his name conjured up a circling forager who would strike when opportunity came, and indeed he did. The son of Mohegan Chief Owenoco, Uncas joined the more powerful Pequot after marrying a daughter of their chief, Sassacus, but rebelled several times against his father-in-law's rule. Banished to the Narragansett, he later subdued them. Uncas sided with English settlers in each fight, including in their successful war against King Philip's coalition in 1675. A monument to Uncas in nearby Norwich honors this alliance.

Uncas Pond nestles into the hills of Niantic State Forest and offers a very pleasant morning or afternoon of paddling—without motors.

Uncas Pond's environs sport a tremendous diversity of trees and shrubs, almost all deciduous, including white, red, and scarlet oaks; black gum; red and sugar maples; beech; gray and yellow birches; sassafras; tulip tree; American chestnut (sprouts from blight-killed trees); a few hemlock; alder; mountain laurel; and swamp azalea. Around most of the pond, the land rises steeply from the water's edge. Laurel, in particular, grows densely along the shore. In some areas you can't even see the actual shoreline, much less get out and walk along the bank. A narrow band of aquatic vegetation—pickerelweed, American white waterlily, watershield, pondweed, and yellow pondlily—protects the shoreline. At the northeast end, floating vegetation grows thicker in a small marshy area. We also found pipewort (*Eriocaulon aquaticum*), with its buttonlike flower heads, poking out of the shallow water. Look for freshwater mussels along the sandy bottom.

Nehantic State Forest offers an extensive trail network and a convenient picnic spot near the pond's north end. From the access, a trail extends along the north side of the pond through a beautiful area of huge boulders, thick carpets of ferns, giant mountain laurel, and feathery flowering dogwoods.

TRIP 84

BABCOCK POND

Babcock Pond lies wholly within the 1,500-acre Babcock Pond Wildlife Management Area. The best paddling is in spring because mats of aquatic vegetation take over the surface in summer. Look for wood duck and other waterfowl and muskrat.

LOCATION Colchester, CT

MAPS *Connecticut/Rhode Island Atlas & Gazetteer*, Map 45: C7, C8; USGS Moodus

AREA 147 acres

TIME 3 hours

HABITAT TYPE Shallow, marshy pond

FISH Largemouth bass, yellow perch, pickerel (see fish advisory, Appendix A)

CAMPING Devil's Hopyard State Park

TAKE NOTE No development; cartop access and shallow, weedy pond limits motors; 8 MPH speed limit

GETTING THERE

From Route 2, Exit 16, go 3.3 miles south on Route 149, and turn left on Route 16. Go 1.0 mile (4.3 miles) to the access on the right. **41° 22.371′ N, 72° 19.334′ W**

From Route 2, Exit 18, go 3.3 miles west on Route 16 to the access on the left.

WHAT YOU'LL SEE

Babcock Pond, although small, offers superb marshland paddling. This shallow pond within the 1,500-acre Babcock Pond Wildlife Management Area sports huge, unbroken rafts of American white waterlily, along with other abundant aquatic vegetation, including pickerelweed, watershield, yellow pondlily, and at least two species of bladderwort: yellow-flowered and purple-flowered. Because of this bounteous vegetation, paddling here can present a challenge, especially late in the season, and works best with the goal of a leisurely visit to study the plants.

If other paddlers have not beaten you to the water, expect to see wood duck, a few other waterfowl, and the occasional muskrat. The undeveloped wooded shoreline consists primarily of deciduous trees, with red maple seeming to be most abundant, along with a shrubby understory.

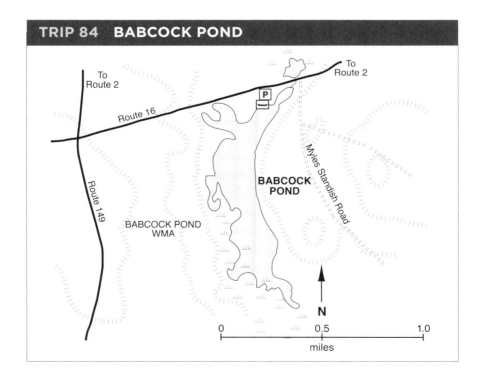

TRIP 84   BABCOCK POND

A muskrat, unconcerned about our preseence, munches on vegetation.

If you paddle under Route 16 onto the small pond north of the road on sunny days, expect to see lots of painted turtles basking in a pond literally ringed with swamp loosestrife. We spent quite some time trying to photograph pollinators on the loosestrife's purple axillary flowers.

TRIP 85

MOODUS RESERVOIR

Moodus is a popular reservoir with a fair amount of development and high-speed boating. The best paddling is in early spring and in fall. For more solitude in summer, head to the deep southeast cove with its dense patches of watershield. Expect to see wood duck, other waterfowl, and green and great blue herons.

LOCATION East Haddam, CT

MAPS *Connecticut/Rhode Island Atlas & Gazetteer*, Map 45: C7, C8; USGS Deep River, Moodus

AREA 486 acres

TIME 5 hours

HABITAT TYPE Shallow, marshy pond with deep coves

FISH Largemouth and calico bass, yellow perch, pickerel (see fish advisory, Appendix A)

INFORMATION Aquatic survey, portal.ct.gov/CAES/OAIS/M/Moodus
-Reservoir-Upper/Upper-Moodus-Reservoir-2016

CAMPING Devil's Hopyard State Park

TAKE NOTE Highly developed on the western half; motors allowed,
35 mph speed limit

GETTING THERE

Launching Area Road Access From Route 9, Exit 7, go 4.9 miles east on Route 82, and turn left on Route 151. Drive 1.2 miles (6.1 miles), and turn right on East Haddam–Colchester Turnpike. Follow it for 2.6 miles (8.7 miles), and turn right on Launching Area Road. Go 0.2 mile (8.9 miles) to the access. **41° 30.248′ N, 72° 24.528′ W**

From Route 2, Exit 18, go 4.3 miles west on Route 16, and turn left on Route 149. Drive 1.7 miles (6.0 miles), and go straight on Eli Chapman Road as Route 149 veers right. Continue 0.4 mile (6.4 miles), and turn left on Mott

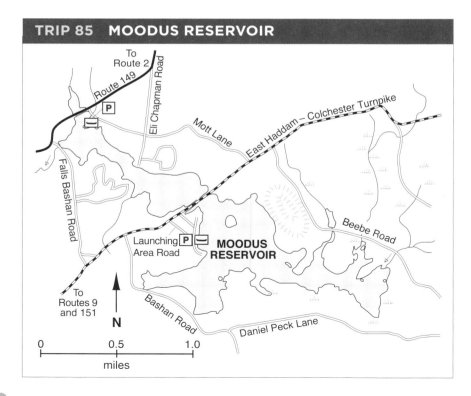

TRIP 85 **MOODUS RESERVOIR**

Lane. In 0.8 mile (7.2 miles), turn right on East Haddam–Colchester Turnpike, and follow it 0.6 mile (7.8 miles), then turn left on Launching Area Road. Go 0.2 mile (8.0 miles) to the access.

From Route 2, Exit 16, go 3.3 miles south on Route 149 to the junction with Route 16, and continue as above.

WHAT YOU'LL SEE

Moodus comes from the Pequot word *machimoodus*, meaning "land of bad noises." The area's loud booms have mystified residents for hundreds or even thousands of years. A deep fault line may cause these noises, which a resident says sound like sonic booms and which generally cannot be felt—only heard. Geologists attribute them to "micro earthquakes." These tremors should have no impact on your paddling (although neither the authors nor AMC can 100 percent guarantee that a huge chasm won't suddenly open up—emptying the reservoir and swallowing you and your boat . . .).

The reservoir provides excellent paddling, particularly on a calm spring day when the shorelines come alive with nesting songbirds and spectacular wood ducks try to hide in the marshy coves. You could easily spend a day on this shallow water, exploring the many long, sinewy coves and watching for painted turtles amid the floating pond vegetation. We recommend that you paddle early or late in the day and avoid busy summer weekends; we paddled here early on a Sunday in July and found plenty of solitude. As boating popularity grows, the best paddling would be in fall and early spring.

Tree swallows nest in standing dead trees on the shallow, marshy east end of Moodus Reservoir.

Don't bother investigating the reservoir's smaller section, northwest of the East Haddam–Colchester Turnpike causeway; detractions include a much more developed shoreline, more water-skiers, and bigger boats than southeast of the causeway. The development that does occur on the larger, southeastern section clusters near the access.

In the marshy coves, keep an eye out for wood ducks, green herons, great blue herons, and painted turtles. You may also see hundreds of tree swallows, which inhabit the standing dead trees in the eastern end of the reservoir and feed on flying insects above the water's surface. In the 30 years since this book's first edition, most of those trees have fallen, leaving fewer nesting cavities for swallows. Typical trees surround the reservoir: red, scarlet, and white oaks; sassafras; yellow and gray birches; red maple; beech; and a few white pine. Along the shores, look for mountain laurel, highbush blueberry, and large patches of swamp azalea, with long, sticky white flowers that bloom in late June.

When we paddled here in July, huge rafts of watershield, with its relatively inconspicuous red flower and gelatinous underwater sheath, filled the deeper coves, particularly in the southeast, covering the surface so densely that we could see no water. In more open areas, the small, white Carolina fanwort flowers and a yellow-flowered bladderwort put on a lovely display.

TRIP 86

SALMON RIVER

This is a prime spot for bird-watchers, with high numbers of birds and high species diversity. Watch osprey dive for fish in the clear water, and look for songbirds in the tall trees on the shore and hillsides. Explore marshy coves harboring wild rice.

LOCATION East Haddam and Haddam, CT

MAPS *Connecticut/Rhode Island Atlas & Gazetteer*, Map 45: C6, D6; USGS Deep River, Moodus

LENGTH 4 miles one way

TIME 4 hours round trip

HABITAT TYPE Shallow, marshy, tidal Connecticut River estuary

FISH Trout (see fish advisory, Appendix A)

CAMPING Devil's Hopyard State Park

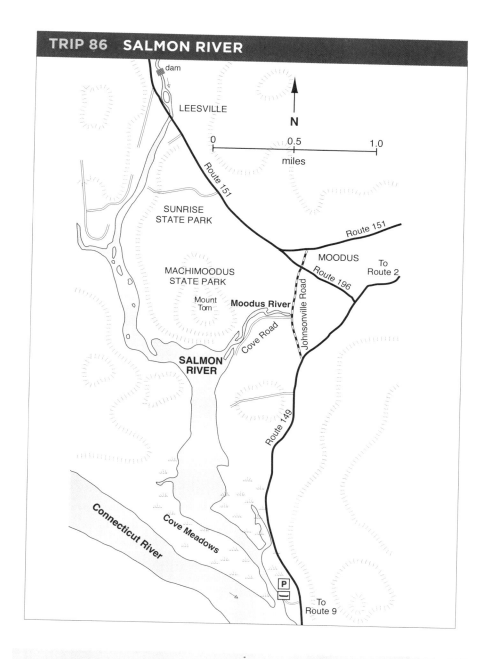

INFORMATION Machimoodus State Park, portal.ct.gov/DEEP /State-Parks/Parks/Machimoodus-State-Park; Goodspeed Opera House, goodspeed.org

TAKE NOTE Some development upstream; motors in lower stretches

GETTING THERE

From Route 9, Exit 7, drive 3.5 miles east on Route 82, and turn left on Route 149. Go 1.0 mile (4.5 miles) to the marked access on the left. Along the way, you will pass the Goodspeed Opera House. **41° 28.03′ N, 72° 28.083′ W**

From Route 2, Exit 18, head 4.3 miles west on Route 16, and turn left on Route 149. Go 7.2 miles (11.5 miles) to the access on the right.

From Route 2, Exit 16, go 10.5 miles south on Route 149 to the access on the right.

WHAT YOU'LL SEE

The Salmon River, popular with canoers and kayakers (we encountered several dozen on a Sunday in July), provides outstanding bird-watching opportunities. A red-tailed hawk soared far overhead as we watched a pair of ospreys hover above the clear water, looking for a meal. Later, we saw an osprey feed on a silvery fish. We paddled through an unconcerned pod of 46 mute swans—an invasive species that competes with native birds—and listened to the songs of many streamside and woodland bird species: red-winged blackbird, grackle, common yellowthroat, yellow warbler, white-throated sparrow, goldfinch, ovenbird, tufted titmouse, robin, catbird, veery, phoebe, great crested flycatcher, brown thrasher, kingfisher, and tree and barn swallows.

Machimoodus State Park, crisscrossed with hiking trails, and Sunrise State Park (under development) protect the river's west side. The marshy lower section near the access, including the cove immediately on the right, has a much different feel from that of the wooded sections upstream near Leesville Dam and its fish ladder. Look for gorgeous patches of swamp rose, particularly in the cove on the right, which also sports vigorous patches of wild rice. Upstream, some lovely stands of hemlock grace the hillsides; mountain laurel and other shrubs fill the shoreline in places, backed up by hillsides clad in a rich diversity of woodland tree species. Although some development occurs upstream, including a small resort that was converted into Sunrise State Park, the shallow water limits motorboat access. We found it well worth the paddle up to Leesville Dam.

If you arrive here from Route 9, you will pass the historical Goodspeed Opera House, built in 1876, which hosted national premieres of musicals such as *Annie* and *Man of La Mancha*. It continues to put on renowned musical theater.

WHALEBONE CREEK AND SELDEN CREEK

Whalebone Creek provides an opportunity for paddlers to enjoy an extensive, pristine freshwater marsh filled with birds and wild rice. Selden Creek offers excellent paddling and also camping on a gorgeous Connecticut River island. Across from the island, more marshlands invite exploration. Novice paddlers should avoid this area.

LOCATION Lyme, CT

MAPS *Connecticut/Rhode Island Atlas & Gazetteer*, Map 57: A7, A8, B7, B8; USGS Deep River

LENGTH Whalebone Creek, 1 mile one way; Selden Creek, 2.7 miles one way

TIME All day

HABITAT TYPE Connecticut River estuaries, marshlands, protected coves

FISH Largemouth, smallmouth, and calico bass; yellow and white perch; walleye; northern pike (see fish advisory, Appendix A)

CAMPING Rocky Neck State Park, Hammonasset Beach State Park, primitive camping on Selden Neck

INFORMATION Selden Neck State Park, portal.ct.gov/DEEP/State-Parks /Parks/Selden-Neck-State-Park; The Nature Conservancy, nature.org; tide charts, usharbors.com

TAKE NOTE No development; motors allowed, 6 MPH speed limit on Selden Creek; use extreme caution off Selden Neck cliffs—novice paddlers should avoid this area; wear your PFD

GETTING THERE

From Route 9, Exit 6, go 2.7 miles east on Route 148, cross the Connecticut River on the Chester–Hadlyme Ferry, and park immediately on the left. If the ferry is not operating, drive north on Route 154, cross the Connecticut on Route 82, go south to Route 148, and turn right to the parking area and access at the ferry. **41° 25.231′ N, 72° 25.702′ W**

From I-95, Exit 70, go 8.4 miles north on Route 156, and turn left on Route 82. Drive 3.2 miles (11.6 miles) to the junction with Route 148. Go straight onto Route 148, and go 1.6 miles (13.2 miles) to the access at the ferry.

WHAT YOU'LL SEE
WHALEBONE CREEK

Just downriver from the access, the inlet to Whalebone Creek provides entry to one of the most pristine tidal freshwater marshes in Connecticut. The Nature Conservancy protects a portion of this important wetland.

How can it be tidal and freshwater at the same time? The incoming tidal rush raises Connecticut River water levels as far north as Hartford, but strong river currents keep salt water from coming much more than about 10 miles upstream. Just south of Whalebone Creek, freshwater and salt water mix to create brackish water conditions; not until Great Island do salt marsh ecosystems dominate.

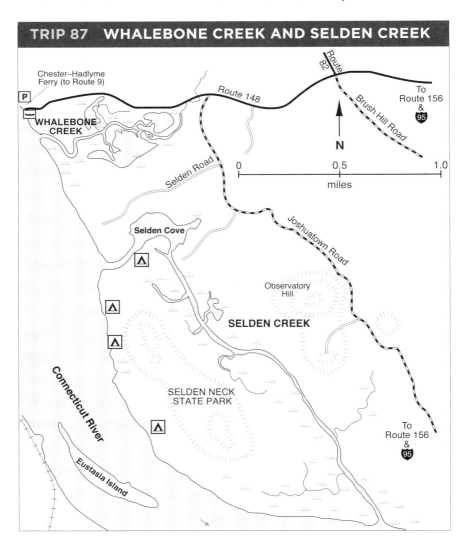

TRIP 87   WHALEBONE CREEK AND SELDEN CREEK

Two signal lights guard the entrance to Whalebone Creek. Entering, you pass a tall granite cliff on the left, festooned with wild grape and other vines— a preferred habitat for the hard-to-see white-eyed vireo. In the early morning light, we watched a raccoon scurry up the rock face, peering down with obvious annoyance. Heavily wooded hillsides occur on the left, but marsh dominates the right, dotted here and there with trees and shrubs adapted to the ever-changing water level.

Farther in, wild rice (*Zizania aquatica*), which reaches 10 feet or more in height, rules the marsh. Its round, jointed, hollow stems grow up to an inch in diameter at the base. The leaves, up to 4 feet long and as much as 2 inches wide, emanate from the stalk, whose top bears flowers and seeds in a form called panicles. Paddling here in late summer, you get a feel for how Ojibwe in Minnesota harvest grain from a closely related species (*Z. palustris*). Carefully bend one of the tall stems down and shake it to release the sheathed seeds. In the thick wild rice marshes of Minnesota, American Indians literally fill their canoes as they harvest the grain.

Along with wild rice, look for bulrush, buttonbush, cattail, pickerelweed, blue iris, and a host of other marsh plants. Birdlife abounds. Even in early autumn, the place seemed alive with red-winged blackbirds, marsh wrens, swallows, kingfishers, black ducks, wood ducks, great blue herons, Canada geese, and mute swans. At high tide—the preferred time to paddle here—you can explore quite far into Whalebone Creek, with winding channels and pools of open water.

SELDEN CREEK

About 0.75 mile south of the access, Selden Creek extends left around a tall, 607-acre hilly island, Selden Neck State Park. It returns to the Connecticut River nearly 3 miles south, forming one of southern New England's true paddling and camping gems. The Nature Conservancy protects the creek's opposite shore, containing wonderful marshlands. A 6 MPH speed limit on Selden Creek keeps down motorboat traffic, but we recommend avoiding busy summer weekends.

Paddling in one of the small side creeks accessible at high tide, we watched schools of small, silvery alewives (or herring) skip along the water's surface, using their strong tails in an apparently defensive response to our disturbance. In some cases, a fish overthrust and flopped back and forth, getting nowhere, but most seemed to dart a foot or two at a time.

When you get to the southern access onto the Connecticut River, we strongly recommend that you turn around and paddle back up Selden Creek. Wakes reflecting off the outer Selden Neck cliffs cause huge waves that can swamp an open boat. As you paddle downriver from the ferry, and any other time you paddle the river, we strongly recommend wearing your PFD. Novice paddlers should avoid this area.

Snowy egrets are a common sight on the lower Connecticut River. We watched this one fish for several minutes before it took flight.

The state permits primitive camping on Selden Neck. Of the four campsites, you reach one from Selden Creek, the others from the Connecticut River. Our favorite remains Quarry Knob—the farthest south—where you camp on a knoll overlooking the river and have easy access to the 226-foot rocky peak of Selden Neck. You may stay for one night after registering and paying a fee. Book your site early.

While in the area, consider a side trip to Gillette Castle, a fascinating stone mansion built between 1914 and 1919 by the eccentric stage actor William Gillette, who became famous for his portrayal of Sherlock Holmes. The state purchased the property in 1943 to create Gillette Castle State Park.

TRIP 88

LORD COVE

Lord Cove offers one of the best places to watch osprey dive for fish. We've seen osprey here every summer trip. The cove also hosts numerous herons and egrets, along with many shorebirds on the mud flats during spring and fall migrations. Try to avoid getting lost in the maze of waterways.

LOCATION Lyme and Old Lyme, CT

MAPS *Connecticut/Rhode Island Atlas & Gazetteer*, Map 57: B8, C8, Map 58: G1, H1; USGS Old Lyme

AREA 351 acres, 5-mile maze of waterways

TIME 5 hours

HABITAT TYPE Connecticut River estuary, brackish marshland, many islands and protected coves

FISH Striped bass (see fish advisory, Appendix A)

CAMPING Rocky Neck State Park, Hammonasset Beach State Park

INFORMATION The Nature Conservancy, nature.org; tide charts, usharbors.com

TAKE NOTE Little development; shallow water limits motors

GETTING THERE

From I-95, Exit 70, go 0.7 mile north on Route 156 to the access on Pilgrim Landing Road on the left, a few feet in. Parking is available for about six vehicles. If the lot is full, leave someone with the boats at the landing, park at the Exit 70 commuter lot, and hike back to the access. **41° 19.782' N, 72° 20.428' W**

Osprey are common in Lord Cove. We watched one dive and catch a large, silvery fish.

WHAT YOU'LL SEE

Lord Cove offers splendid paddling through a 5-mile maze of waterways, particularly during shorebird and waterfowl migrations. The Nature Conservancy, Old Lyme Land Trust, and the Connecticut Department of Energy and Environmental Protection preserve the cove from development and have instituted a program to remove invasive phragmites and to protect ten threatened or endangered native plant species.

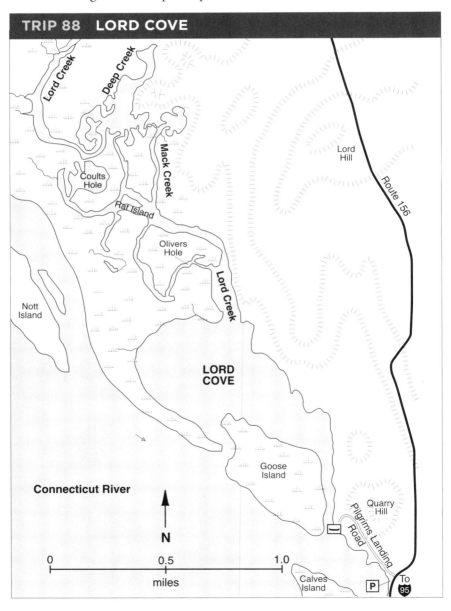

TRIP 88 LORD COVE

Lord Creek

Deep Creek

Lord Hill

Mack Creek

Coults Hole

Route 156

Rat Island

Olivers Hole

Lord Creek

Nott Island

LORD COVE

Connecticut River

Goose Island

Quarry Hill

N

Pilgrims Landing Road

0   0.5   1.0

miles

Calves Island

P

To 95

Brackish marshes dotted with low, grassy islands take at least half a day to explore fully. Though you won't see as many shorebirds, we recommend paddling here around high tide to avoid exposed mud flats. To access more northern reaches, you have to paddle over a large, shallow expanse of open water. When winds from the south whip up whitecaps, paddle nearby Powers Lake (Trip 82) or Uncas Pond (Trip 83).

We saw ducks and laughing gulls, along with many snowy egrets. Look for marsh wren nests in—and muskrats harvesting—narrow-leaved cattails. You can paddle way back into the marsh, twisting and turning among the many islands. We sat still and observed an osprey hover over the marsh, eventually diving talons-first on a fish, submerging completely beneath the surface. Popping up, it beat its wings furiously, first against the water, then against the sky, straining to gain altitude with a heavy-bodied, silvery fish, fully as long as the osprey, clutched in its talons. We watched the two sail out of sight, gulls in hot pursuit, hoping to make the osprey drop its prized possession.

TRIP 89

GREAT ISLAND ESTUARY AND ROGER TORY PETERSON WILDLIFE AREA

Great Island Estuary offers an extraordinary paddling opportunity, and that's reflected in the large kayak groups that converge here on weekends. Escape the crowds by paddling into the estuary's side channels. Birdlife abounds, which is why Roger Tory Peterson, the famed naturalist, chose to live in Old Lyme for a while. The wildlife area now bears his name.

LOCATION Old Lyme, CT

MAPS *Connecticut/Rhode Island Atlas & Gazetteer*, Map 58: C1, D1; USGS Old Lyme

AREA/LENGTH Wildlife area, 588 acres; Lieutenant River, 3.5 miles one way; Blackhall River, 3.0 miles one way

TIME: All day; shorter trips possible

HABITAT TYPE Shallow saltwater estuary; grassy marshlands, many islands and protected bays

FISH Striped bass, bluefish (see fish advisory, Appendix A)

CAMPING Rocky Neck State Park, Hammonasset Beach State Park

INFORMATION Tide charts, usharbors.com

TAKE NOTE Little development; no motors allowed in wildlife area

GETTING THERE

Lieutenant River From I-95 northbound, Exit 70, go 0.4 mile south on Route 156 to the access on the right, just before the bridge. From I-95 southbound, Exit 70, go 0.7 mile west on Route 1, and turn left on Route 156 south. Go 0.5 mile (1.2 miles) to the access on the right. **41° 18.851' N, 72° 20.238' W**

Smith Neck Go 1.4 miles south on Route 156 from the Lieutenant River access, and turn right on Smith Neck Road. In 0.8 mile (2.2 miles) the access is at road's end. **41° 17.243' N, 72° 19.438' W**

WHAT YOU'LL SEE

This shallow saltwater estuary draws large groups of sea kayakers on summer weekends. Paddling here on a Sunday in late August, we saw more kayaks than we have seen anywhere else in the Northeast. You can get away from the crowds, however, by paddling into the twisting channels of Roger Tory Peterson Wildlife Area. Note that the Griswold Point sandspit washed away in a storm and no longer offers a protected place to paddle. Threatened piping plovers and least terns still nest on sand dunes.

On one trip, with fall shorebird migration in full swing, we saw hundreds of sandpipers and plovers, including least and semipalmated sandpipers, black-bellied and semipalmated plovers, and greater and lesser yellowlegs. Soras (a type of rail), as well as saltmarsh sharp-tailed and seaside sparrows, skulked in the dense stands of cordgrass and phragmites. We also noted a large number of mute swans.

Scientists discovered osprey eggshell thinning caused by DDT here in the 1960s, which resulted in a lawsuit that ultimately led to the banning of DDT. Having exhibited a remarkable recovery, twenty or more osprey pairs now nest in the refuge, and we watched them hover and dive for fish.

The Blackhall, a beautiful, marshy river, provides wonderful paddling. Red, scarlet, and white oaks line the banks, along with sassafras, black gum, cedar, blueberry, and the occasional mountain laurel. Phragmites, which gives way to narrow-leaved cattails upstream, creeps out from the shore. Look for marsh wren nests in the cattails. We saw green herons, snowy and great egrets, osprey, and cormorants here.

Up on the Lieutenant River, we watched barn swallows snatch insects on the wing while we listened to numerous catbirds and cardinals call from the

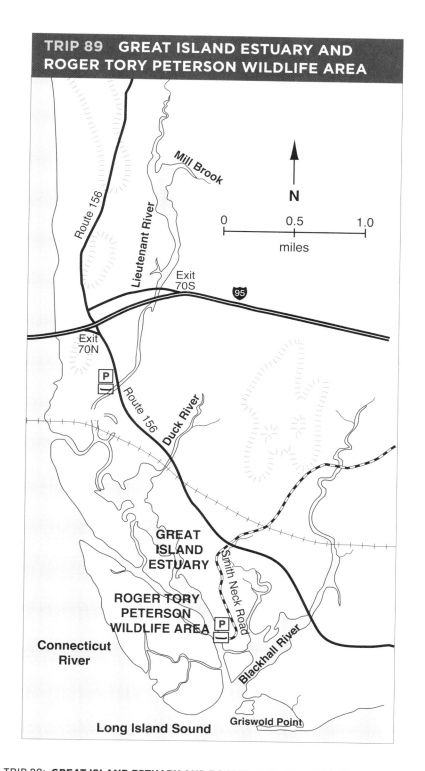

TRIP 89 GREAT ISLAND ESTUARY AND ROGER TORY PETERSON WILDLIFE AREA

Mill Brook

Route 156

Lieutenant River

Exit 70S

95

N

0   0.5   1.0
miles

Exit 70N

P

Route 156

Duck River

GREAT
ISLAND
ESTUARY

Smith Neck Road

ROGER TORY
PETERSON
WILDLIFE AREA

P

Connecticut
River

Blackhall River

Griswold Point

Long Island Sound

dense shoreline vegetation. Kingfishers darted before us up the river, while flocks of ducks took wing or fled into high grass. A fish ladder installed on a tributary, Mill Brook, provides spawning access for alewives to a series of small ponds and, someday, with another ladder, to Rogers Lake.

SALT MARSH: WHERE RIVER AND SEA MEET

The salt marsh ecosystem enjoys tremendous biological productivity, yet stresses its inhabitants—plants especially—so severely with constant change that few species can survive. Incoming tides flood the marsh, saturating the peaty soil. As tides recede, the exposed surface may actually dry out on a hot, breezy day, but changing salinity, even more than fluctuating water level, determines what can survive.

As sea water surges into the marsh, salinity increases, reaching a peak at high tide. As the tide drops, so does the salinity, reaching a minimum at low tide when incoming freshwater from inlet streams dilutes the sea water. Salinity conditions often vary markedly in different portions of a salt marsh—from nearly pure freshwater at one end to salinity nearly matching that of the ocean at the other. The volume of freshwater flowing into the marsh, the tidal differential along that section of coastline, and the size and configuration of the connection to the sea each control salinity.

Such salinity conditions allow just two species of grass—*Spartina alterniflora* (smooth cordgrass) and *S. patens* (salt-meadow cordgrass)—to dominate this ecosystem. In the largest salt marshes, the *Spartinas* compose a rare natural monoculture as far as the eye can see. The instability inherent in monocultures has apparently not affected the *Spartina* marshes, which have exhibited little evidence of disease or significant die-off over many thousands of years.

Spartina alterniflora occupies the lower ground, where twice-daily flooding inundates it with salt water. In ideal conditions, *S. alterniflora* reaches 10 feet in height, though more commonly it reaches less than half that. *S. patens*, which grows to 2 feet, dominates the high marsh—the firmer land flooded only irregularly, at spring tides and during storms. Generations of coastal New England farmers harvested this species as feed for their livestock (an acre of salt marsh produces twice as much hay as the best dry-land hayfields). You can recognize *S. patens* by the broad "cowlicks" that form on the marsh as swaths of the grass get matted down. A lower, flexible stem section defends against wave forces and strong current.

Glasswort (*Salicornia depressa*), a succulent species able to withstand salt marsh rigors, grows upright with swollen, jointed stems. Its name may derive from its onetime use in making glass (the ash is very high in sodium carbonate, an ingredient in older glassmaking processes). Amid the *S. patens* you may also see the delicate flowers of Carolina sea lavender (*Limonium carolinianum*), a plant long collected for dried-flower arrangements. Pressure from collectors has reduced Carolina sea lavender abundance considerably; please enjoy it from your boat. Look for other specialists here—seaside goldenrod with thick, fleshy leaves, sea aster, sea plantain, and sea purslane among them.

Complex mechanisms allow plants to adapt to high and constantly changing salinity levels. Organisms maintain a fairly precise balance of fluid and dissolved substances in their cells. When concentrations of dissolved compounds vary across cell membranes, water tends to flow from the less concentrated to the more concentrated to equalize the "osmotic gradient." Water in plant cells that is more dilute than sea water—the case with

most plants—flows out through the cell membrane, drying and killing the plant cells. This drying is why most plants cannot survive in the salt marsh. *Spartina* can survive through a complex series of evolutionary adaptations, of which the book *Life and Death of the Salt Marsh* (see Appendix B) contains an excellent discussion.

In the less saline areas, you may see wild rice and other less salt-tolerant species. On tidal rivers, sea water can only penetrate upriver a short distance before freshwater dilutes it to such an extent that freshwater plants and animals can survive. Paddling up these rivers, you can watch the progression of species—and species diversity. On a large-volume river such as the Connecticut, salt water cannot penetrate far upstream. The tidal rush, however, slows the river's flow and raises the water level for many miles upstream without increasing its salinity.

Most animals, unlike plants, can move to counter changing water levels. Many mollusks and invertebrates either bury themselves deep in the muck or swim in the current, like the fish that live or spawn here. Mussels and barnacles attach tightly to rocks, pilings, or other solid objects and so do not shift about. To survive the twice-daily drying at low tide, these mollusks close up tightly. Some salt marsh fish can regulate their osmotic balance with changing salinity. Some lower invertebrates actually bloat up in lower-salinity water and then shrink as salinity increases.

The fiddler crab (named for its large claw-size difference) has several adaptations to salt marsh life. Like all crabs, it has gills, but it also has a primitive lung, enabling it to breathe air as long as it keeps the lung moist. It also can survive without oxygen for long periods when it tunnels down into oxygen-deficient mud. In addition, the fiddler crab maintains constant osmotic equilibrium in diluted sea water and in water more concentrated than sea water, as found in briny tidal ponds where water has evaporated.

The rich salt marsh birdlife needs to adapt less to the environment. At low tide, dozens of wading birds feed on insect larvae and crustaceans in exposed mud flats. Clapper rails and marsh wrens nest amid the *Spartina*. Harriers weave back and forth low over the marsh in search of mice, and ospreys scan the deeper water for fish. Snowy and great egrets and green and great blue herons patrol the marsh for small fish and other prey. During spring and fall migrations, many waterfowl species make stopovers in salt marshes before winging southward. Early morning paddlers may see raccoons and an occasional river otter.

Insects also play an important role in the salt marsh, and efforts to control them—chiefly mosquitoes—have caused some of the most significant human impact on this ecosystem. In the 1930s, the Civilian Conservation Corps drained vast areas of salt marsh. Evidence of this only modestly successful effort to eliminate standing water can still be seen clearly today. After 50 years, you can still paddle a short way into some of these long, straight, mosquito-control ditches at high tide.

Many commercially important fish and shellfish species depend on the salt marsh ecosystem. A full two-thirds of the eastern U.S. commercial fish and shellfish catch—including oysters, scallops, clams, blue crabs, shrimp, bluefish, flounder, and striped bass—depend on the salt marsh for at least some phase of their life cycle.

Sustaining nutrients, borne on incoming rivers and streams, support this productivity. Inflowing freshwater spreads out and deposits its sediment, rich with minerals and nutrients. Unfortunately, this same water carries pollutants as well. All too often we see signs warning of polluted water off-limits to shellfishing. But the salt marsh also plays a vitally important role in breaking down many of these pollutants. Like a giant sewage treatment plant, it purifies water and extracts toxins, making the organisms toxic in the process. The long-lasting pesticide DDT, used from the late 1940s until the early 1970s, concentrated in salt marsh organisms from crustaceans and fish up the food chain to ospreys, bald eagles, and other predators. By the time of DDT's banning, the osprey and bald eagle had almost vanished from New England's salt marshes.

Hundreds of thousands of acres of coastal salt marsh, though vitally important to us economically and biologically, have been lost to development during the past hundred years. The relatively small remnants of these once vast stretches are still threatened by development and pollution. Feeling the tidal current under a boat while watching *Spartina* wave in the breeze and an osprey fish overhead helps us appreciate the importance of these resources.

Those of us who value the salt marsh's unique beauty and who understand this ecosystem's fragile nature must guarantee that additional salt marsh acreage will not be lost to development and pollution. Learn about the salt marsh environments in your area, and talk to local planning officials to find out how you can help protect these special places.

TRIP 90

PATTACONK RESERVOIR

Undeveloped Pattaconk Reservoir sits amid Connecticut's second-largest state forest and does not allow motors. Although a great place to paddle surrounded by gorgeous hillsides, it also draws large crowds for hiking, biking, swimming, and paddling, particularly on weekends.

LOCATION Chester, CT

MAPS *Connecticut/Rhode Island Atlas & Gazetteer*, Map 57: A5; USGS Haddam

AREA 56 acres

TIME 2 hours

HABITAT TYPE Shallow, marshy pond

FISH Brown trout, largemouth bass, pickerel (see fish advisory, Appendix A)

CAMPING Rocky Neck State Park, Hammonasset Beach State Park

INFORMATION Cockaponset State Forest, portal.ct.gov/DEEP/State -Parks/Forests/Cockaponset-State-Forest

TAKE NOTE No development; no motors

GETTING THERE

From Route 9, Exit 6, drive 1.5 miles west on Route 148, and turn right on Cedar Lake Road. Go 1.6 miles (3.1 miles), and turn left into Pattaconk Lake State Recreation Area. Continue for 0.3 mile (3.4 miles) to the large parking area. Carry your boat about 75 yards down to the water. **41° 24.534′ N, 72° 31.525′ W**

WHAT YOU'LL SEE

Pattaconk Reservoir in south-central Connecticut is hidden away in Cockaponset State Forest, the state's second-largest state forest. A small but stunning undeveloped body of water in an area known more for tidal river paddling, Pattaconk offers a refreshing alternative with a real mountain pond feel. If you visit in summer, you will see dozens of people paddling, swimming, hiking, and off-road bicycling. If you prefer more solitude, paddle similar, but larger, nearby Messerschmidt Pond (Trip 91).

Deciduous trees dominate the surrounding woods, including four different oak species (red, white, chestnut, and scarlet), three birch species (gray, black, and yellow), red maple, sassafras, beech, shagbark hickory, black gum, American chestnut, and tulip tree. Mountain laurel, highbush blueberry, and sweet pepperbush grow densely along the shore, overhanging the water in many places, making the shoreline mostly inaccessible. Where you can get onto the shore, the open woods beyond offer great hiking.

Some plant life floats on the water (American white waterlily, pondweed, watershield, yellow pondlily). When we paddled here in 1992, very little vegetation appeared underwater. When we returned ten years later, an infestation of watermilfoil had begun to fill the void, literally. The clean water with sandy bottom supports freshwater mussels and patches of what we think are small, nodding white orchids in the shallows. Occasional boulders dot the shoreline of this beautiful pond.

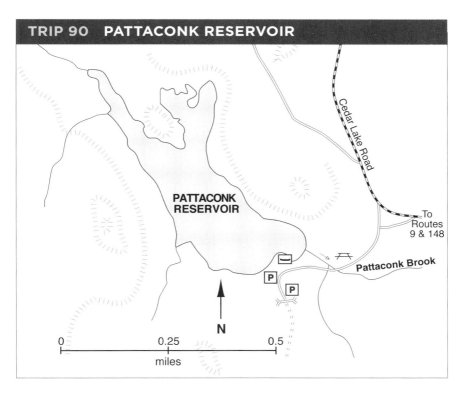

TRIP 90   PATTACONK RESERVOIR

TRIP 91

MESSERSCHMIDT POND

Quiet Messerschmidt Pond, surrounded by a wildlife management area, is an excellent place to paddle. On our visits, we've seen painted and snapping turtles and listened to many birds calling from the woods. We found large patches of relatively rare little floating heart here.

LOCATION Deep River and Westbrook, CT

MAPS *Connecticut/Rhode Island Atlas & Gazetteer*, Map 57: C6; USGS Essex

AREA 73 acres

TIME 2 hours

HABITAT TYPE Shallow, marshy pond

FISH Largemouth bass, yellow perch, pickerel (see fish advisory, Appendix A)

CAMPING Rocky Neck State Park, Hammonasset Beach State Park

TAKE NOTE No development; no motors

GETTING THERE

From Route 9, Exit 5, go 3.6 miles west on Route 80, and turn left on Route 145 (Stevenstown Road). Go 1.3 miles (4.9 miles) to the access on the left. **41° 20.424′ N, 72° 29.578′ W**

From I-95, Exit 64, go 3.0 miles north on Route 145 to the access on the right.

WHAT YOU'LL SEE

Although small, Messerschmidt Pond offers an opportunity for a wonderful morning of paddling. Lying wholly within Messerschmidt Wildlife Management Area, the pond's low earthen dam at the south end and a couple of groves of Norway spruce provide the only evidence of human presence. Paddling the entire shoreline takes much more time than the pond's acreage would suggest because of undulating deep coves, peninsulas, and a couple of very large wooded islands.

Shrubs line the shore, leading to hillsides covered with deciduous trees, many of them oaks. A large patch of buttonbush, its fluffy, ball-like flowers festooned with bees in mid-July, covers the backside of one island, while stands of swamp azalea and mountain laurel—both of which put on showy displays in June—dominate stretches of shoreline.

Though American white waterlily and watershield rule the surface, a yellow-flowered bladderwort and Carolina fanwort fill much of the underwater volume. Carolina fanwort is now crowding out the five species of bladderwort found in this pond. Surprisingly, we also found some fairly large patches of little floating heart (*Nymphoides cordata*), an uncommon aquatic plant, in bloom in mid-July.

As we paddled into the northern cove, eastern kingbirds chased a red-tailed hawk, while catbirds, cardinals, and hermit thrushes called from the undergrowth. We had a very relaxing visit here, away from the motorboats and development that characterize most bodies of water in the area.

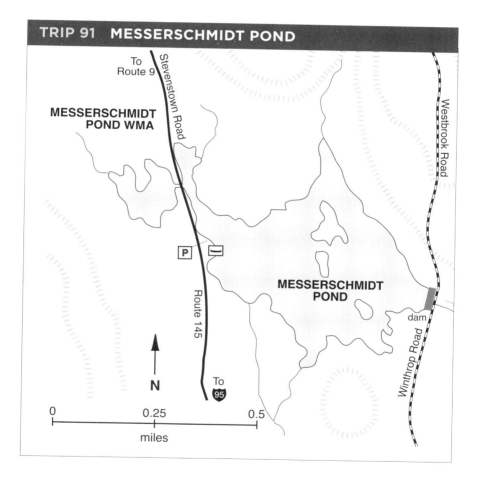

TRIP 91   MESSERSCHMIDT POND

TRIP 92

EAST RIVER

The East River offers a marvelous opportunity to explore an extensive Spartina *salt marsh, or you can paddle upriver away from Long Island Sound. Look for fiddler crabs, herons, egrets, osprey, northern harrier, and many other bird species.*

LOCATION Guilford and Madison, CT

MAPS *Connecticut/Rhode Island Atlas & Gazetteer*, Map 56: C2, D2, D3; USGS Guilford

LENGTH 6 miles one way

TIME 5 hours round trip, more if you explore side streams

HABITAT TYPE Salt marsh estuary and tidal river

FISH Trout, striped bass (see fish advisory, Appendix A)

INFORMATION Tide charts, usharbors.com; Guilford Salt Meadows Audubon Sanctuary, guilford.audubon.org

CAMPING Hammonasset Beach State Park

TAKE NOTE Limited development with areas protected by the Connecticut Audubon Society; motors allowed; plan your paddle around wind and tides

GETTING THERE

From I-95, Exit 59, go 1.6 miles east on Route 1, and turn right on Neck Road. Bear right after a few hundred yards, and go 2.1 miles (3.7 miles) to the access on the right; follow boat launch signs. **41° 16.166' N, 72° 39.42' W**

You can also launch from the northeast parking lot off Route 1 where it crosses the river. **41° 17.149' N, 72° 38.811' W**

WHAT YOU'LL SEE

The East River—the boundary between Guilford and Madison—provides superb tidal salt marsh paddling. From the access on Grass Island, the river extends about 6 miles inland in a fairly wide, gently winding channel, with lots of small tributary streams. Near the boat launch, the Neck River bears to the right but heads into a more populated area. You could easily spend a full day exploring this location, observing the many changes caused by rising and falling tides.

At high tide you can look out over the broad expanses of *Spartina* (salt marsh cordgrass). As the tide falls, the horizon disappears behind high sod banks clad with mussels and alive with fiddler crabs and other generally hidden salt marsh creatures. Look for herons and egrets hunting small crabs and fish in the network of water-filled drainage ditches that extends through the marsh.

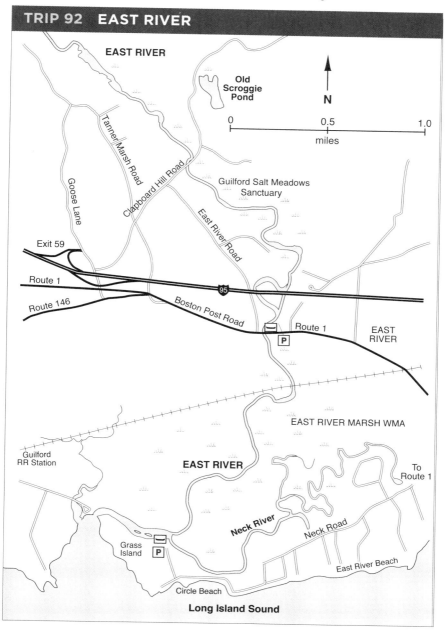

TRIP 92   EAST RIVER

EAST RIVER

Old Scroggie Pond

N

0   0.5   1.0
miles

Tanner Marsh Road

Clapboard Hill Road

Goose Lane

Guilford Salt Meadows Sanctuary

East River Road

Exit 59

Route 1

Route 146

95

Boston Post Road

Route 1

P

EAST RIVER

Guilford RR Station

EAST RIVER MARSH WMA

EAST RIVER

To Route 1

Neck River

Neck Road

Grass Island

P

East River Beach

Circle Beach

Long Island Sound

In the 1930s and 1940s, drainage ditches were dug throughout coastal salt marshes in an effort to eliminate mosquito-breeding stagnant water pools. Although only marginally successful, the effort put hundreds of people to work during the Great Depression. At high tide, you can squeeze your boat into some of these long, straight ditches, getting away from the main tidal river current and permitting close examination of salt marsh flora and fauna.

Pass under several bridges, including one for Amtrak on the heavily traveled Northeast Corridor, about 1.5 miles upstream. A quarter-mile past that, you can stop at the Route 1 bridge to visit one of the stores along the highway—on an incoming tide, make sure to tie your boat securely. The I-95 bridge follows just

Spartina alterniflora dominates the banks of the East River. Look for cedars and oaks on higher ground.

after the Route 1 bridge, and highway noise here can detract somewhat from this peaceful stretch of water, but it gradually fades as you paddle upriver.

A short distance north of I-95, the Connecticut Audubon Society protects land known as the Guilford Salt Meadows Audubon Sanctuary on both sides of the river. At high tide you can explore numerous small inlet streams teeming with birdlife, including osprey, northern harrier, heron, and egret. Red and white oak, sassafras, sumac, cedar, flowering dogwood, and a few black gum trees grow along the high ground. Watch out for poison ivy and Lyme disease–carrying deer ticks if you decide to explore on foot.

By timing your visit, you can paddle upriver from the access on an incoming tide, enjoy traveling around the salt marsh at high tide, and then paddle back after the tide turns. Several miles up the East River, high tide occurs quite a bit later than at the coast, which is about twenty minutes before Bridgeport. The wind, however, may cause more difficulty than the modest current. Visit in early morning or early evening to avoid the typical afternoon wind.

TRIP 93

CHARLES E. WHEELER WILDLIFE MANAGEMENT AREA, HOUSATONIC RIVER ESTUARY

This salt marsh is a birder's paradise, especially during shorebird migration in August. More than 300 bird species have been observed here. The area is off-limits to motors from March until September 1, making for delightful paddling in the extensive channels that crisscross the marsh. Paddle here near high tide.

LOCATION Milford, CT

MAPS *Connecticut/Rhode Island Atlas & Gazetteer,* Map 67: B5, B6; USGS Milford

AREA Wildlife management area, 812 acres

TIME 4 hours or more

HABITAT TYPE Housatonic River estuary, brackish marshland, many protected waterways

FISH Striped bass, bluefish (see fish advisory, Appendix A)

INFORMATION Connecticut Audubon Society Coastal Center, ctaudubon.org/coastal-center-home; tide charts, usharbors.com

CAMPING Kettletown State Park, Hammonasset Beach State Park

TAKE NOTE Little development; motors limited to after August 31; in the river and on Long Island Sound, winds, tides, and wakes can be dangerous; wear your PFD; best to paddle within two hours either side of high tide

GETTING THERE
From I-95, Exit 34, turn right (west) on Route 1, go 0.5 mile, and turn left on Naugatuck Avenue. Continue 0.6 mile (1.1 miles), and turn right on Milford Point Road. Go 0.8 mile (1.9 miles), and turn right on Court Street. In 0.2 mile (2.1 miles), continue straight onto the access road. **41° 16.166′ N, 72° 39.42′ W**

WHAT YOU'LL SEE
Charles E. Wheeler Wildlife Management Area's protected waters harbor a wide array of interesting bird species. A number of long, broad passageways, each with several side channels, penetrate the heart of the marsh, which extends a little over a mile in both the north–south and east–west directions. If you can, paddle here in August during peak shorebird migration. From March until September 1, the access is limited to cartop boats, and the marsh remains off-limits to motorized boats. From September 1 through February, the gate is opened to trailered boats for waterfowl hunting.

As we explored the *Spartina*-lined waterways, we saw many bird species, including herring, great black-backed, and ring-billed gulls; double-crested cormorant; great blue heron; snowy and common egrets; semipalmated and piping plovers; short-billed dowitcher; lesser and greater yellowlegs; unidentified peeps (probably semipalmated sandpiper and possibly others); black duck; mute swan; Canada goose; cardinal; kingfisher; osprey; red-winged blackbird; and swamp, song, and saltmarsh sparrows. Two rather tame clapper rails—normally very elusive—stepped out into plain view as we lingered nearby, begging to be photographed. Look also for yellow-crowned night heron, glossy ibis, willet, and marsh wren, all of which breed here. The Connecticut Audubon Society has a webcam on an osprey nest in spring; check the society's website.

Paddling is best within a few hours of high tide. At other times, some side channels become difficult, if not impossible, to paddle.

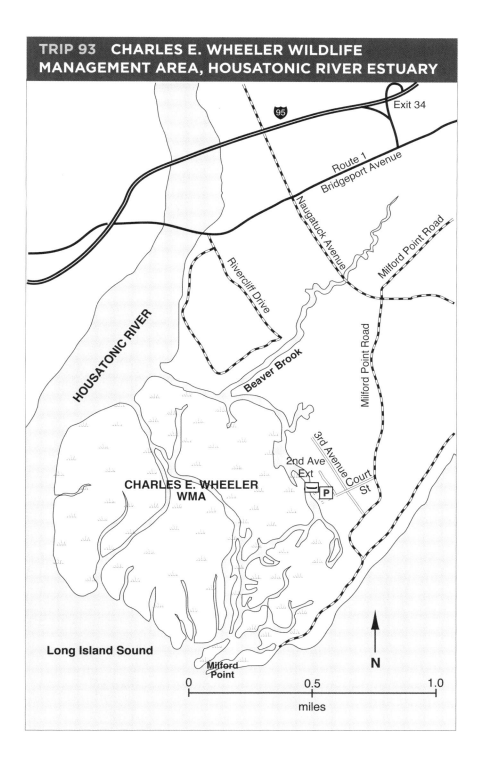

Exit 34

95

Route 1
Bridgeport Avenue

Naugatuck Avenue

Milford Point Road

Rivercliff Drive

Milford Point Road

HOUSATONIC RIVER

Beaver Brook

CHARLES E. WHEELER
WMA

3rd Avenue

2nd Ave
Ext

Court
St

P

N

Long Island Sound

Milford
Point

0   0.5   1.0

miles

SECTION 9

WESTERN CONNECTICUT

Western Connecticut includes long sections of four rivers: the Housatonic, Mattabesset, Coginchaug, and Bantam. It also includes seven ponds and lakes. The Housatonic River, flowing lazily down from the Massachusetts border, is justifiably very popular for canoeing and kayaking. Tree species diversity along the river is high, with lots of basswood and silver maple lining the banks.

The Mattabesset and Coginchaug rivers end at Cromwell Meadows, a wetlands of global significance, teeming with wildlife. We watched muskrats, deer, and many bird species amid the acres and acres of wild rice, feathery golden tips swaying in the light breeze. The Bantam River represents one of the preeminent paddling resources in western Connecticut. Flowing through a 4,000-acre nature preserve protected by the White Memorial Foundation, it's a superb location to see wildlife, such as osprey, beaver, deer, and possibly bald eagle.

Wood Creek Pond exudes a northern wilderness feel, especially on the north end where the red spruce Holleran Swamp begins. Look for nesting Canada goose and other waterfowl species here. West Branch Reservoir impounds a section of the West Branch Farmington River, just below much larger Colebrook River Lake. Scenic, tree-clad hillsides flow upward from the water's edge. We can't decide if we prefer paddling Lake Winchester in spring with abundant mountain laurel in bloom or in late summer when the highbush blueberries ripen. At either time, we love this lake's varied shoreline, rocky coves, gorgeous hillsides, and abundant spring wildflowers. You will likely see beaver in the evening, and you should see birdlife everywhere.

A popular recreation destination, Lake McDonough, with its long, narrow profile and exceptionally clear water, nestles among gorgeous wooded hillsides. You can cruise down this waterway unimpeded, getting lots of exercise.

TRIP 94

HOUSATONIC RIVER

This slow-moving section of the Housatonic River is popular, especially on summer weekends. The biological diversity—both on the banks and at nearby Bartholomew's Cobble—is remarkable. However, the area does have a significant amount of PCB contamination.

LOCATION Canaan, North Canaan, Salisbury, CT, and Sheffield, MA

MAPS *Connecticut/Rhode Island Atlas & Gazetteer*, Map 16: A4, B4, Map 17: A5; *Massachusetts Atlas & Gazetteer*, Map 44: C1; USGS Ashley Falls, South Canaan

LENGTH 11.5 miles one way

TIME All day; shorter trips possible

HABITAT TYPE Broad, tree-lined river

FISH The river holds 45 species of fish, but they cannot be eaten from this portion of the river because of PCB contamination (see fish advisory, Appendix A).

INFORMATION Bartholomew's Cobble: thetrustees.org/place /bartholomews-cobble

CAMPING Housatonic Meadows State Park, Macedonia Brook State Park

TAKE NOTE Little development; few motors; lots of canoes and kayaks on summer weekends

GETTING THERE

Falls Village, CT From Canaan, go south on Route 7, and turn right on Route 126 (Main Street). Go 0.3 mile, and fork right on Brewster Road/Route 126. Drive 0.3 mile (0.6 mile), and go left at the T. Turn immediately right on Water Street, go 0.5 mile (1.1 miles), and just after crossing the iron bridge, turn right on Housatonic River Road. The access is in 0.5 mile (1.6 miles) on the right at the dam. **41° 57.83′ N, 73° 22.313′ W**

Ashley Falls, MA From Ashley Falls at the junction of Route 7A and Rannapo Road, go 0.8 mile west on Rannapo Road to the access at the bridge. From the north, when Routes 7 and 7A split, go 0.6 mile south on Route 7A, and turn right on Rannapo Road. Continue 1.6 miles (2.2 miles) to the access on the left, just before the bridge. **42° 3.53′ N, 73° 20.952′ W**

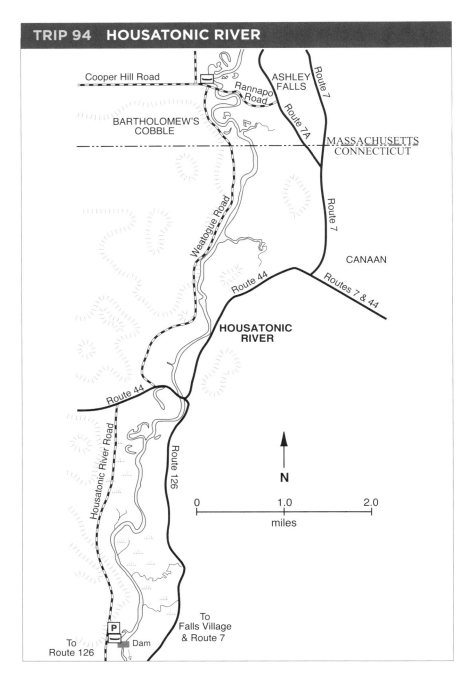

TRIP 94 HOUSATONIC RIVER

Cooper Hill Road

ASHLEY FALLS

Route 7

Rannapo Road

Route 7A

BARTHOLOMEW'S COBBLE

MASSACHUSETTS
CONNECTICUT

Weatogue Road

Route 7

CANAAN

Route 44

Routes 7 & 44

HOUSATONIC RIVER

Route 44

Housatonic River Road

Route 126

N

0   1.0   2.0
miles

To Falls Village & Route 7

P

To Route 126

Dam

Bartholomew's Cobble From the Ashley Falls access, go 0.1 mile west on Rannapo Road, and turn left on Weatogue Road. **42° 3.449′ N, 73° 21.054′ W**

WHAT YOU'LL SEE

When we paddled here on an August weekend, dozens of canoes floated by us as we traveled upstream through the lazy current. If you crave solitude, stay away from this section of the Housatonic River on summer weekends. Little development marks the river's shores, but for one short section of a little more than a mile, busy Route 44 parallels the water.

Though we did not see large numbers of wildlife because of boat traffic, tree-species diversity along the river impressed us; we quit identifying species after fifteen. Basswood and silver maple appeared in profusion. This section of the Housatonic Valley features hundreds of rare native plants, drawing scores of naturalists. The northern section of the Housatonic River included here, just over the border in Massachusetts, flows along Bartholomew's Cobble, arguably the most important plant preserve in the Northeast.

Because of PCB contamination, no one should eat the fish from this section of the river. We also recommend limiting children's contact with the water here. See the Housatonic River entry for Massachusetts (Trip 50) for more information.

BARTHOLOMEW'S COBBLE

The 329 acres of Bartholomew's Cobble—a National Natural Landmark— host an extraordinary number of rare plant species. Several trails wind through the woods along the Housatonic River and up over limestone and

Maidenhair spleenwort (*Asplenium trichomanes*) is one of the many species of fern that grow at Bartholomew's Cobble.

marble outcroppings. Because you must stay on the trails, binoculars may be advantageous if you want to scan the cliffs for rare ferns.

More than 50 species of ferns and fern allies grow here, along with 800 plant species from nearly a hundred families. You will need a plant guide, available at the visitor center, if you hope to distinguish purple-stemmed cliff brake from maidenhair spleenwort. You can download a trail map from the Bartholomew's Cobble website. For anyone with a strong interest in north-eastern plants, Bartholomew's Cobble represents an unparalleled resource.

TRIP 95

WOOD CREEK POND

Although you can see a few houses on its shores, Wood Creek Pond exudes a northern wilderness feel, especially on the north end where the red spruce Holleran Swamp begins. Look for nesting Canada goose and other waterfowl species here. Surface vegetation can make paddling slow, especially in summer.

LOCATION Norfolk, CT

MAPS *Connecticut/Rhode Island Atlas & Gazetteer*, Map 17: A8; USGS South Sandisfield

AREA 151 acres

TIME 3 hours

HABITAT TYPE Shallow, marshy pond

FISH Largemouth bass, yellow perch, pickerel (see fish advisory, Appendix A)

CAMPING American Legion State Forest

TAKE NOTE No development; vegetation and shallowness limit motors

GETTING THERE

From Route 44 in Norfolk, go 1.4 miles north on Route 272, and turn right on Ashpohtag Road at the Wood Creek Pond launch sign. Go 0.4 mile (1.8 miles) to the access road on the left. **42° 1.101′ N, 73° 11.599′ W**

WHAT YOU'LL SEE

In an out-of-the-way setting near Connecticut's northwest tip, Wood Creek Pond offers a very pleasant morning or afternoon of paddling in a shallow, marshy, heavily vegetated pond about a mile long. Near the south end, you may see nesting Canada geese. As you approach the geese, if they have young, notice the adults' defensive posturing, ruffling their neck feathers to look more forbidding to would-be aggressors.

As you paddle north, hillsides rise steeply from the shore, heavily wooded with mountain laurel, red maple, and other deciduous trees interspersed with hemlock and white pine. The pond's surface vegetation of American white waterlily, watershield, pondweed, and yellow pondlily can get quite thick, especially in late summer; coontail and a yellow-flowered bladderwort hang

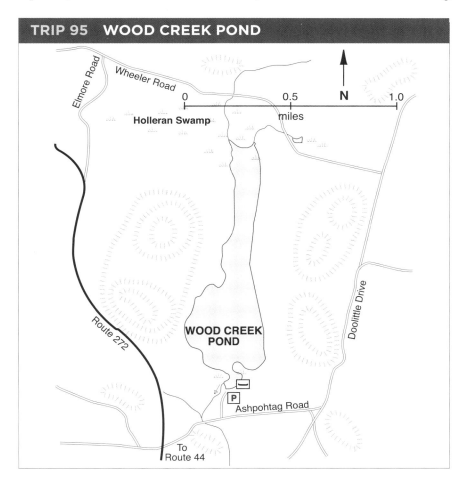

TRIP 95   WOOD CREEK POND

Very shallow and thick with vegetation, Wood Creek Pond provides hours of exploration and discovery for the quietwater paddler.

in large masses beneath the surface. Take a few minutes to look at the yellow pondlily flowers. The waxy yellow "petals" are actually sepals; the smaller true petals look more like stamens. A wide pistil with a yellow cap and reddish sides covers the middle of the flower.

The shallow north end, adjacent to the important red spruce Holleran Swamp, can be almost impenetrable, with thick, soupy muck a few inches beneath the surface, made up of decades-old, partially decomposed vegetation on its way to becoming peat. Methane, hydrogen sulfide, and other gases bubble out with the odor of anaerobic digestion. Wend your way carefully around stumps and submerged logs camouflaged by the murky water.

Look for the shallow, bowl-shaped depressions that pumpkinseed sunfish make for depositing eggs in the sandy bottom. The aggressive male stands guard over the eggs, fanning them with his tail until they hatch, and then defends the young until they're large enough to survive on their own. The males show such perseverance that you can hover right over them, watching them from inches away.

WEST BRANCH RESERVOIR

Undeveloped West Branch Reservoir nestles among scenic hillsides, with nearby mountains visible in the surrounding state forests. Its deep, cool waters contain a trout fishery. Bald eagles nest in the area, and you have a good chance of seeing them here.

LOCATION Colebrook and Hartland, CT

MAPS *Connecticut/Rhode Island Atlas & Gazetteer*, Map 18: A3, B3; USGS Tolland Center, Winsted

AREA 201 acres

TIME: 3 hours

HABITAT TYPE Deep, forested mountain reservoir

FISH Brown and rainbow trout, smallmouth bass, yellow perch (see fish advisory, Appendix A)

CAMPING American Legion State Forest

TAKE NOTE No development; cartop access only

GETTING THERE

From Route 20 northbound in Riverton, turn left on Robertsville Road where Route 20 goes right. Go 1.2 miles, and turn right on End Hill Road. Drive 0.7 mile (1.9 miles), and turn right on Durst Road. Go 0.8 mile (2.7 miles) to the access on the left, just before the dam. **41° 59.332′ N, 73° 1.351′ W**

WHAT YOU'LL SEE

West Branch Reservoir, also called Hogsback Reservoir, offers a different environment from most trips in this book. Its location in a scenic, deep mountain valley surrounded by northern deciduous forest, coupled with its 90-foot depth, distinguishes it from the many shallow, marshy ponds and streams you'll find throughout this book. The reservoir supports a coldwater fishery, mainly trout, but anglers catch smallmouth bass here as well.

The Metropolitan District of Hartford owns 6,000 acres surrounding West Branch Reservoir and enormous Colebrook River Lake, whose dam looms over the reservoir's north end. Currently used for flood control by the U.S. Army Corps of Engineers, these two bodies of water could eventually supply water to a growing population. Fortunately, the scenic hillsides and nearby mountains, some in the Algonquin and Tunxis state forests, will remain protected for generations to come.

Occasional white pine and eastern hemlock infiltrate the predominately deciduous forest. Look for red oak; sugar and red maples; black, yellow, and white birches; ash; shagbark and pignut hickories; and black cherry on the steep hillsides.

When we paddle in this out-of-the-way water, we often couple it with a trip to nearby Upper Spectacle Pond (Trip 52), which offers a contrasting marshy paddling experience. No matter where you paddle in this area, keep your eye out for soaring, majestic bald eagles that nest near Colebrook River Lake; their nest was the first in this location in 100 years. In our travels to Colebrook River Lake and West Branch Reservoir and other nearby bodies of water over the last twenty years, we've seen them on most trips, including high above Upper Spectacle Pond.

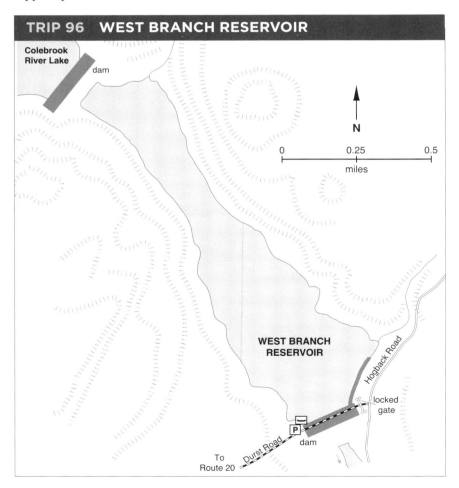

The surrounding forest harbors the usual woodland bird species—we especially enjoy listening to thrushes calling from the understory in the evening—and you may notice an occasional great blue heron patrolling the shoreline. We've also seen Canada geese here, and if you're lucky, you could see a flock of wild turkeys.

TRIP 97

LAKE WINCHESTER

We can't decide if we prefer paddling this wonderful place in spring with abundant mountain laurel in bloom or in late summer when the highbush blueberries ripen. At either time, we love paddling Lake Winchester because of the varied shoreline, rocky coves, gorgeous hillsides, and abundant spring wildflowers. You will likely see beaver in the evening, and you should see birdlife everywhere.

LOCATION Winchester, CT

MAPS *Connecticut/Rhode Island Atlas & Gazetteer*, Map 17: C8, Map 18, C1; USGS Norfolk

AREA 246 acres

TIME 3 hours

HABITAT TYPE Shallow reservoir, shrubby marshlands, protected bays

FISH Largemouth and calico bass, yellow perch, pickerel, northern pike (see fish advisory, Appendix A)

CAMPING American Legion State Forest

INFORMATION Aquatic plant survey, ct.gov/CAES/OAIS/Office-of -Aquatic-Invasive-Species

TAKE NOTE No development; motors limited to 8 MPH; watch out for submerged rocks and tree stumps

GETTING THERE

From the northern terminus of Route 8 in Winsted, go 1.4 miles west on Route 44, and turn left on Route 263. Drive 4.5 miles (5.9 miles), and as Route 263 curves left, go straight on West Road at the Winchester Lake sign. Continue 0.6 mile (6.5 miles) to the access on the right. **41° 54.466′ N, 3° 9.121′ W**

WHAT YOU'LL SEE

Lake Winchester's beautiful setting—coupled with limited development—makes it one of our favorite destinations in northwestern Connecticut. You could easily spend half a day exploring this small, shallow lake's highly varied shoreline and rocky coves. We prefer paddling here in spring when the abundant mountain laurel blooms and in summer when the highbush blueberries ripen. In spring, also look for pink lady's slipper, trillium, Solomon's seal, and other spring wildflowers. By midsummer, American eelgrass, watershield, and

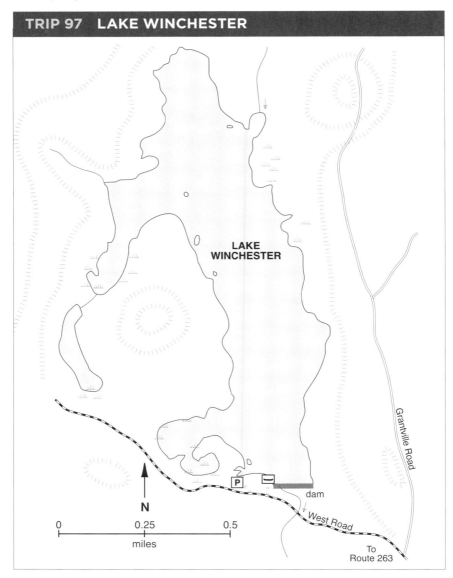

TRIP 97   LAKE WINCHESTER

LAKE WINCHESTER

Grantville Road

P   dam

N

West Road

0   0.25   0.5

miles

To
Route 263

waterlilies begin to cover the water's surface in shallower areas. In August, look for the purple blossoms of the abundant eastern purple bladderwort (*Utricularia purpurea*). An aquatic survey in 2007 found no invasive species, but that certainly could have changed in the intervening years.

Paddling here in the evening, expect to see beaver swimming about, especially in the coves. The clean water supports freshwater mussels and good fishing. We also enjoyed the abundant birdlife in the lake's more hidden reaches. Look for red maple, beech, red oak, and black and gray birches among the large pines and hemlocks along the shore. As you paddle, watch out for rocks lurking just below the water's surface, along with old stumps from trees cut off at ice level after the reservoir's formation.

TRIP 98

LAKE McDONOUGH

Lake McDonough is a popular recreation destination. This long, narrow lake with exceptionally clear water nestles among gorgeous wooded hillsides. This is a great place for a picnic and for swimming. It lacks the marshy areas loaded with plants that characterize other entries in this book, but lack of plants also means that you can cruise down the waterway unimpeded, getting lots of exercise.

LOCATION Barkhamsted, CT

MAPS *Connecticut/Rhode Island Atlas & Gazetteer*, Map 18: C4, D4; USGS New Hartford

AREA 391 acres

TIME 5 hours

HABITAT TYPE Forested oligotrophic reservoir

FISH Trout, largemouth and smallmouth bass, yellow perch, northern pike (see fish advisory, Appendix A)

CAMPING American Legion State Forest

INFORMATION For up-to-date fees and days and hours of operation, themdc.org/lake-mcdonough

TAKE NOTE Development limited to park facilities; 10 MPH speed limit, northwest arm off-limits to motors; fee to launch

GETTING THERE

From Route 8 northbound in Winsted, go 3.1 miles east on Route 44, and turn left on Route 318. In 2.9 miles (6.0 miles), just after crossing Barkhamsted Reservoir's Saville Dam, turn right on Route 219, and follow it for 0.5 mile (6.5 miles) to Lake McDonough Recreation Area on the right. **41° 54.302' N, 72° 57.411' W**

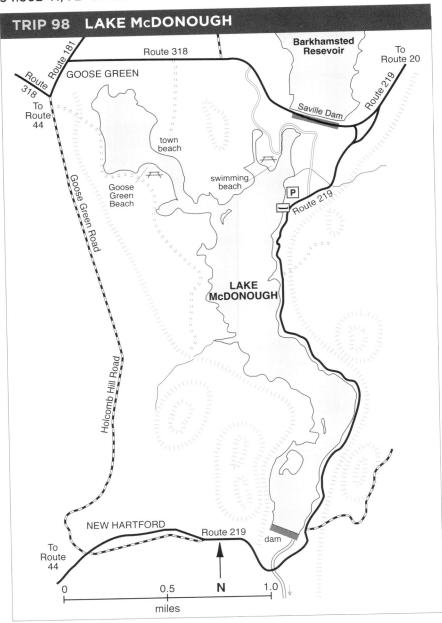

TRIP 98   LAKE McDONOUGH

From I-91, Exit 40, drive 12.7 miles west on Route 20, and turn left on Route 219. Go 6.9 miles (19.6 miles) to the access on the right, just past the junction with Route 318.

WHAT YOU'LL SEE

Lake McDonough lies just to the south of enormous Barkhamsted Reservoir, which supplies drinking water to the Hartford area. The Metropolitan District of Hartford maintains both reservoirs, although Lake McDonough does not supply drinking water. Even though visitors must pay to get in and to launch a boat, anglers and recreational boaters flock to the exceptionally clear waters of this lovely place on sunny summer weekends. You can get a real workout here, paddling on open water along gorgeous forested hillsides.

Make sure to paddle the northwest arm, the most pleasant section because of a ban on motors and a greater distance from Route 219, which extends along the east side of the lake's north–south axis. Grassy shores, clear water, and a generally sandy bottom characterize this section. Surprisingly, we could find no floating vegetation anywhere on the lake; the Metropolitan District may lower the water level each fall, which would discourage aquatic plants from getting established. With so little natural vegetation, the lake seems somewhat sterile. We saw no turtles and only a few birds—including a family of Canada geese. The one beaver lodge appeared old and long abandoned. On warm days, you should be able to find northern water snakes.

The larger portion of the lake extending to the south sports a few attractive islands that provide inviting picnic spots. We found the west shore—with its many coves and small inlets—a lot more interesting than the east shore.

TRIP 99

MATTABESSET RIVER, COGINCHAUG RIVER, AND CROMWELL MEADOWS STATE WILDLIFE AREA

Cromwell Meadows is a wetlands of global significance, teeming with wildlife. We watched muskrats, deer, and many bird species amid the acres and acres of wild rice, with feathery golden tips swaying in the light breeze.

LOCATION Cromwell and Middletown, CT

MAPS *Connecticut/Rhode Island Atlas & Gazetteer*, Map 44: B2, B3; USGS Middletown

LENGTH Mattabesset River, 5 miles one way; Coginchaug River, 2 miles one way

TIME 6 hours round trip; shorter trips possible

HABITAT TYPE River through extensive marshland, many bays and side channels

FISH Trout, largemouth and smallmouth bass, pickerel, northern pike (see fish advisory, Appendix A)

TAKE NOTE No development; motors allowed; because of wind, waves, and wakes on the Connecticut River, wear your PFD; novice paddlers should avoid the Connecticut River

GETTING THERE

Connecticut River Access From downtown Middletown, head south on Main Street, and turn left on Union Street at the stoplight. Go 0.1 mile, pass under Route 9, veer left for 100 feet, and turn right into the Harbor Park parking area. **41° 33.546′ N, 72° 38.63′ W**

Mattabesset River Access From downtown Middletown, drive north on Route 3. When Berlin Road goes left, continue on Route 3 for 100 yards, and turn right into the gravel parking lot. **41° 35.985′ N, 72° 40.574′ W**

WHAT YOU'LL SEE

Though some road noise emanates from numerous four-lane divided highways that ring Middletown, Cromwell Meadows State Wildlife Area still represents an extraordinary paddling resource, all the more so because of its metropolitan location. Huge numbers of nesting and migrating waterfowl congregate here, and nowhere else in our exploration of Connecticut have we seen so much wild rice (*Zizania aquatica*).

If you paddle north from the Connecticut River Harbor Park access, nominally upstream—the tidal surge travels this far upriver—you may have to paddle against the current in either direction. The current presents little problem, however, compared with motorboat wakes and wind-driven waves that pile up over a couple of miles of open water. Because the Connecticut bends and bows, the winds cause less havoc here than on straighter stretches of river. Under windy conditions, we strongly recommend that you wear your PFD, or better yet, paddle elsewhere. Novice paddlers should avoid the Connecticut River.

You could also use the Mattabesset River access off Route 3, but that gets pretty muddy at low tide. According to the Mattabesset River Watershed Association, the incoming tide at the Mattabesset's mouth lags the incoming tide at the Saybrook Jetty at the Connecticut River mouth by two hours and 45 minutes. The Route 3 access gets the incoming tide 45 minutes later, for a total incoming tide lag of three and a half hours. This might be helpful in trying to avoid the mud.

On a late August afternoon, the first time we paddled under the Route 9 bridge and into the Mattabesset River, a big surprise unfolded before us: the vast, wild, Cromwell marshlands, full of wood ducks, kingfishers, and cardinals. The area teems with wildlife and interesting plants. Chimney swifts and

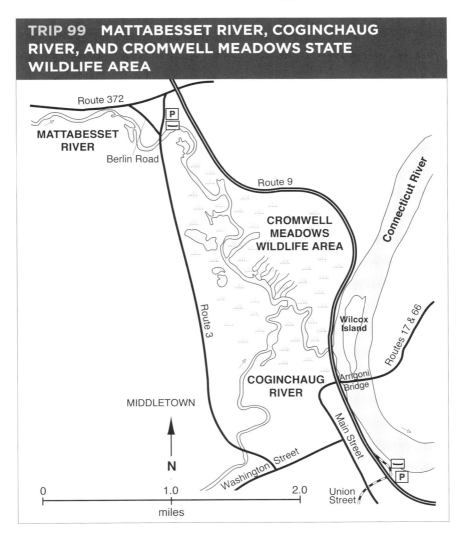

TRIP 99 MATTABESSET RIVER, COGINCHAUG RIVER, AND CROMWELL MEADOWS STATE WILDLIFE AREA

barn swallows darted over the water's surface, while spotted sandpipers and great blue herons stalked the shores. The gorgeous golden tops of wild rice, backlit in the setting sun, swayed in the light breeze. Deer came down for an evening drink, and muskrats swam by, towing grasses destined for winter stores. We lingered, reluctant to leave this enchanted place. (We and the waterfowl would return to watch spring unfold.)

BANTAM RIVER, BANTAM LAKE, AND LITTLE POND

The Bantam River is one of the preeminent paddling resources in western Connecticut. Flowing through a 4,000-acre nature preserve protected by the White Memorial Foundation, it abounds with wildlife. You will see osprey and should see beaver in the evening. Deer come to the water to drink, and many bird species frequent the shore and the woods. You might see bald eagles here as well.

LOCATION Litchfield and Morris, CT

MAPS *Connecticut/Rhode Island Atlas & Gazetteer*, Map 29: C7, C8, D7; USGS Litchfield

AREA/LENGTH Bantam Lake, 933 acres; Bantam River, 2 miles one way

TIME 3 hours for entire river, through Little Pond, round trip

HABITAT TYPE Large natural lake; meandering river, shrubby marshlands

FISH Largemouth, smallmouth, and calico bass; yellow and white perch; northern pike (see fish advisory, Appendix A)

CAMPING White Memorial Foundation, Black Rock State Park

INFORMATION White Memorial Foundation, whitememorialcc.org

TAKE NOTE Development and motors on lake; no development or internal combustion motors on river

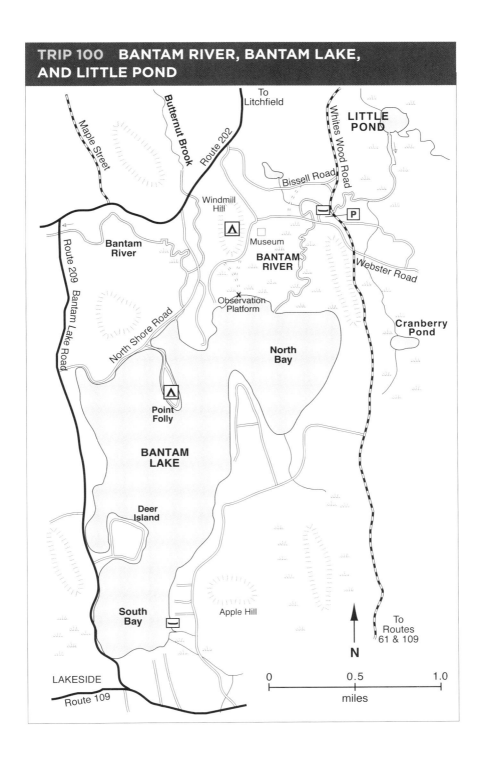

GETTING THERE

From Litchfield, at the junction of Routes 63 north and 202, go 2.1 miles west on Route 202, and turn left on Bissell Road. In 0.7 mile (2.8 miles), veer right on Whites Wood Road, and go 0.1 mile (2.9 miles) to the access on the right, just over the bridge. **41° 43.509' N, 73° 12.334' W**

WHAT YOU'LL SEE

At 933 acres—the largest natural body of water in Connecticut—Bantam Lake draws many motorboaters, especially on weekends. We much prefer the lake's north end and the motor-free Bantam River inlet that flows through a marshland owned by the White Memorial Foundation. Though you will not paddle alone on Bantam River, especially on weekends, it offers one of the premier paddling destinations in western Connecticut.

The White Memorial Foundation, founded in 1913, protects one of southern New England's finest nature preserves. The 4,000-acre tract includes upland hardwood forests, fields, marshlands, and open water. The foundation manages some land for forest production or wildlife habitat but leaves some untouched for research on natural succession. More than 35 miles of trails crisscross the property, including 1,700 feet of elevated boardwalk around Little Pond. The foundation stocks many publications about the natural history of the area at the White Memorial Conservation Center.

On the winding Bantam River, expect to see osprey, kingfisher, great blue heron, and many other bird species. Look for beaver near dusk; each time we paddled here, we had to portage over small beaver dams. We watched many basking painted turtles splash into the water as we cruised by. The barely noticeable current does not impede upstream paddling as this wonderful river passes through a sparse red maple swamp, the shores festooned with alder, willow, viburnum, dogwood, buttonbush, winterberry, cattail, bulrush, burreed, pickerelweed, and grasses galore.

Few locations in Connecticut boast as much bird diversity as found here, with nearly 250 recorded species (115 nesting here). Highlights for us included an osprey perched in a dead tree over the river, feeding on a fish clutched in its talons, and a normally secretive swamp sparrow, with its bright rufous cap and prominent white throat patch, hopping around in plain view.

Paddling around to the right as you enter North Bay from the river, note the old concrete piers left over from a railroad spur used to cart away blocks of ice sawed from the frozen lake. Some of the piers now hold a bird observation platform. Farther down the lake, Point Folly hosts a White Memorial Foundation campground, complete with another bird observation platform.

APPENDIX A:
FISH ADVISORIES

The information below includes Massachusetts, Connecticut, and Rhode Island advisories from public health departments for safely eating fish. A variety of toxins show up in game fish in each state, usually specific to certain bodies of water, for which the states provide consumption guidelines. The states do not list every body of water but issue general guidelines on eating fish from the state's unlisted waters. See the web pages below for more information.

MASSACHUSETTS
The Massachusetts Department of Public Health (DPH) produces a table that lists bodies of water with advisories on fish consumption. For example, for the Charles River section included in this book, the DPH cautions that children younger than age 12, pregnant women, nursing mothers, and women of childbearing age should not eat any fish. All others should limit fish meals to a maximum of two per month. The toxins accumulated in Charles River fish: mercury, chlordane, and DDT.

General advisory for unlisted bodies of water. Guidelines for pregnant women, women who may become pregnant, nursing mothers, and children younger than age 12: Do not eat freshwater fish caught in streams, rivers, lakes, and ponds; bluefish caught off the coast; and lobsters, flounder, soft-shell clams, and bivalves from Boston Harbor. Safe to eat: fish stocked in streams, rivers, lakes, and ponds. Guidelines for everyone, including the groups listed above: Do not eat fish, shellfish, or lobsters from Area I of New Bedford Harbor; lobsters or bottom-feeding fish from Area II of New Bedford Harbor; lobsters from Area III of New Bedford Harbor; or lobster tomalley from any location.

See mass.gov/lists/fish-consumption-advisories for updates. Also see mass.gov/info-details/eating-fish-safely-in-massachusetts for how to eat fish safely.

CONNECTICUT
The Connecticut Department of Public Health maintains a website that lists bodies of water with advisories on fish consumption. For example, for the Housatonic River section included in this book, and indeed all of the Housatonic upstream of Lake Lillinonah, no one should eat trout, catfish, eel, carp, and northern pike (other fish have restrictions, as well). The toxin present in fish is PCBs.

General advisory for unlisted bodies of water. High Risk Group: pregnant women, women who could become pregnant, nursing women, and children younger than age 6 should eat no more than one fish meal per month of most freshwater fish from local waters. Low Risk Group: should limit eating most freshwater fish to once a week. Most trout are not part of any advisory and are safe to eat unless otherwise noted.

See portal.ct.gov/fish for descriptions of how to eat fish safely and for advisories for specific bodies of water.

RHODE ISLAND

Because Rhode Island does not have advisories for specific bodies of water, we refer you to a brochure on mercury that includes recommendations on which fish to eat and not to eat: health.ri.gov/publications/brochures/FishIs GoodMercuryIsBad.pdf.

We also believe it's worth becoming familiar with EPA and FDA fish consumption guidelines, contained here: epa.gov/fish-tech/epa-fda -advice-about-eating-fish-and-shellfish and here: fda.gov/food/consumers /advice-about-eating-fish.

APPENDIX B: FURTHER READING

Brame, Rich, and David Cole. *Soft Paths: How to Enjoy the Wilderness without Harming It.* 4th ed. Mechanicsburg, PA: Stackpole Books, 2011.

Burk, John S. *AMC's Best Day Hikes in Central Massachusetts: Four-Season Guide to 50 of the Best Hikes from Pioneer Valley to the Worcester Hills.* 2nd ed. Boston: Appalachian Mountain Club Books, 2024.

Burk, John S. *Massachusetts Trail Guide: AMC's Comprehensive Guide to Hiking Trails Massachusetts, from the Berkshires to Cape Cod.* 11th ed. Boston: Appalachian Mountain Club Books, 2021.

Carroll, David. *The Year of the Turtle: A Natural History.* New York: St. Martin's Press, 1996.

Cole, Jim. *Paddling Connecticut and Rhode Island: Southern New England's Best Paddling Routes.* Guilford, CT: Falcon, 2009.

Connecticut and Rhode Island Atlas & Gazetteer. 5th ed. Yarmouth, ME: DeLorme, 2020.

Connecticut River Joint Commission. Connecticut River maps. crjc.org /boating/boating1.htm.

Connecticut River Watershed Council. *The Connecticut River Boating Guide: Source to Sea.* 3rd ed. Guilford, CT: Falcon, 2007.

Daugherty, Michael. *AMC's Best Sea Kayaking in New England: 50 Coastal Paddling Adventures from Maine to Connecticut.* Boston: Appalachian Mountain Club Books, 2016.

Evans, Lisa. *Sea Kayaking Coastal Massachusetts: From Newburyport to Buzzards Bay.* Boston: Appalachian Mountain Club Books, 2000.

Fagin, Steve, René Laubach, and Charles W. G. Smith. *AMC's Best Day Hikes in Connecticut and Rhode Island: Four-Season Guide to 60 of the Best Trails from the Highland to the Coast.* Boston: Appalachian Mountain Club Books, 2024.

Hutchinson, Derek. *The Basic Book of Sea Kayaking.* 2nd ed. Guilford, CT: Falcon, 2007.

Jacobs, Robert, and Eileen O'Donnell. *A Fisheries Guide to Lakes and Ponds of Connecticut, Including the Connecticut River and Its Coves.* 2nd ed. Hartford, CT: Connecticut Department of Energy and Environmental Protection, 2002.

Jacobson, Cliff. *Canoeing and Camping: Beyond the Basics.* 3rd ed. Guilford, CT: Falcon, 2007.

Laubach, René, and John S. Burk. *AMC's Best Day Hikes in the Berkshires: Four-Season Guide to 50 of the Best Trails in Massachusetts.* 3rd ed. Boston: Appalachian Mountain Club Books, 2020.

Leave No Trace information and materials, Leave No Trace Center for Outdoor Ethics, lnt.org.

Lessels, Bruce, and Karen Blom. *Paddling with Kids: AMC Essential Handbook for Fun and Safe Paddling.* Boston: Appalachian Mountain Club Books, 2002.

Massachusetts Atlas & Gazetteer. 6th ed. Yarmouth, ME: DeLorme, 2022.

McAdow, Ron. *The Charles River: Exploring Nature and History on Foot and by Canoe: A Guide to Canoeing, Wildlife, and History.* Bliss Publishing, 1999.

McAdow, Ron. *The Concord, Sudbury, and Assabet Rivers: A Guide to Canoeing, Wildlife, and History.* 2nd ed. Bliss Publishing, 2000.

O'Connor, Michael. *Discover Cape Cod: AMC's Guide to the Best Hiking, Biking, and Paddling.* Boston: Appalachian Mountain Club Books, 2009.

Older, Julia, and Steve Sherman. *Nature Walks along the Seacoast: Massachusetts, New Hampshire, and Maine.* Boston: Appalachian Mountain Club Books, 2003.

Roberts, Harry, and Steve Salins. *Basic Essentials Canoe Paddling.* 3rd ed. Guilford, CT: Falcon, 2006.

Seidman, David. *The Essential Sea Kayaker: A Complete Guide for the Open-Water Paddler.* 2nd ed. Camden, ME: Ragged Mountain Press, 2001.

Sinai, Lee. *Discover Martha's Vineyard: AMC's Guide to the Best Hiking, Biking, and Paddling.* Boston: Appalachian Mountain Club Books, 2009.

Smith, Charles, and Susan Smith. *Discover the Berkshires of Massachusetts: AMC Guide to the Best Hiking, Biking, and Paddling.* Boston: Appalachian Mountain Club Books, 2003.

Spring, Sue. *Appalachian Trail Guide to Massachusetts–Connecticut.* 14th ed. Harpers Ferry, WV: Appalachian Trail Conservancy, 2018.

Teal, John, and Mildred Teal. *Life and Death of the Salt Marsh.* New York: Ballantine Books, 1983.

Tougias, Michael, Alison O'Leary, and John S. Burk. *AMC's Best Day Hikes near Boston: Four-Season Guide to 60 of the Best Trails in Eastern Massachusetts.* 4th ed. Boston: Appalachian Mountain Club Books, 2022.

LIST OF WATERWAYS

ABOUT THE AUTHORS

ALEX WILSON has been exploring quiet waters of the Northeast for decades and in 1992 published the first in this series of guides to quietwater paddling destinations for AMC. He is also the founder of BuildingGreen, a company that has been publishing information on environmentally responsible design and construction since 1985. In 2012, he launched the nonprofit Resilient Design Institute to focus on how to design buildings and communities to bounce back from disruption and be better adapted to climate change. He is a widely published author, focusing primarily on building technology, energy, and the environment. Besides the Quiet Water series, he has authored or co-authored *The Consumer Guide to Home Energy Savings*, 10th edition (ACEEE, 2012), *Your Green Home* (New Society Publishing, 2006), and *Green Development: Integrating Ecology and Real Estate* (Wiley, 1998). Before starting Building-Green, he worked for a solar organization in New Mexico and was executive director of the Northeast Sustainable Energy Association. He was the first recipient of the NESEA Lifetime Achievement Award in 1993, and received the U.S. Green Building Council's Leadership Award for Education in 2008 and the Hanley Award for Vision and Leadership in Sustainable Housing in 2010. He lives with his wife in southern Vermont.

JOHN HAYES is a retired professor of environmental science at Marlboro College in Vermont and former Director of Sustainability at Pacific University in Oregon. Besides exploring the lakes and rivers of his new home in the Northwest, he has paddled Minnesota's Boundary Waters Canoe Area, Georgia's Okefenokee Swamp, and Florida's Everglades, as well as throughout the Northeast. Hayes has written for *National Geographic Traveler* and has edited numerous solar energy conference proceedings. He was book review editor of the *Passive Solar Journal* and served as vice chair of the American Solar Energy Society. He has led natural history field trips to Central America, Mexico, Southwest deserts, the Rockies, the Everglades, Borneo, and Africa. He and Alex Wilson are co-authors of paddling guides to all New England states and New York.

ABOUT AMC IN SOUTHERN NEW ENGLAND

MASSACHUSETTS

The Appalachian Mountain Club has four active chapters in Massachusetts: Boston, Southeastern Massachusetts, Worcester, and Western Massachusetts. Each offers a range of activities, from rock climbing and backpacking to local walks, skiing, paddling, and cycling. Each chapter also offers social and young member events. A complete listing of upcoming events is available on activities.outdoors.org.

Chapter volunteers are active in maintaining the state's long trails, including the Appalachian, New England, Midstate, and Bay Circuit trails. Volunteers also manage the self-service Ponkapoag Camp in the Blue Hills Reservation near Boston.

AMC works closely with youth agencies in Boston and Worcester through its Educator Outdoors program, offering leadership training, equipment, and support to agency staff. AMC also advocates on behalf of sound land conservation, energy, climate, and clean air policies in the Commonwealth.

CONNECTICUT

The AMC Connecticut Chapter has more than 8,000 members and offers hundreds of trips each year. Well-trained and dedicated leaders guide hiking, paddling, skiing, and climbing excursions, in addition to family activities. The chapter is also active in trail work and conservation projects and maintains Northwest Camp, a rustic and secluded cabin in a remote section of the northwestern corner of Connecticut.

RHODE ISLAND

Established in 1921, the AMC Narragansett Chapter consists of more than 2,500 members. In order to provide people with a clear path to the enjoyment of new outdoor pursuits, the chapter puts on bicycling, paddling, hiking, camping, cross-country skiing, technical climbing, and other outdoor activities for adventurers of all levels of experience and skill. In addition to conservation efforts, they host social events for members and non-members alike.

You can learn more about these chapters by visiting outdoors.org/chapters. To view a list of AMC activities in Massachusetts, Connecticut, Rhode Island, and other parts of the Northeast, visit outdoors.org/activities.

AMC BOOK UPDATES

AMC Books strives to keep our guidebooks as up-to-date as possible to help you plan safe and enjoyable adventures. If we learn after publishing a book that relevant trails have been relocated or route or contact information has changed, we will post the updated information online. Before you hit the trail, visit outdoors.org/books-maps and click the "Book Updates" tab.

While using this book, if you notice discrepancies with the trip descriptions or maps, or if you find any other errors in the book, please let us know by submitting them to amcbookupdates@outdoors.org or to Books Editor, c/o AMC, 10 City Square, Suite 2, Boston, MA 02129. We will verify all submissions and post key updates each month. AMC Books is dedicated to being a recognized leader in outdoor publishing. Thank you for your participation.

AMC Books are published by the Appalachian Mountain Club (AMC), a nonprofit with the mission to foster the protection, enjoyment, and understanding of the outdoors. **Since 1876** we have been working to protect the mountains, forests, waters, and trails you love in the Northeast and Mid-Atlantic regions.

Join us in this work by becoming an AMC member! **When you join AMC, you can:**

- Take pride in knowing that you are supporting outdoor recreation and conservation in the Northeast and Mid-Atlantic
- Enjoy thousands of outdoor activities
- Receive up to 20% off merchandise, books & maps, and stays at AMC destinations

Scan the QR code to sign up!